Advances in Computing Communications and Informatics

(Volume 5)

Data Science and Interdisciplinary Research: Recent Trends and Applications

Edited by

Brojo Kishore Mishra
Department of Computer Science & Engineering
NIST Institute of Science and Technology (Autonomous)
Institute Park, Pallur Hills, Golanthara
Berhampur-761008, Odisha, India

Advances in Computing Communications and Informatics

(Volume 5)

Data Science and Interdisciplinary Research: Recent Trends and Applications

Series Editors: Pradeep Kumar Singh, Bharat Bhargava & Wei-Chiang Hong

Volume Editor: Brojo Kishore Mishra

ISSN (Online): 2737-5730

ISSN (Print): 2737-5722

ISBN (Online): 978-981-5079-00-5

ISBN (Print): 978-981-5079-01-2

ISBN (Paperback): 978-981-5079-02-9

©2023, Bentham Books imprint.

Published by Bentham Science Publishers Pte. Ltd. Singapore. All Rights Reserved.

First published in 2023.

need for a court order if at any point you breach any terms of this License Agreement. In no event will any delay or failure by Bentham Science Publishers in enforcing your compliance with this License Agreement constitute a waiver of any of its rights.

3. You acknowledge that you have read this License Agreement, and agree to be bound by its terms and conditions. To the extent that any other terms and conditions presented on any website of Bentham Science Publishers conflict with, or are inconsistent with, the terms and conditions set out in this License Agreement, you acknowledge that the terms and conditions set out in this License Agreement shall prevail.

Bentham Science Publishers Pte. Ltd.
80 Robinson Road #02-00
Singapore 068898
Singapore
Email: subscriptions@benthamscience.net

BENTHAM SCIENCE

CONTENTS

PREFACE

Data science has recently gained much attention for a number of reasons, Big Data is the most significant among them. Scientists (from almost all disciplines including physics, chemistry, biology, and sociology, among others) and engineers (from all fields including civil, environmental, chemical, and mechanical, among others) are faced with challenges posed by data volume, variety, and velocity, or Big Data.

The book contains quantitative research, case studies, conceptual papers, and model papers, review papers, theoretical backing, *etc*. This book will cover data science and its application to interdisciplinary science.

This book will prove valuable for graduate students, researchers, academicians, and professionals in information science, business, health, planning, manufacturing, and other areas who are interested in exploring the ever-expanding research on Data Science.

Chapter-01 provides a detailed survey and comparative analysis of various methodologies in the prediction of rainfall over multiple countries.

Chapter -02 focuses on applying clustering for gaining the benefits of evolutionary computation to process large-scale data and based on optimality, the performance of the datasets can be measured.

Chapter-05 presents an investigation of the data obtained from IoT sensors and observed that a huge amount of work can be done in the reliability analysis of the data from the sensors deployed in the agricultural fields.

Chapter-06 says that - Smart devices have rapidly started intruding our lifestyles with the technological promotion of the Internet of Things. One of the most used smart devices is the electric meter. Urban areas witness power theft as well as un-proportionate billing, both incurring tremendous losses to the respective exchequers. We thought that if a system may be designed which can predict power utilization and also classify the current usage, it would be beneficial to both the service providers as well as the consumers. Equipped with such thoughts, thorough research was conducted to monitor electric consumption and fault detection in the devices.

Chapter-08 focused on undertaking a quick analysis of socio-economic conditions. Information on the aforementioned parameters was gathered in order to get insight into the research area's socio-economic profile.

In the end, we thank the contributory authors, reviewers and my family members for their support. Special thanks to Prof. (Dr.) Pradeep Kumar Singh for his best support as a Book Series Editor. The editors are also thankful to all members of Bentham Science Publication house.

Brojo Kishore Mishra
Department of Computer Science & Engineering
NIST Institute of Science and Technology (Autonomous)
Institute Park, Pallur Hills, Golanthara
Berhampur-761008, Odisha, India

List of Contributors

Adrija Dasgupta	Department of Computer Science and Engineering, Meghnad Saha Institute of Technology, Kolkata, India
A. Kavitha	Department of Computer Science, Kongunadu Arts and Science College, Coimbatore, Tamil Nadu, India
C. Kishor Kumar Reddy	Stanley College of Engineering and Technology for Women, Hyderabad, India
Diganta Sengupta	Department of Computer Science and Engineering, Meghnad Saha Institute of Technology, Kolkata, India
D. Alamelu	KGiSL Institute of Technology, Coimbatore, Tamil Nadu, India
Debasish Swapnesh Kumar Nayak	Department of Computer Science & Engineering, Institute of Technical Education and Research, Siksha 'O' Anusandhan Deemed to be University, Bhubaneswar, India
Das Jayashankar	Avior Genomics, Mumbai, India
Fahmina Taranum	Computer Science and Engineering Department, Muffakham Jah College of Engineering and Technology, Hyderabad, India
Gouri C. Khadabadi	Department of CSE, KLS Gogte Institute of Technolgy, Belagavi, India
Jyoti Prakash Mishra	Gandhi Institute for Education and Technology, Baniatangi, hubaneswar, Affiliated to BijuPatnaik University of Technology, Rourkela, Odisha, India
Jayashankar Das	Avior Genomics, Mumbai, India
K. Manimekalai	Department of Computer Applications, Sri GVG Visalakshi College for Women, Udumalpet, Tamil Nadu, India
K. Sridevi	Computer Science and Engineering Department, Muffakham Jah College of Engineering and Technology, Hyderabad, India
Manjunath Managuli	Department of ECE, KLS Gogte Institute of Technology, Belagavi, India
Nguyen Gia Nhu	Dean, Graduate School, Duy Tan University, Da Nang, Vietnam
N. Venugopal	Sri Krishna College of Technology, Coimbatore, Tamil Nadu, India
P.R. Anisha	Stanley College of Engineering and Technology for Women, Hyderabad, India
Pankaja S. Kadalgi	Department of CSE, KLS Gogte Institute of Technolgy, Belagavi, India
Sambit Kumar Mishra	Gandhi Institute for Education and Technology, Baniatangi, hubaneswar, Affiliated to BijuPatnaik University of Technology, Rourkela, Odisha, India
Sudha Slake	Department of CSE, KLS Gogte Institute of Technolgy, Belagavi, India
Subhash Mondal	Department of Computer Science and Engineering, Meghnad Saha Institute of Technology, Kolkata, India
Samrat Podder	Department of Computer Science and Engineering, Meghnad Saha Institute of Technology, Kolkata, India
Suharta Banerjee	Department of Computer Science and Engineering, Meghnad Saha Institute of Technology, Kolkata, India

Sugata Ghosh   Department of Computer Science and Engineering, Meghnad Saha Institute of Technology, Kolkata, India

T. Padmavati   Department of Marine Sciences, Berhampur University, Odisha, India

Tripti Swarnkar   Department of Computer Application, Institute of Technical Education and Research, Siksha 'O' Anusandhan Deemed to be University, Bhubaneswar, India

V. Kalaiarasi   PSG College of Arts and Science, Coimbatore, Tamil Nadu, India

Zdzislaw Polkowski   Department of Humanities and Social Sciences, The Karkonosze University of Applied Sciences in Jelenia Góra, Jelenia Góra, Poland

CHAPTER 1

A Comprehensive Study and Analysis on Prediction of Rainfall Across Multiple Countries using Machine Learning

C. Kishor Kumar Reddy[1,*], **P.R. Anisha**[1] and **Nguyen Gia Nhu**[2]

[1] *Stanley College of Engineering and Technology for Women, Hyderabad, India*

[2] *Dean, Graduate School, Duy Tan University, Da Nang, Vietnam*

Abstract: Rainfall is one of the most considerable natural occurrences, which is important for both human beings and living beings. Since the environment is changing and there is a huge change in weather, it is noted that the rainfall cycles are also varying and the earth's temperature is increasing day-by-day. The changes in weather conditions like humidity, pressure, wind speed, dew point and temperature affect the agriculture, industry, production, and construction and also lead to floods and landslides. Hence it is one of the important factors to be noted for human beings to keep track of the natural occurrences in order to survive. In order to overcome these issues, a system is required which is able to forecast and predict the rainfall using statistical techniques which is the most popular tool in modern technology. This paper provides a detailed survey and comparative analysis of various methodologies used in the prediction of rainfall over multiple countries. Comparison is made in terms of various performance measures: accuracy, precision, recall, RMSE, specificity, sensitivity, MAE, F-Measure, ROC and RAE. Further, the drawbacks with existing approaches applied so far in the prediction are discussed.

Keywords: Artificial Neural Networks, Classification Techniques, Decision Trees, Naïve Bayes, Rainfall, Random Forest, SVM.

INTRODUCTION

Weather forecasting has become one of the most serious problems in the world and many researchers, governments, industries, risk management communities and scientific communities are looking into this issue. Weather is a natural and climatic characteristic that affects the daily routine of human activities such as farming in agriculture, production, construction, generation of electricity, forest and many more factors. Weather forecasting is one of the most important factors

* **Corresponding author C. Kishor Kumar Reddy:** Stanley College of Engineering and Technology for Women, Hyderabad, India; E-mail: kishoar23@gmail.com.

Brojo Kishore Mishra (Ed.)
All rights reserved-© 2023 Bentham Science Publishers

because if the weather changes, then it may lead to natural calamities such as landslides, volcanoes, earthquakes, hurricanes, *in situ.*, which lead to a lot of loss to society. Therefore, it is suggested to have a proper approach for the prediction of rainfall with which we can take preventive measures for these natural calamities. This forecasting helps in supervising human activities such as agriculture, production, construction, tourism, and many more. This forecasting also helps disaster prevention agencies with proper predictions regarding the weather with which they can take corrective measures and make a decision in order to prevent society from natural calamities.

Weather forecasting has the highest impact on human life and activities. Changes in the weather are rapidly increasing, hence it is crucial to conduct research on weather prediction and provide precipitation data for the prediction of weather timely and give early warning to avoid natural disasters. Rainfall prediction is one of the most crucial areas in the field of weather forecasting. Rainfall is one of the essential occurrences within the climatic system, whose disordered nature has the highest impact on water resources, agricultural and biological systems. Hence rainfall prediction is important for agricultural farming, tourism, navigation, and sailing. The collection of data related to weather has become very easy and sorted and moreover meteorological data can also be collected due to innovation and research in the fields of science and technology. A large amount of meteorological data should be collected for weather forecasting and it is very difficult to attain good accuracy. Science and development have improved in the field of information technology and computers with which researchers are able to analyse large amounts of data using big data analytics, which have found hidden relationships using machine learning techniques.

Numerous natural disasters across the world are correlated to meteorological phenomena. In the most recent years, lots of machine intelligent learning techniques have been proposed to undertake, unlike issues in the world. In this paper, multiple intelligent learning models are discussed for precipitation forecasting across different parts of the earth. It is pragmatic that intelligent learning methods are able to make predictions with a smaller amount of error rate. An additional improvement in machine intelligent learning methods is computational performance, and it executes more rapidly with much lesser computer resources than methods based on differential equations that are presently used in operational centers. Henceforth, it is significant to consider intelligent machine learning models for precipitation forecasts in operational centres as a method to advance prediction quality and decrease computational costs. The utilization of machine intelligent learning methods coupled with meteorological science has encouraged scientists, academicians, and researchers to apply machine intelligent learning methods to classify and predict events in different climatic conditions.

Predictions can be made using several of methods such as machine learning techniques for classification and prediction, soft computing, and complex methodologies such as artificial neural networks (ANN). These are the most common techniques used for the prediction of weather. The functional correlation between data, and the correlation that is not known or difficult can be made using ANN's since they learn from examples and are based on self-adaptive mechanism. Problems that are complex can be solved using deep learning techniques. Deep learning refers to a series of several multilayers that are trained using unsupervised methodologies. Learning dense, valid and non-linear data using unsupervised methodologies results in knowledge development and we can be able to predict new data. The above methodology is used in the fields of natural language processing, bioinformatics, object recognition and computer vision. Deep learning has been promising for modelling time series data through methods such as Conditional RBM, Autoencoder, Restricted Boltzmann Machine (RBM), Recurrent neural networks, Convolution and pooling, and Hidden Markov Models. The main idea behind this paper is to present a wide survey of traditional statistical methodologies along with modern methodologies of Machine Learning in the prediction of rainfall accurately. Further, a comparison on rainfall predictions that used different approaches is made. Some reasonable solutions for predicting weather efficiently are also recommended.

RELEVANT WORK

Prediction of rainfall is a tedious work particularly when we expect accurate and exact values for predicting the rainfall. Rainfall prediction is trending research in the field of scientific research areas of technology and innovation in the modern world, since it has a large impact on the socio-economic life of human beings and all living beings.

Du *et al.* [1] researched and proposed deep belief networks methodology to be used in forecasting weather precipitation. A one year meteorological data is collected and used which is taken from Nanjing station. The author discussed the applications of big data processing methodologies in the field of meteorology for meteorological datasets. The proposed methodology is based on deep belief networks that develop a statistical model between precipitation characteristics and other meteorological information. Abhisheka *et al.* [2] conducted an experiment on the capability of ANN methodology by developing an efficient and consistent non-linear predictive model for analyzing weather. The authors have made comparison and assessed the performance of the model using diverse transfer functions, hidden layers, temperature of 365 days and neurons for maximal forecasting.

Sun *et al.* [3] researched on the feasible development of decadal predicting models for autumn rainfall (RA) in central Vietnam by using a published tree-ring reconstruction of October to November rainfall data obtained from the early wood width measurements. Harvey *et al.* [4] experimented on how the rainfall patterns relate with normal climatic conditions and the rate of occurrence of rainfall cycles. To assess the behaviour of rainfall, the authors have collected the data from certain regions of Brazil that frequently suffer from droughts. The authors have used theoretical rotational methodology that allows rotational components to be modelled unambiguously. The authors discovered that the cyclic parts are random rather than deterministic models.

Kuo and Sun [5] used an intervention model to experiment on typical 10 day stream forecast. The authors have experimented and synthesized the characteristics which influence the unusual situation originated by storms and rigorous diverse asymmetry in the climate near Tanshui river valley located in Taiwan. Chiew *et al.* [6] made an estimation on 6 rainwater surplus modelling methodologies to replicate every day, monthly and yearly streams in 8 irregular watershed areas. The authors have discovered that time series methodology is good and it efficiently evaluates the monthly and yearly yield inside the water resources of the watershed area.

Langu *et al.* [7] used time series methodology to spot the alterations in rainwater and the surplus design. The designs that were identified helped in identifying considerable alterations in rainwater timings. The authors applied statistical methodologies to inspect the alterations in rainwater and surplus designs which identify significant transformations in rainwater statistics. The authors researched and developed approaches for statistic modelling inside univariate cases, which is referred to as Univariate Box-Jenkins (UBJ) ARIMA modelling in early 1970s. Based on this approach, several scientists and researchers have developed many different methodologies *i.e.*, time series disintegration methodology, augmented smoothening methodology, vector ARIMA, and ARNAx, *etc.*

Carter and Elsner [8] accompanied the result commencing the characteristic investigation of decentralization of non-tropical rainstorm convectional rainwater on the isle of Puerto Rico. The authors have involved statistical methodologies in order to discover the capability to calculate rainwater in certain localities. Isle decentralization was applied to 15-year datasets. A data file that contains 3 years of exterior and rainwater data were used in this methodology for prediction. Exterior data is taken from the two first class locations and these were taken as input to partial adaptive categorization tree to predict the occurrence of intense rain on new data.

Al-Ansari and Baban [9] have anticipated a functional mathematical investigation for measuring rainwater in 3 meteorological locations in Jordan such as Amman aerodrome (central Jordan), Irbid (northern Jordan) and Mafraq (eastern Jordan). Conventional functional mathematics, power band analysis and ARIMA models were applied onto the variable annual measurement of rainfall from 3 locations. The outcome shows that the capable intervals in the sequence of 2.3-3.45, 2.5-3.4 and 2.44-4.1 years for Amman, Irbid and Mafraq locations correspondingly were achieved. A statistical methodology for every location was accustomed, organized, and checked analytically and at last, the ARIMA methodology was developed for each location with an assurance intermission of 95% and the methodology was able to predict the yearly rainwater digits for 5 years for Amman, Irbid and Mafraq meteorological locations.

Al-Ansari *et al.* [10] performed a statistical investigation on records of rainfall at 3 key meteorological locations in Jordan. The authors have applied certain approaches like ordinary statistics, harmonic and power band examination, and time series evaluation. At every location, an ARIMA methodology was developed with an assurance intermission of 95%. The model has shown the outcomes with reducing trends in predicting rainfall at all the stations. Ingsrisawang *et al.* [11] performed three statistical methods First-order Markov Chain, Logistic model, and Generalized Estimating Equation (GEE) in modelling rainwater forecasting in the eastern location of Thailand. 2 data files called Meteor and GPCM were gathered daily all throughout the years 2004 to 2008. GPCM dataset and Meteor dataset were combined in order to get GPCM+Meteor dataset. Using the Meteor data file, the First-order Markov Chain methodology was performed.

Seyed *et al.* [12] tuned the specifications of weather by applying arbitrary methodologies such as the ARIMA methodology. The author involved time series approach to tune the parameters of climate in Abadeh located in Iran and suggested ARIMA (0,0,1), (1,1,1) methodology is appropriate for monthly rainwater and ARIMA(2,1,0), (2,1,0) for average monthly temperature for Abadeh location. Mahsin *et al.* [13] applied Box-Jenkins method for the creation of a seasonal ARIMA model for monthly rainwater information that is taken from Dhaka station, located in Bangladesh. The data contains information from 1981 to 2010 *i.e.*, 30 years. In this paper, the ARIMA (0,0,1),(0,1,1) methodology was discovered to be satisfactory and can be applied for predicting monthly rainwater.

Neural networks are widely used for tuning a wide range of non-linear hydrological processes like forecasting the climate. The ASCE task board has shown few facts regarding the uses of ANNs in the geophysical science area [14]. Hu *et al.* [15] applied the idea of ANN for predicting the climate. This was the foremost effort made to put into operation the soft computing methodology in this area which led as a base for the latest facet in the climate allied research. French *et al.* [16] recommended two-dimensional model which forecasts rainfall 1 hour earlier. The author used ANN methodology which is essentially a mathematical methodology for predicting rainfall. The obtained end product of this model is further used as input for future forecasting. The first drawback of this model is that the contact interface and the training time are unbalanced. The second drawback of this model is the contrast between the input and output nodes, and the amount of concealed layers and concealed nodes that are not sufficient. These were needed in order to keep the higher order correlation for effectively evolving the methodology. With this model, the authors faced huge amount of issues, but this model was the primary effort made to use the ANN methodology on geophysical operations. Michaelides *et al.* [17] conducted an experiment to analyze the performance of the ANN model and determined it in opposition to multiple regressions. The authors worked on the Cyprus region where there was missing rainfall data and evaluated on that.

Kalogirou *et al.* [18] applied the ANN model using time series information in order to recreate the rainwater data for the Cyprus region. Adyaland Collopy [19] presented 11 strategies to evaluate the ANN model. The authors have applied their theoretical neural networks for commercial forecasting and prediction of rainfall. From 1988 to 1994, they administered 48 investigations. For each examination, the authors have evaluated the efficiency of the model in contrast with substitutes like the efficiency of validation. They also worked on the efficiency of performance of the model. In their investigation, they discovered that 11 studies were efficiently validated and applied, and other 11 investigations were efficiently justified and obtained affirmative outcomes. From these 22 investigations, better results were found using neural networks in 18 studies.

Pucheta *et al.* [20] developed a feed-forward neural network based NAR methodology for time series forecasting. The Levenberg-Marquardt methodology was implemented for examining rules to fine-tune the neural network weights. The methodology evaluated 5 time series that were acquired from the Mackey-Glass delay differential equation and from monthly growing rainwater. 3 sets of specifications were used for the Mackey-Glass equation. The monthly growing rainfall data is taken from two different locations and time slots. They are La Perla from 1962 to 1971 and Santa Francisca from 2000 to 2010 and these places are located in Cordoba, Argentina. This methodology predicts 18 values for each new time series data replicated by 500 Monte Carlo trials to denote the discrepancy using fractional Gaussian noise.

Adhikari and Agarwal [21] systematically investigated the stupendous ability of ANNs in identifying and forecasting tough seasonal patterns without deleting them from the unprocessed data. Six real world time series data along with prevailing seasonal variations were applied in this work. Practical results showed outstanding efficiency in forecasting tough seasonal fluctuations if the ANN is designed perfectly and the three statistical models for the six time series data were found to be performing well.

Nanda *et al.* [22] experimented on several ANN models, along with Functional link ANN (FLANN), Legendre Polynomial Equation (LPE), and Multi Layer Perceptron (MLP). After experimenting on these models MLP, FLANN, and LPE, they found that these three models were performing outstandingly for the time series data. The authors suggested ARIMA method along with the ANN methodology. A performance examination was made using MATLAB and was approved by the use of the information gathered from Indian meteorological sector from June to September in the year 2012. The authors stated that the FLANN methodology forecasting improved in contrast to ARIMA with very small Absolute average percentage error (AAPE). Sethi *et al.* [23] brought up a Multi linear regression (MLR) model for predicting the rainwater. The authors have applied empirical statistical methodology on the 30 years of weather data such as temperature, cloud coverage, vapour pressure, and precipitation from Udaipur city, Rajasthan India. The authors conducted an experiment on the prediction accuracy of rainfall data. They recognized the features of MLR and made a contrast prediction with the concrete data. The authors analyzed the data and showed them in graphs so as to confirm that their model is performing better and be able to obtain the values that are nearer to concrete data. Prasad and Neeraj [24] conducted an investigation on the prediction of weather by applying 9 years' information collected from Basara city. The authors used different techniques of data mining like association rule mining, classification, aggregation and outlier analysis for prediction of weather.

Helen *et al.* [25] developed one of the best models for accurate rainfall prediction in the south western Nigeria. The authors developed neural network and fuzzy logic models for prediction. They applied mean squared error, root mean squared error, mean absolute error and accuracy metrics onto these two models for checking their performance. The neural network model performed better with an accuracy of 77.17% than the fuzzy logic model having 68.92% of accuracy. Manandhar *et al.* [26] recommended an organized methodology for analyzing various specifications that influence precipitation in the environment. Diverse ground-based climatic characteristics such as temperature, humidity, dew point, solar radiation, PWV, seasonal variables and diurnal variables were recognized and a comprehensive characteristic relational study is presented. For rainfall classification, all the climatic characteristics play a key role, but for rainfall prediction, only a few features such as PWV, solar radiation, seasonal and diurnal features play a significant role. On the basis of these, a set of finest characteristics were used in machine learning algorithm for prediction of rainfall. The authors have experimented on 4-year data from 2012 to 2015 and found that the model is able to correctly evaluate 80.4% data and incorrect predictions were found to be 20.3% and the accuracy was found to be 79.6 %. In contrast with the existing relevant work, this methodology outperforms by reducing incorrect predictions.

Manandhar *et al.* [27] recommended a comprehensive study on PWV values of rainfall using a simple and efficient algorithm for prediction of the beginning of the rainfall in the tropical region. The authors implemented the recommended algorithm on a seasonal dependent PWV threshold value that is enhanced by taking into account the time of the day when most of the rainfall occurs in diverse seasons and an SD threshold is used to predict the beginning of the rainfall in the next 5 minutes using the information from past 30 minutes in a tropical region. The data is collected from Singapore, NTUS GPS station and the algorithm is developed from this data. The authors have experimented on the NTUS data and found that the model has 87.7% evaluation accuracy and incorrect predictions were found to be 38.6%. The authors also collected the data from two more tropical stations SNUS and SALU and applied this algorithm to this data individually. They found that the algorithm performed well and gave good accuracy based on these data. Hence the derived algorithm presents that the PWV and SD are good features for forecasting the rainfall.

Agboola *et al.* [28] evaluated the performance of fuzzy rules/logic for modelling rainfall in the south western Nigeria. The fuzzy logic model is derived from two efficient components; one is the knowledge base and the other is fuzzy reasoning or decision making unit. The operations that were carried out on the fuzzy logic model are fuzzification and defuzzification. The predicted results were compared with the original rainfall data. Simulation results were found to be good for prediction and were in good agreement with the measured data. Performance metrics like accuracy, root mean squared error, mean absolute error, and prediction error were calculated on the model and it was found that the fuzzy logic methodology was effective and efficient for handling scattered data. The fuzzy logic model was found to be flexible and capable of modelling irregular relationship between input and output variables.

David Saur [29] aimed to fetch large data on numerical models that have the highest accuracy for convective forecasting of precipitation that is based on the examination of 30 situations in the year 2014. These predictions can be helpful when there is a situation of crisis in the Zlin region in unusual natural calamities. Urmay Shah *et al.* [30] predicted the rainfall using a mixture of diverse machine learning and forecasting algorithms. Rainfall is dependent on many specifications, but we could get good classification accuracy using certain amount of specifications only. The authors classified the rainfall into eight different parts, and discovered that the accuracy was outstanding. Validation was made on the forecasted specifications using the RMSE measure. The authors conducted research on various algorithms and found that the results of ARIMA model for maximal temperature, of Neural network for minimal temperature and of SVR for humidity and wind speed were better. Using the performance metrics like accuracy, precision and recall, the validation is made on the classification model. ROC curve is drawn for all the classifiers and Random forest classifier outperforms in classifying rainfall.

Razeef Mohd *et al.* [31] made a comparative analysis on most popular data mining methodologies for prediction of rainfall. The climatic data was collected from Srinagar, J&K, India. The authors compared the performance metrics such as recall, F-measure score, ROC and accuracy of different algorithms and found that the Random forest algorithm outperformed with an accuracy of 87.76% with the highest values of performance metrics.

Anochi *et al.* [43] showed the capability of neural networks for seasonal precipitation forecasting over South America. In this research, a large dataset from 1980 to 2016 was used for training the neural network model and testing was performed on 2018 and 2019. Chalachew *et al.* [44] proposed a study to classify the applicable atmospheric features that cause rainfall and predict the intensity of daily rainfall using machine learning techniques. The Pearson correlation technique was used to select relevant environmental variables which were used as an input for the machine learning model. The dataset was collected from the local meteorological office at Bahir Dar City, Ethiopia to measure the performance of three machine learning techniques (Multivariate Linear Regression, Random Forest, and Extreme Gradient Boost). Root mean squared error and Mean absolute Error methods were used to measure the performance of the machine learning model. The result of the study revealed that the Extreme Gradient Boosting machine learning algorithm performed better than others.

DISCUSSION

Classification accuracy is the ratio of the total number of true predictions to the sum of true and false predictions. Accuracy is a performance metric which is inapt for unfair categorization issues. The devastating figures of instances from the mainstream classes will devastate the figures of instances in the low stream class, which determines that amateur methodologies may also achieve an accuracy of 90% to 99% which depends on how rigorous is the class unevenness.

The proportional investigation of the accuracy is shown in equation 1 on diverse methodologies from India that are shown in Table (**1**). Graphical representation is shown in Fig. (**1**). Multiple locations are shown in Table (**2**) and their graphical representation is shown in Fig. (**2**), with the details such as location, data collection period, proposed methodology, accuracy in % and the year of proposal of model. In Table (**1**), the outcomes evidently show that Intensified Long short term memory (ILSTM) proposed by [39] yields an accuracy of 88%, Random forest proposed by [31], yields an accuracy of 87.76%, and Support vector machine (SVM) proposed by [26], yields an accuracy of 87.7%, that are better for large amounts of data when compared to other algorithms. In Table (**2**), the column location gives the details regarding which countries data is used for predictions. The outcomes show that CART model proposed by [35] yields an accuracy of 84.62%. Considering Tables (**1** & **2**), it can be stated that the accuracy depends on the data and the period of data considered.

$$Accuracy = (TP+TN)/(TP+TN+FP+FN) \qquad\qquad (1)$$

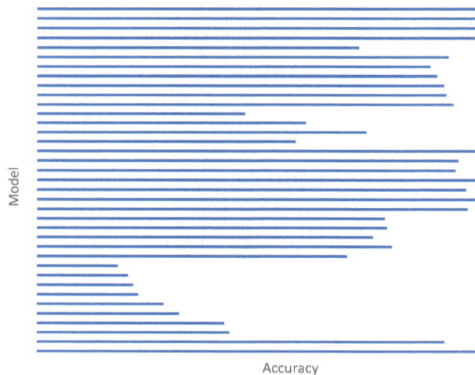

Fig. (1). Accuracy performance measure of various models over India.

Fig. (2). Accuracy performance measure of various models over multiple locations.

Table 1. Accuracy Performance Measure Of Various Models Over India.

S.No	Authors	Location	Period	Model	Accuracy	Year
1	Shilpa Manandhar *et al.* [26]	India	2012-15	SVM	87.70	2019
2	Shilpa Manandhar *et al.* [27]	India	2012-15	SVM	80.40	2018
3	David Šaur [29]	India	2014	MM5	38.00	2015
4	David Šaur [29]	India	2014	ALADIN CR	37.00	2015
5	David Šaur [29]	India	2014	ALADIN SR	28.00	2015
6	David Šaur [29]	India	2014	EURO4	25.00	2015
7	David Šaur [29]	India	2014	RHMC	20.00	2015
8	David Šaur [29]	India	2014	NAVGEM	19.00	2015
9	David Šaur [29]	India	2014	GFS	18.00	2015
10	David Šaur [29]	India	2014	COAMPS	16.00	2015
11	Urmay Shah *et al.* [30]	India	1979-2014	Decision Tree	61.21	2018
12	Urmay Shah *et al.* [30]	India	1979-2014	Random Forest	70.09	2018
13	Urmay Shah *et al.* [30]	India	1979-2014	KNN	66.35	2018
14	Urmay Shah *et al.* [30]	India	1979-2014	SVM	69.15	2018
15	Urmay Shah *et al.* [30]	India	1979-2014	Neural Network	68.69	2018
16	Razeef Mohd *et al.* [31]	India	2015-16	Naïve Bayes	85.01	2018

(Table 1) cont.....

S.No	Authors	Location	Period	Model	Accuracy	Year
17	Razeef Mohd *et al.* [31]	India	2015-16	Simple Logistic	87.15	2018
18	Razeef Mohd *et al.* [31]	India	2015-16	IBK	84.70	2018
19	Razeef Mohd *et al.* [31]	India	2015-16	Bagging	86.85	2018
20	Razeef Mohd *et al.* [31]	India	2015-16	PART	82.56	2018
21	Razeef Mohd *et al.* [31]	India	2015-16	J48	83.18	2018
22	Razeef Mohd *et al.* [31]	India	2015-16	Random Forest	87.76	2018
23	Essays [32]	India	1901-2013	SVM	51.00	2018
24	Essays [32]	India	1901-2013	Random Forest	65.00	2018
25	Essays [32]	India	1901-2013	Naïve Bayes	53.00	2018
26	Essays [32]	India	1901-2013	Multilayer Perceptron	41.00	2018
27	Gupta *et al.* [34]	India	1996-2014	Neural Network	82.10	2015
28	Gupta *et al.* [34]	India	1996-2014	KNN	80.70	2015
29	Gupta *et al.* [34]	India	1996-2014	CART	80.30	2015
30	Gupta *et al.* [34]	India	1996-2014	Naïve Bayes	78.90	2015
31	Poornima *et al.* [39]	India	1980-2014	Holt-Winters	77.55	2019
32	Poornima *et al.* [39]	India	1980-2014	ARIMA	81.15	2019
33	Poornima *et al.* [39]	India	1980-2014	ELM	63.51	2019
34	Poornima *et al.* [39]	India	1980-2014	RNN with Relu	86.44	2019
35	Poornima *et al.* [39]	India	1980-2014	RNN with Silu	86.91	2019
36	Poornima *et al.* [39]	India	1980-2014	LSTM	87.01	2019
37	Poornima *et al.* [39]	India	1980-2014	ILSTM	88.00	2019

Classification accuracy is extensively used as a performance metric.

Table 2. accuracy performance measure of various models over multiple locations.

S.No	Authors	Country	Period	Model	Accuracy	Year
1	Helen *et al.* [25]	Nigeria	2007-10	Neural network	77.17	2016
2	Agboola A.H *et al.* [28]	Nigeria	2007-10	Fuzzy Logic	68.92	2013
3	Agboola *et al.* [28]	Nigeria	-	Fuzzy Inference System	68.92	2013
4	Nabila *et al.* [35]	Malaysia	2009-16	CHAID	82.69	2018
5	Nabila *et al.* [35]	Malaysia	2009-16	CART	84.62	2018
6	Nabila *et al.* [35]	Malaysia	2009-16	ANN	83.83	2018
7	Nabila *et al.* [35]	Malaysia	2009-16	Naïve Bayes	81.78	2018
8	Pedro *et al.* [38]	Portugal	2011-15	NARX	71.9	2019

(Table 2) cont.....

S.No	Authors	Country	Period	Model	Accuracy	Year
9	Chibuzo *et al.* [40]	Nigeria	2015	NCEP-GFS	55	2017
10	Chibuzo *et al.* [40]	Nigeria	2015	ECMWF	69	2017
11	Chibuzo *et al.* [40]	Nigeria	2015	UKMET	55	2017
12	Chibuzo *et al.* [40]	Nigeria	2015	WRF	69	2017
13	Ricardo *et al.* [41]	Canary	1976-2016	Logistic Model Trees	75	2019
14	Ricardo *et al.* [41]	Canary	1976-2016	Linear Discriminant Analysis	65	2019
15	Ricardo *et al.* [41]	Canary	1976-2016	Generalized Linear Model	64	2019
16	Ricardo *et al.* [41]	Canary	1976-2016	SVM	73	2019
17	Ricardo *et al.* [41]	Canary	1976-2016	Random Forest	77	2019
18	Ricardo *et al.* [41]	Canary	1976-2016	Stochastic Gradient Boosting	76	2019
19	Ricardo *et al.* [41]	Canary	1976-2016	Extreme Gradient Boosting	77	2019

Precision, shown in equation 2, is the ratio of total number of true positives to the sum of true positives and false positives. The proportional investigation of the precision on diverse models across multiple locations is shown in Table (**3**) and graphical representation is shown in Fig. (**3**), which contains the details such as the location, data period, proposed methodology, precision in % and the year of proposal of the model. The outcomes show that Random forest model yields a precision of 87.4% and is found to be the best algorithm compared to other algorithms.

$$Precision = TP/(TP+FP) \qquad\qquad (2)$$

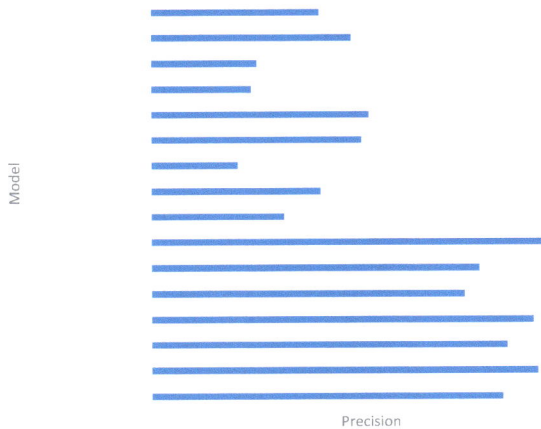

Fig. (3). Precision performance measure of various models over multiple locations.

Table 3. Precision performance measure of various models over multiple locations.

S.No	Authors	Location	Period	Model	Precision	Year
1	Razeef Mohd *et al.* [31]	India	2015-16	Naïve Bayes	84.1	2018
2	Razeef Mohd *et al.* [31]	India	2015-16	Simple Logistic	86.5	2018
3	Razeef Mohd *et al.* [31]	India	2015-16	IBK	84.4	2018
4	Razeef Mohd *et al.* [31]	India	2015-16	Bagging	86.2	2018
5	Razeef Mohd *et al.* [31]	India	2015-16	PART	81.5	2018
6	Razeef Mohd *et al.* [31]	India	2015-16	J48	82.5	2018
7	Razeef Mohd *et al.* [31]	India	2015-16	Random Forest	87.4	2018
8	Urmay Shah *et al.* [30]	India	1979-2014	KNN	69.1	2018
9	Urmay Shah *et al.* [30]	India	1979-2014	Tree	71.6	2018
10	Urmay Shah *et al.* [30]	India	1979-2014	SVM	65.9	2018
11	Urmay Shah *et al.* [30]	India	1979-2014	Random Forest	74.4	2018
12	Suhaila Zainudin *et al.* [33]	Malaysia	2010-14	Decision Trees	74.9	2016
13	Suhaila Zainudin *et al.* [33]	Malaysia	2010-14	Naïve Bayes	66.8	2016
14	Suhaila Zainudin *et al.* [33]	Malaysia	2010-14	SVM	67.2	2016
15	Suhaila Zainudin *et al.* [33]	Malaysia	2010-14	Neural Network	73.7	2016
16	Suhaila Zainudin *et al.* [33]	Malaysia	2010-14	Random Forest	71.5	2016

Recall, shown in equation 3, is the ratio of total number of true positives to the sum of true positives and false negatives. The proportional investigation of the recall on diverse models across multiple locations is shown in Table (**4**) and graphical representation is shown in Fig. (**4**) which contains details such as the location, data period, proposed methodology, recall in % and the year of proposal of the model. The outcomes show that the Random forest yields a recall of 87.8% and is found to be the best algorithm compared to other algorithms.

$$Recall=TP/(TP+FN) \qquad\qquad (3)$$

Table 4. recall performance measure of various models over multiple locations.

S.No	Authors	Location	Period	Model	Recall	Year
1	Razeef Mohd *et al.* [31]	India	2015-16	Naïve Bayes	85.00	2018
2	Razeef Mohd *et al.* [31]	India	2015-16	Simple Logistic	87.20	2018
3	Razeef Mohd *et al.* [31]	India	2015-16	IBK	84.70	2018
4	Razeef Mohd *et al.* [31]	India	2015-16	Bagging	86.90	2018
5	Razeef Mohd *et al.* [31]	India	2015-16	PART	82.60	2018

(Table 4) cont.....

S.No	Authors	Location	Period	Model	Recall	Year
6	Razeef Mohd *et al.* [31]	India	2015-16	J48	83.20	2018
7	Razeef Mohd *et al.* [31]	India	2015-16	Random Forest	87.80	2018
8	Urmay Shah *et al.* [30]	India	1979-2014	KNN	72.1	2018
9	Urmay Shah *et al.* [30]	India	1979-2014	Tree	72.1	2018
10	Urmay Shah *et al.* [30]	India	1979-2014	SVM	53.9	2018
11	Urmay Shah *et al.* [30]	India	1979-2014	Random Forest	76.0	2018
12	Suhaila Zainudin *et al.* [33]	Malaysia	2010-14	Decision Trees	72.9	2016
13	Suhaila Zainudin *et al.* [33]	Malaysia	2010-14	Naïve Bayes	71.1	2016
14	Suhaila Zainudin *et al.* [33]	Malaysia	2010-14	SVM	71.9	2016
15	Suhaila Zainudin *et al.* [33]	Malaysia	2010-14	Neural Network	74.7	2016
16	Suhaila Zainudin *et al.* [33]	Malaysia	2010-14	Random Forest	73.8	2016
17	Nabila *et al.* [35]	Malaysia	2009-16	CHAID	56.00	2018
18	Nabila *et al.* [35]	Malaysia	2009-16	CART	58.00	2018
19	Nabila *et al.* [35]	Malaysia	2009-16	ANN	51.00	2018
20	Nabila *et al.* [35]	Malaysia	2009-16	Naïve Bayes	46.00	2018

Fig. (4). Recall performance measure of various models over multiple locations.

F-measure, shown in equation 4, is a score obtained by merging precision and recall into a single metric that encapsulates both the properties. Neither precision nor recall alone can show the performance of the model. It can be seen that either precision or recall is good, but both might not be good . Hence, F-measure is used which presents both properties within a single score. If the precision and recall are calculated for binary or multiclass classification, then the two scores can be combined in order to calculate F-measure. The proportional investigation of the F-measure on diverse models across multiple locations is shown in Table (**5**) and graphical representation is shown in Fig. (**5**) which contains details such as the location, data period, proposed methodology, F-measure in % and the year of proposal of the model. The outcomes show that the Random forest yields the F-measure of 87.5% and is found to be the best algorithm compared to other algorithms.

$$\text{F-Measure} = (2 * \text{Precision} * \text{Recall}) / (\text{Precision} + \text{Recall}) \qquad \textbf{(4)}$$

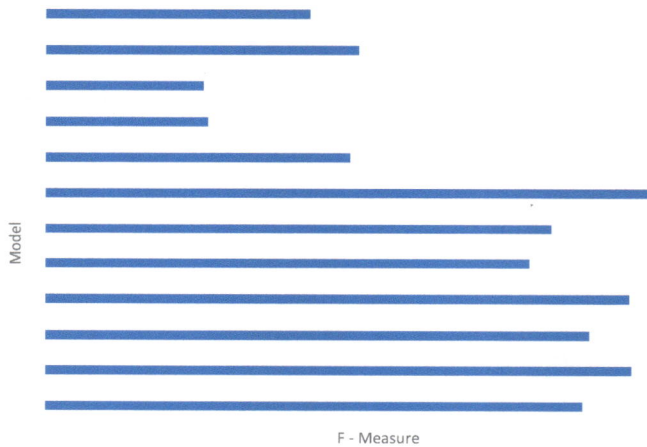

Fig. (5). F-Measure comparison of various models over multiple locations.

Table 5. F-Measure performance measure of various models over multiple locations.

S.No	Authors	Location	Period	Model	F- Measure	Year
1	Razeef Mohd *et al.* [31]	India	2015-16	Naïve Bayes	84.2	2018
2	Razeef Mohd *et al.* [31]	India	2015-16	Simple Logistic	86.4	2018
3	Razeef Mohd *et al.* [31]	India	2015-16	IBK	84.5	2018
4	Razeef Mohd *et al.* [31]	India	2015-16	Bagging	86.3	2018
5	Razeef Mohd *et al.* [31]	India	2015-16	PART	81.8	2018
6	Razeef Mohd *et al.* [31]	India	2015-16	J48	82.8	2018

(Table 5) cont.....

S.No	Authors	Location	Period	Model	F- Measure	Year
7	Razeef Mohd *et al.* [31]	India	2015-16	Random Forest	87.5	2018
8	Suhaila Zainudin *et al.* [33]	Malaysia	2010-14	Decision Trees	73.7	2016
9	Suhaila Zainudin *et al.* [33]	Malaysia	2010-14	Naïve Bayes	67.3	2016
10	Suhaila Zainudin *et al.* [33]	Malaysia	2010-14	SVM	67.1	2016
11	Suhaila Zainudin *et al.* [33]	Malaysia	2010-14	Neural Network	74.1	2016
12	Suhaila Zainudin *et al.* [33]	Malaysia	2010-14	Random Forest	71.9	2016

Mean absolute error (MAE), shown in equation 5, calculates the standard magnitude of the errors found in a set of predictions without taking their direction. It is the average across the test set of absolute difference between predicted and actual results where each and every individual difference has an equal weight. The proportional investigation of the MAE on diverse models across multiple locations is shown in Table (**6**) and graphical representation is shown in Fig. (**6**) which contains details such as the location, data period, proposed methodology, MAE in % and the year of proposal of the model. The outcomes show that the Meyer Wavelet + SANN model yields less MAE of 0.09% and is found to be the best algorithm compared to other algorithms since it has less MAE.

$$MAE = \text{True values} - \text{Predicted values} \qquad \textbf{(5)}$$

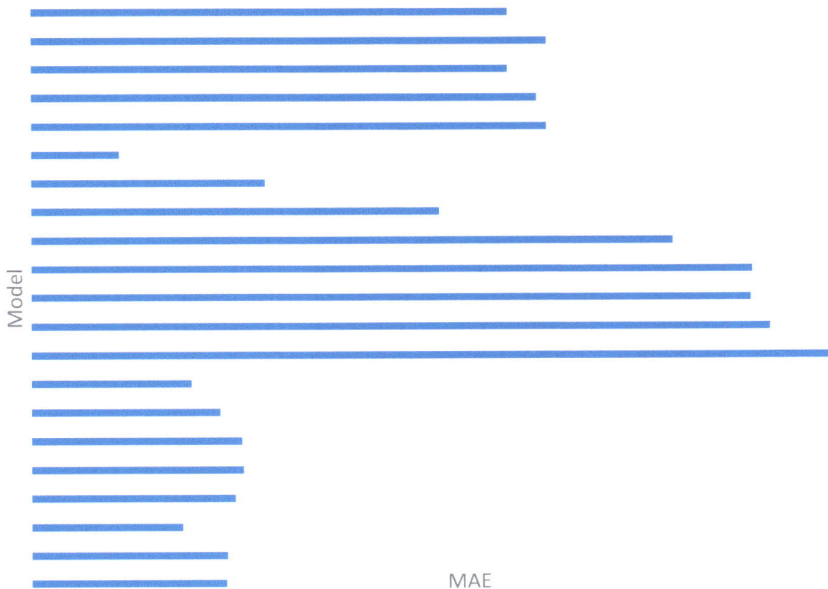

Fig. (6). MAE performance measure of various models over multiple locations.

Table 6. Mae Performance Measure Of Various Models Over Multiple Locations.

S.No	Authors	Location	Period	Model	MAE	Year
1	Razeef Mohd *et al.* [31]	India	2015-16	Naïve Bayes	0.2002	2018
2	Razeef Mohd *et al.* [31]	India	2015-16	Simple Logistic	0.201	2018
3	Razeef Mohd *et al.* [31]	India	2015-16	IBK	0.1552	2018
4	Razeef Mohd *et al.* [31]	India	2015-16	Bagging	0.2094	2018
5	Razeef Mohd *et al.* [31]	India	2015-16	PART	0.2175	2018
6	Razeef Mohd *et al.* [31]	India	2015-16	J48	0.2161	2018
7	Razeef Mohd *et al.* [31]	India	2015-16	Random Forest	0.1938	2018
8	Agboola A.H [28]	Nigeria	2007-10	Fuzzy Logic	0.164	2013
9	Duong *et al.* [36]	Vietnam	1971-2010	ARIMA	0.83	2019
10	Duong *et al.* [36]	Vietnam	1971-2010	GA-SA	0.76	2019
11	Duong *et al.* [36]	Vietnam	1971-2010	ANN	0.7405	2019
12	Duong *et al.* [36]	Vietnam	1971-2010	SANN	0.7422	2019
13	Duong *et al.* [36]	Vietnam	1971-2010	SD+ANN	0.66	2019
14	Duong *et al.* [36]	Vietnam	1971-2010	SD+SANN	0.42	2019
15	Duong *et al.* [36]	Vietnam	1971-2010	Meyer Wavelet + ANN	0.24	2019
16	Duong *et al.* [36]	Vietnam	1971-2010	Meyer Wavelet + SANN	0.09	2019
17	Mohit [42]	India	1961-2010	MLR	0.53	2012
18	Mohit [42]	India	1961-2010	ARIMA	0.52	2012
19	Mohit [42]	India	1961-2010	ANN	0.49	2012
20	Mohit [42]	India	1961-2010	MLR_ARIMA	0.53	2012
21	Mohit [42]	India	1961-2010	MLR_ANN	0.49	2012

Root mean square error (RMSE) is a quadratic scoring rule which calculates the average magnitude of the errors. It is the square root of the average of squared differences between predicted and actual results. The proportional investigation of the RMSE on diverse models across India is shown in Table (**7**) and graphical representation is shown in Fig. (**7**) which contains details such as the location, data period, proposed methodology, RMSE in % and the year of proposal of the model. The outcomes show that the ARIMA model proposed by [30] yields less RMSE value of 0.0345% and is found to be the best algorithm compared to other algorithms. The proportional investigation of the RMSE on diverse models across multiple locations is shown in Table (**8**) and graphical representation is shown in Fig. (**8**) which contains details such as the location, data period, proposed methodology, RMSE in % and the year of proposal of the model. The outcomes show that the Meyer Wavelet + SANN proposed by [36] yields less RMSE value of 0.12% and is found to be the best algorithm compared to other algorithms.

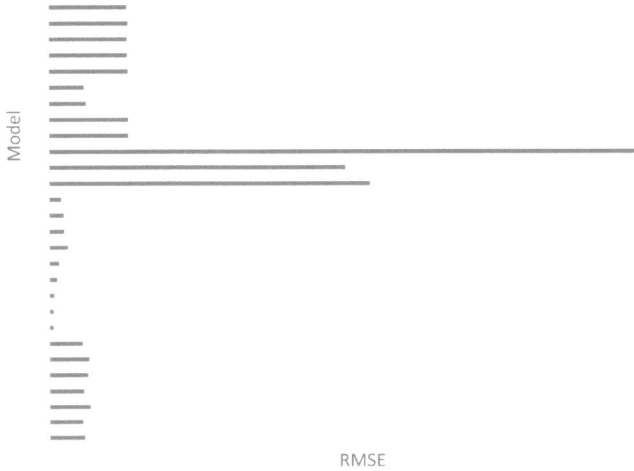

Fig. (7). RMSE performance measure of various models over India.

Table 7. RMSE performance measure of various models over multiple India.

S.No	Authors	Location	Period	Model	RMSE	Year
1	Razeef Mohd *et al.* [31]	India	2015-16	Naïve Bayes	0.3353	2018
2	Razeef Mohd *et al.* [31]	India	2015-16	Simple Logistic	0.3151	2018
3	Razeef Mohd *et al.* [31]	India	2015-16	IBK	0.3897	2018
4	Razeef Mohd *et al.* [31]	India	2015-16	Bagging	0.325	2018
5	Razeef Mohd *et al.* [31]	India	2015-16	PART	0.3705	2018
6	Razeef Mohd *et al.* [31]	India	2015-16	J48	0.3811	2018
7	Razeef Mohd *et al.* [31]	India	2015-16	Random Forest	0.3138	2018
8	Urmay Shah *et al.* [30]	India	1979-2014	ARIMA	0.0345	2018
9	Urmay Shah *et al.* [30]	India	1979-2014	TBATS	0.0353	2018
10	Urmay Shah *et al.* [30]	India	1979-2014	Naïve Method	0.0433	2018
11	Urmay Shah *et al.* [30]	India	1979-2014	Moving Avg.	0.0693	2018
12	Urmay Shah *et al.* [30]	India	1979-2014	Neural Network	0.0866	2018
13	Urmay Shah *et al.* [30]	India	1979-2014	Holt Winters Additive	0.1747	2018

(Table 7) cont.....

14	Urmay Shah *et al.* [30]	India	1979-2014	Holt Winters Multiplicative	0.1357	2018
15	Urmay Shah *et al.* [30]	India	1979-2014	Linear Regression	0.1345	2018
16	Urmay Shah *et al.* [30]	India	1979-2014	SVM	0.1116	2018
17	Poornima *et al.* [39]	India	1980-2014	Holt-Winters	3.08	2019
18	Poornima *et al.* [39]	India	1980-2014	ARIMA	2.84	2019
19	Poornima *et al.* [39]	India	1980-2014	ELM	5.68	2019
20	Poornima *et al.* [39]	India	1980-2014	RNN with Relu	0.76	2019
21	Poornima *et al.* [39]	India	1980-2014	RNN with Silu	0.76	2019
22	Poornima *et al.* [39]	India	1980-2014	LSTM	0.35	2019
23	Poornima *et al.* [39]	India	1980-2014	ILSTM	0.33	2019
24	Mohit [42]	India	1961-2010	MLR	0.7558	2012
25	Mohit [42]	India	1961-2010	ARIMA	0.749	2012
26	Mohit [42]	India	1961-2010	ANN	0.7474	2012
27	Mohit [42]	India	1961-2010	MLR_ARIMA	0.755	2012
28	Mohit [42]	India	1961-2010	MLR_ANN	0.7434	2012

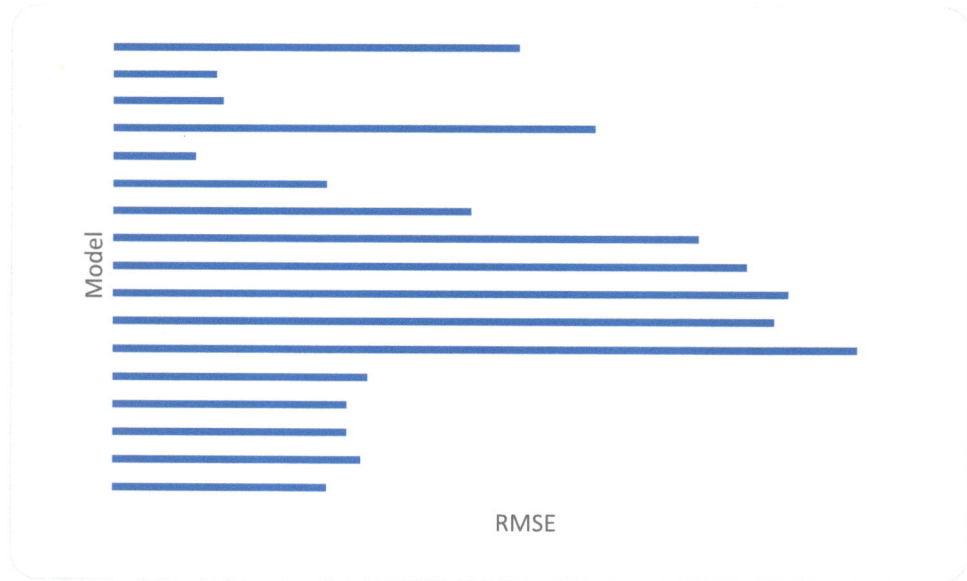

Fig. (8). RMSE performance measure of various models over multiple locations.

Table 8. RMSE performance measure of various models over multiple locations.

S.No	Authors	Location	Period	Model	RMSE	Year
1	Agboola A.H [28]	Nigeria	2007-10	Fuzzy Logic	0.3107	2013
2	Nabila *et al.* [35]	Malaysia	2009-16	CHAID	0.36	2018
3	Nabila *et al.* [35]	Malaysia	2009-16	CART	0.34	2018
4	Nabila *et al.* [35]	Malaysia	2009-16	ANN	0.34	2018
5	Nabila *et al.* [35]	Malaysia	2009-16	Naïve Bayes	0.37	2018
6	Duong *et al.* [36]	Vietnam	1971-2010	ARIMA	1.0807	2019
7	Duong *et al.* [36]	Vietnam	1971-2010	GA-SA	0.96	2019
8	Duong *et al.* [36]	Vietnam	1971-2010	ANN	0.98	2019
9	Duong *et al.* [36]	Vietnam	1971-2010	SANN	0.92	2019
10	Duong *et al.* [36]	Vietnam	1971-2010	SD+ANN	0.85	2019
11	Duong *et al.* [36]	Vietnam	1971-2010	SD+SANN	0.52	2019
12	Duong *et al.* [36]	Vietnam	1971-2010	Meyer Wavelet + ANN	0.31	2019
13	Duong *et al.* [36]	Vietnam	1971-2010	Meyer Wavelet + SANN	0.12	2019
14	Phanit Mab *et al.* [37]	Cambodia	1997-99	GIS vs GEE	0.7	2019
15	Phanit Mab *et al.* [37]	Cambodia	1997-99	GEE vs OBS	0.16	2019
16	Phanit Mab *et al.* [37]	Cambodia	1997-99	GIS vs OBS	0.15	2019
17	Pedro *et al.* [38]	Portugal	2011-15	NARX	0.589	2019

The proportional investigation of the Relative absolute error (RAE) on diverse models across India is shown in Table (**9**) and graphical representation is shown in Fig. (**9**) which contains details such as the location, data period, proposed methodology, RAE in % and the year of proposal of the model. The outcome shows that the IBK proposed by [31] yields less RAE of 45.51% and is found to be the best algorithm compared to other algorithms.

Table 9. RAE performance measure of various models over India.

S.No	Authors	Location	Period	Model	RAE	Year
1	Razeef Mohd *et al.* [31]	India	2015-16	Naïve Bayes	58.69	2018
2	Razeef Mohd *et al.* [31]	India	2015-16	Simple Logistic	58.92	2018
3	Razeef Mohd *et al.* [31]	India	2015-16	IBK	45.51	2018
4	Razeef Mohd *et al.* [31]	India	2015-16	Bagging	61.38	2018
5	Razeef Mohd *et al.* [31]	India	2015-16	PART	63.76	2018
6	Razeef Mohd *et al.* [31]	India	2015-16	J48	63.37	2018

(Table 9) cont.....

| 7 | Razeef Mohd *et al.* [31] | India | 2015-16 | Random Forest | 56.82 | 2018 |

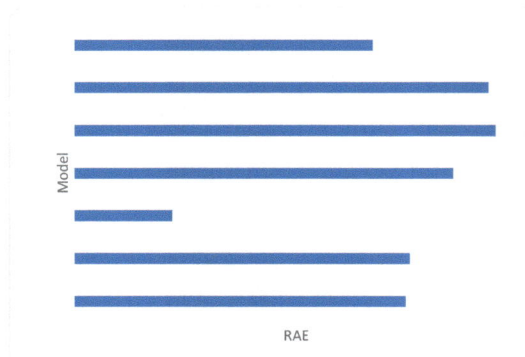

Fig. (9). RAE performance measure of various models over India.

Specificity, shown in equation 6, is defined as the ratio of actual negatives, which got predicted as the negative (or true negative). This implies that there will be another proportion of actual negative, which got predicted as positive and could be termed as false positives. This proportion could also be called a false positive rate. The sum of specificity and false positive rate would always be 1. The proportional investigation of the Specificity on diverse models across Malaysia is shown in Table (**10**) and graphical representation is shown in Fig. (**10**) which contains details such as the location, data period, proposed methodology, specificity in % and the year of proposal of model. The outcomes show that the CART proposed by [35] yields a specificity of 93.0% and is found to be the best algorithm compared to other algorithms.

$$\text{Specificity} = TN/(TN+FP) \tag{6}$$

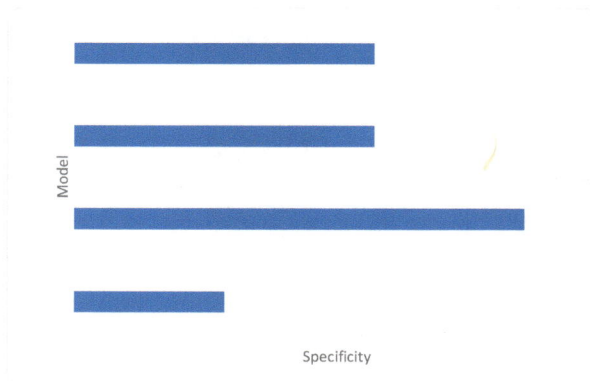

Fig. (10). Specificity performance measure of various models over Malaysia.

Table 10. specificity performance measure of various models over Malaysia.

S.No	Authors	Location	Period	Model	Specificity	Year
1	Nabila *et al.* [35]	Malaysia	2009-16	CHAID	91.00	2018
2	Nabila *et al.* [35]	Malaysia	2009-16	CART	93.00	2018
3	Nabila *et al.* [35]	Malaysia	2009-16	ANN	92.00	2018
4	Nabila *et al.* [35]	Malaysia	2009-16	Naïve Bayes	92.00	2018

From Tables (**1** to **10**) [26 - 28, 30 - 34, 39 - 41], it is observed that the decision trees are giving promising results in terms of various performance metrics such as Accuracy, Precision, Recall, F-Measure, MAE, RMSE, RAE, and Specificity. Though the decision trees are giving best performance results, it can be further improvised by introducing the concepts of splitting points, various attribute selection measures and also cascading with clustering mechanisms.

Table 11. notations used in the research.

S.No.	Notations	Explanation
1	TP	True Positives
2	TN	True Negatives
3	FP	False Positives
4	FN	False Negatives
5	RAE	Relative Absolute error
6	RMSE	Root Mean Square error

CONCLUSION

This chapter presents a detailed study on statistical techniques for prediction of rainfall and analysis of data. Based on the study made above, the subsequent problems are acknowledged as unconsidered:

1. The mentioned research works applied decision trees in the prediction of rainfall. Among all the models proposed so far, decision trees are giving more promising results. The accuracy of prediction can be improvised by cascading clustering mechanism with decision tree approaches.

2. Huge amounts of historical numerical rainfall data are available at meteorological departments that can be used for accurate predictions along with decision trees.

3. The mentioned research works used artificial neural networks most of the time,

but they have not concentrated on other methodologies such as genetic algorithm, swarm optimization and many more. These algorithms may also work better and give good results.

4. Accuracy is one of the most important metrics for analyzing the performance of the model. There is a concrete proof regarding precise forecasting.

5. Every part of the investigation is made for certain locations. The atmosphere, weather and environment are diverse for every area. The outcomes of one area can be used as a base for other areas.

6. Every method gives prediction for diverse cycles of instants. Therefore it is complicated to recognize which methodology is good for predicting rainwater.

7. The study is merely based on rainwater forecasting. Other natural calamities like rainfall surplus patterns, effects of weather change, tsunami, *etc.*, are not focused.

CONSENT FOR PUBLICATION

Not applicable.

CONFLICT OF INTEREST

The authors declare no conflict of interest, financial or otherwise.

ACKNOWLEDGEMENT

Declared none.

REFERENCES

[1]   J. Du, Y. Liu, and Z. Liu, *Study of Precipitation Forecast Based on Deep Belief Networks, Algorithms.* MDPI, 2018.

[2]   M.P. Kumar Abhisheka, *Singha, Saswata Ghoshb and Abhishek Anandc, Weather forecasting model using Artificial Neural Network.* Elsevier Procedia Technology, 2012.

[3]   Y. Sun, *Simon Wang, Rong Li, Brendan M.* Buckley, Robert Gillies and Kyle G. Hansen, Feasibility of Predicting Vietnam's Autumn Rainfall Regime Based on the Tree-Ring Record and Decadal Variability, Climate MDPI, 2018.

[4]   A.C. Harvey, R.C. Souza, and R.C. Souza, "Assessing and Modeling the Cyclical Behavior of Rainfall in Northeast Brazil", *J. Clim. Appl. Meteorol.*, vol. 26, no. 10, pp. 1339-1344, 1987.
        [http://dx.doi.org/10.1175/1520-0450(1987)026<1339:AAMTCB>2.0.CO;2]

[5]   J.T. Kuo, and Y.H. Sun, "An intervention model for average 10 day streamflow forecast and synthesis", *J. Hydrol. (Amst.),* vol. 151, no. 1, pp. 35-56, 1993.
        [http://dx.doi.org/10.1016/0022-1694(93)90247-7]

[6]   F.H.S. Chiew, M.J. Stewardson, and T.A. McMahon, "Comparison of six rainfall-runoff modelling approaches", *J. Hydrol. (Amst.),* vol. 147, no. 1-4, pp. 1-36, 1993.

[http://dx.doi.org/10.1016/0022-1694(93)90073-I]

[7]   E.M. Lungu, "Detection of changes in rainfall and runoff patterns", *J. Hydrol. (Amst.),* vol. 147, no. 1-4, pp. 153-167, 1993.
        [http://dx.doi.org/10.1016/0022-1694(93)90079-O]

[8]   M.M. Carter, and J.B. Elsner, "A Statistical Method for Forecasting Rainfall over Puerto Rico", *Weather Forecast.,* vol. 12, no. 3, pp. 515-525, 1997.
        [http://dx.doi.org/10.1175/1520-0434(1997)012<0515:ASMFFR>2.0.CO;2]

[9]   N.A. Al-Ansari, and S. Baban, "Rainfall Trends in the Badia Region of Jordan", *Surveying and Land Information Science,* vol. 65, no. 4, pp. 233-243, 2005.

[10]   N.A. Al-Ansari, B. Al-Shamali, and A. Shatnawi, "Statistical Analysis at Three Major Meteorological Stations, Jordan", *Al Manara Journal for Scientific Studies and Research,* vol. 12, pp. 93-120, 2006.

[11]   L. Ingsrisawang, S. Ingsriswang, P. Luenam, P. Trisaranuwatana, S. Klinpratoom, P. Aungsuratana, and W. Khantiyanan, "Applications of Statistical Methods for Rainfall Prediction over The Eastern Thailand", Proceedings of the International MultiConference of Engineers and Computer Scientists 2010, IMECS 2010. 2010. 2024-2027.

[12]   A. Seyed, M. Shamsnia, S. Naeem, and L. Ali, *International conference on Environment and Industrial innovation IPCBEE.,* 2011.

[13]   M.D. Mahsin, A. Yesmin, and B. Monira, "Modeling Rain in Dacca (National Capital) Division of Bangladesh Using Time Series Analysis", *Journal of Mathematical Modelling and Application,* vol. 1, no. 5, pp. 67-73, 2012.

[14]   "ASCE Task Committee on Application of Artificial Neural Networks in Hydrology", *J. Hydrol. Eng.,* vol. 5, no. 2, pp. 115-123, 2000.
        [http://dx.doi.org/10.1061/(ASCE)1084-0699(2000)5:2(115)]

[15]   Hu, M.J.C., Application of ADALINE System to Weather Forecasting, Technical Report, Master Thesis, Technical Report 6775-1, Stanford Electronic Laboratories, Stanford, United States, 1964.

[16]   French, M.N., Krajewski, W.F. & Cuykendall, R.R., Rainfall Forecasting in Space and Time Using Neural Network, Journal of Hydrology, 137(1), pp. 1-31, 1992.
        [http://dx.doi.org/10.1016/0022-1694(92)90046-X]

[17]   Michaelides, S.C., Neocleous, C.C. & Schizas, C.N., Artificial Neural Networks and Multiple Linear Regression in Estimating Missing Rainfall Data, Proceedings of the DSP95 International Conference on Digital Signal Processing, X. Limassol, Cyprus, pp. 668-673, 1992.

[18]   S.A. Kalogirou, C.C. Neocleous, and C.N. Schizas, "Artificial Neural Networks for the Estimation of the Performance of a Parabolic Trough Collector Steam Generation System", *Proceedings of the International Conference EANN'97,* pp. 227-232, 1997.Stockholm, Sweden

[19]   M. Adya, and F. Collopy, "How Effective are Neural Networks at Forecasting and Prediction?", *A Review and Evaluation, J. Forecast,* vol. 17, no. 5- 6, pp. 481-495, 1998.

[20]   J.A. Pucheta, C.M.R. Rivero, M.R. Herrera, H.D. Patiño, and B.R. Kuchen, "A Feed-Forward Neural Networks-Based Nonlinear Autoregressive Model for Forecasting Time Series", *Comput. Sist.,* vol. 14, no. 4, pp. 423-435, 2011.

[21]   R. Adhikari, and R.K. Agrawal, "Forecasting Strong Seasonal Time Series with Artificial Neural Network", *J. Sci. Ind. Res. (India),* vol. 71, no. 10, pp. 657-666, 2012.

[22]   S.K. Nanda, and D.P. Tripathy, "Nayak, S.K., & Mohapatra, S", *Prediction of Rainfall in India Using Artificial Intelligent Systems and Applications,* vol. 12, pp. 1-22, 2013.

[23]   N. Sethi, and K. Garg, "Exploiting Data Mining Technique for Rainfall Prediction", *Int. J. Comput. Sci. Inf. Technol.,* vol. 5, no. 3, pp. 3982-3984, 2014.

[24]   R.K. Prasad, and S.M. Nejres, "Use of Data Mining Techniques for Weather Data in Basra City", *Int.*

J. Adv. Res. Comput. Sci. Softw. Eng., vol. 5, no. 12, pp. 135-139, 2015.

[25]   A.A. Helen, A.O. Bolanle, and O. F. Samuel, "Comparative Analysis of Rainfall Prediction Models Using Neural Network and Fuzzy Logic, *Int. J. Soft. Comput. Eng.,* vol. 5, no. 6, pp. 4-7, 2016.

[26]   S. Manandhar, S. Dev, Y.H. Lee, Y.S. Meng, and S. Winkler, "A Data-Driven Approach for Accurate Rainfall Prediction", *IEEE Trans. Geosci. Remote Sens.,* vol. 57, no. 11, pp. 9323-9331, 2019.
       [http://dx.doi.org/10.1109/TGRS.2019.2926110]

[27]   S. Manandhar, Y.H. Lee, Y.S. Meng, F. Yuan, and J.T. Ong, "GPS-Derived PWV for Rainfall Nowcasting in Tropical Region", *IEEE Trans. Geosci. Remote Sens.,* vol. 56, no. 8, pp. 4835-4844, 2018.
       [http://dx.doi.org/10.1109/TGRS.2018.2839899]

[28]   A.H. Agboola, A.J. Gabriel, E.O. Aliyu, and B.K. Alese, "Development of a Fuzzy Logic Based Rainfall Prediction Model", *IACSIT Int. J. Eng. Technol.,* 2013.

[29]   D. Šaur, *Evaluation of the accuracy of numerical weather prediction models.* Springer Advances in Intelligent Systems and Computing, 2015.

[30]   U. Shah, N. Dube, S. Garg, S. Sharma, and R. Prediction, "Accuracy Enhancement Using Machine Learning and Forecasting Techniques", *5th IEEE International Conference on Parallel, Distributed and Grid Computing,* 2018 Solan, India.

[31]   Razeef Mohd, Muheet Ahmed Butt, and MajidZaman Baba, "Comparative Study of Rainfall Prediction Modeling Techniques (A Case Study on Srinagar, J&K, India)", *Asian Journal of Computer Science and Technology,* 2018.

[32]   U.K.   Essays,   *Rainfall   Prediction   Using   Machine   Learning   Algorithms.,*   2018.
       https://ukdiss.com/examples/rainfall-prediction-machine-learning.php?vref=1

[33]   S. Zainudin, D.S. Jasim, and A. Abu Bakar, "Comparative Analysis of Data Mining Techniques for Malaysian Rainfall Prediction", *Int. J. Adv. Sci. Eng. Inf. Technol.,* vol. 6, no. 6, p. 1148, 2016.
       [http://dx.doi.org/10.18517/ijaseit.6.6.1487]

[34]   D. Gupta and U. Ghose, A comparative study of classification algorithms for forecasting rainfall, 4th International Conference on Reliability, Infocom Technologies and Optimization (ICRITO) (Trends and Future Directions), 2015.

[35]   Nabila Wardah Zamani and Siti Shaliza Mohd Khairi , A Comparative Study on Data Mining Techniques for Rainfall Prediction in Subang, AIP Conference Proceedings, 2018.

[36]   D.T. Anh, T.D. Dang, S.P. Van. Improved Rainfall Prediction Using Combined Pre-Processing Methods and Feed-Forward Neural Networks. *J.,* vol. 2, no. 1, pp. 65-83, 2019.

[37]   P. Mab, S. Ly, C. Chompuchan, and E. Kositsakulchai, "Evaluation of Satellite Precipitation from Google Earth Engine in Tonle Sap Basin, Cambodia", *THA International Conference on Water Management and Climate Change towards Asia's Water-Energy-Food Nexus and SDGs,* 2019 Thailand.

[38]   P. Benevides, J. Catalao and G. Nico, Neural Network Approach to Forecast Hourly Intense Rainfall Using GNSS Precipitable Water Vapor and Meteorological Sensors. *Remote Sensing,* vol. 11, no. 8, p. 966, 2019.

[39]   S. Poornima, and M. Pushpalatha, Prediction of Rainfall Using Intensified LSTM Based Recurrent Neural Network with Weighted Linear Units. *Atmosphere,* vol. 10, no. 11, p. 668, 2019.
       [http://dx.doi.org/10.3390/atmos10110668]

[40]   N.C. Agogbuo, M.O. Nwagbara, E. Bekele and A. Olusegun, Evaluation of Selected Numerical Weather Prediction Models for a Case of Widespread Rainfall over Central and Southern Nigeria, *J. Environ. Anal. Toxicol.,* vol. 7, no. 4, pp. 1-9, 2017.

[41]   D. Castellanos-Nieves and M. Méndez, Comparative Analysis of Rainfall Prediction Models Using Machine Learning in Islands with Complex Orography: Tenerife Island. *Appl. Sci.* vol. 9, no. 22, p.

4931, 2019.

[42]   Mohit Anand Sharma, Comparative Study of Forecasting Models Based on Weather Parameters, PhD Thesis Shobhit University, 2012.

[43]   Juliana Aparecida Anochi, Vinicius Albuquerque de Almedia and Harlodo, Machine Learning for Climate Precipitation Prediction Modelling over South America", MDPI Remote Sensing, 2021.

[44]   Chalachew Muluken Liyew and Haileyesus, Machine Learning Techniques to Predict Daily Rainfall Amount, Springer Journal of Big Data, 2021.

CHAPTER 2

A Novel Approach for Clustering Large-scale Cloud Data using Computational Mechanism

Zdzislaw Polkowski[1], Jyoti Prakash Mishra[2] and **Sambit Kumar Mishra[2,*]**

[1] *Department of Humanities and Social Sciences, The Karkonosze University of Applied Sciences in Jelenia Góra, Jelenia Góra, Poland*

[2] *Gandhi Institute for Education and Technology, Baniatangi, Bhubaneswar, Affiliated to BijuPatnaik University of Technology, Rourkela, Odisha, India*

Abstract: In the present situation, with the enhancement of virtualization techniques, it is very essential to keep track of accumulated large-scaled heterogeneous data in every respect. In addition to that, it is also necessary to prioritize the processing mechanisms when being linked with clustered data. Sometimes it has been observed that the large scaled datasets are too complex and therefore, the normal computation mechanisms are not sufficient or adequate for the specific applications. But it is highly required to observe the significance of each individual dataset and focus on the responses being accumulated from other aspects to make a suitable decision and generation of efficient analytical clustered data. The main aim of such applications is to apply the clustering gaining merits from evolutionary computation to process the large-scaled data and based on optimality, the performance of datasets can be measured.

Keywords: Clustered data, Entity integrity, Heterogeneity, Query term, Resource prioritization.

INTRODUCTION

Nowadays, the complexities linked to the large scaled heterogeneous data in general have been increased due to somehow incorporating virtual machines. In fact, it is very difficult to analyze either the complexities or the processing abilities using normal mining mechanisms or computational methods. As the application of these clustered datasets is quite relevant to the extraction of meaningful information as well as making decisions, specific tools and computation mechanisms may be deployed which in return may be more computationally efficient and adaptive to the situation. Of course, the integrity of

* **Corresponding author Sambit Kumar Mishra:** Gandhi Institute for Education and Technology, Baniatangi, Bhubaneswar, affiliated to BijuPatnaik University of Technology, Rourkela, Odisha, India; E-mail: sambitmishra@giet.edu.in

data resembles complete accuracy along with its consistency. In a similar situation, the accumulation of processes can be maintained by having associated rules during the conceptualization stage. Also the suitable validation of data with check parameters can ensure the categorization of sensitive data while maintaining its integrity. Prioritizing both physical and logical integrity constrained, it has been observed that not only it will provide accuracy of data but also it will focus on unique parameters of data adopting entity integrity. Sometimes a group of similar processes intend to provide uniform storage with no provisioning commonalities. So, it is essential to adopt referential integrity rules to overcome the situation. Sometimes to preserve the accuracy, it is also required to prioritize the domain values and quantify the constraints. There are many mechanisms to search and obtain user-defined patterns as far as the large scaled data is concerned. In fact, specific classification mechanism can also be applied prioritizing the decomposition of fixed-length data. Somehow the primary purpose of this application is to obtain merits from evolutionary computation to process the large scaled data. Accordingly, the optimality linked to the datasets can be measured based on the performance.

REVIEW OF LITERATURE

Reiss *et al.* [1] in their work have focused on the criteria of cloud computing services specifically on scientific computations. They observed the importance of specific computations during the accumulation of resources from data centers.

Zhang *et al.* [2] in their work prioritized WSDF framework to observe the performance of transfer of data specifically linked with workflows on web services. Somehow it is provisioned with the involvement of data within services associated with web application. Also, it is associated with providing better performance with enhanced speed of transfer of data in the application.

Liu *et al.* [3] in their work have given more importance to clustered data and tried to obtain the machine response. Also they observed the performance of machines that have a storage capacity value of 0.5 In fact, the temporal locality of machine events is required to be considered in such situations.

Reiss *et al.* [4] in their work have discussed resource heterogeneity of the Google clusters. In fact, they observed considerable heterogeneity in different available resources along with resource allocation.

Yousif *et al.* [5] in their work have focused on clustered mechanisms linked to the cloud tasks which are intended to support the scheduler of the data center in the cloud. Probably this is directly linked to the replacement of virtual machines. In their work, they have prioritized k means as well as density-based clustering.

Reiss *et al.* [6] in their work tried to obtain the facts related to the utility of resources within the clusters and simultaneous requests on accompanying the tasks. In fact, the prediction of usage of resources during task execution can be judged with the actual usage of resources and probably the performance can be measured with not much difficulty. Accordingly, the authors tried to determine the actual implementation of tasks within the clusters.

Al-Dulaimy *et al.* [7] in their research focused on the enhancement of utilization of resources prioritizing the performance and minimizing the consumption of energy associated with data centers. In fact, the authors analyzed the large scaled tasks along with clustering.

Tayal *et al.* [8]. in their work focused on concepts of optimization linked to the scheduling of tasks toward cloud computing system using fuzzy genetic algorithms. They observed the appropriateness of the decision on scheduling of tasks during the entire process. In fact, these are quite modeled to imprecise scheduling parameters to attain the objectives.

Evangelinos *et al.* [9] in their research analyzed the implications associated with virtualized resources. As per their analysis, the performance achievement implied the complexities linked to specified applications on cloud resources. The enhancements in the process applications reflect mapping in the processors associated with clusters.

Raicu *et al.* [10] in their work prioritized the structure of managing data provisioned during the implementation of retrieval of data. They focused their work on grid computing towards handling the data. In fact, they observed that encapsulation as well as virtualization can be implemented quite efficiently in grid computing.

Agrawal *et al.* [11] in their work focused on complexities associated with the application of data science and business intelligence. They observed the importance of optimization criteria in specifically adopting the cross-platform systems and to some extent the machine learning models. The uniqueness lies in the encapsulation of the entire enumeration of plans. Initially the cost linked to transformation of queries can be avoided and then permitting to speed up the entire enumeration process by exploiting the processing elements for quantification.

Agrawal *et al.* [12] in their application discussed the rules based as well as cost based optimizers. They observed that these may require minimum support from the system administrators to exhibit efficient execution plans.

Lin *et al.* [13] in their research focused on the centralized as well as distributed data. The reason for inclusion of this is physical localization with proper maintenance. Somehow, though the distributed data propagates to different locations, still it is logically connected to a database and even implemented while linked to a network environment.

Lakshmi *et al.* [14] in their work discussed on the concepts of query optimization and the criteria of implementation techniques to obtain the optimality of query process focusing on the access points' complete accelerated time period. Citing the specific example, they focused on the join dependencies of the relations which will help minimize the tuples managed in the join dependencies.

Bouros *et al.* [15] in their work prioritized on the join interval mechanism linked to multiple domains mainly spatial databases, uncertain and real data. In their study, they have also focused on the intervals calculation operation evaluation to classify intervals as per the number of semi-joins.

Padia *et al.* [16] in their work focused on the optimization criteria of distributed queries linked to the highest level process evaluation. During the experimentation, it has been seen that the strategies can be enhanced as per the demand of efficiency. Also the processing strategies of the intermediate data depend on the cost of network communication.

Samaddar *et al* [17] during their work intend on the classic problems related to the automatic optimization of queries. Somehow, by observing the complexities and challenges, the quality as well as the key differentiation can be maintained within the databases.

Mohsin *et al.* [18] in their study focused on the performance evaluation as well as the accuracy of their proposed model and compared it with the traditional optimization mechanisms. Also, they have considered the classical distributed database query optimization techniques adopting the ACO implementation procedures.

Rana *et al.* [19] in their work have observed that the specified search mechanism in the desired application is the key component of the query within the optimizer. Particularly, in the distributed database system, sometimes, the processing of transactions may affect the query optimizer which may result an inconsistent database query. So to ensure correctness, recovery mechanisms must be in place to ensure transaction atomicity and durability.

Adriana J *et al.* [20]. in their work prioritized on the execution of structured queries towards the processing of data for NoSQL databases. In fact, they focused on the approach for translation of queries from SQL to NoSQL format. Cited for example, a web translator can generate equivalent DB queries from the existing SQL queries which may not require any specific format of data or schema.

IMPLEMENTATION USING GENETIC ALGORITHM

Generally, implementation mechanisms linked with the genetic algorithm are provisioned with initialization, selection, recombination, mutation and process generation of offspring. In fact, in initialization, the entire population associated with the process can be accumulated and can be processed through semantic analysis. Then subsets can be thought of based on the categorization of the data which may contain multiple sets of large-scaled data. The principle of the crossover technique can be applied based on a genetic algorithm that may result in the exchange of behavior setting a logical relationship within the genes or query terms in this application. Of course, the mutation is also very much essential to maintaining individuality and accumulation of various parameters of genes or query terms. During the generation of the offspring, the candidate solution of the successors can be linked up to evaluate the percentage of acceptability of genes or query terms.

STRATEGIES OF EVALUATION OF QUERY PLANS RELATED TO LARGE SCALE DATA

The main concern of implementation of complex query plans linked to large scaled data is the architectural aspects of search engines. In fact, the complex queries require the mechanisms toward query optimization to work together as shown in Fig. (**1**). The intention of the search optimization is to provide suitable methods for query evaluation retrieved from the query optimizer for simultaneous execution. In fact, the basic approach is to parallelize the search optimization process associated with the query plans and apply the generic process on data to obtain results at any point of time. It is understood that the mechanism of mapping is well-driven through the schema information which is usually linked to logical as well as physical levels. Also, the mapping from logical to physical query plan may not need any further schema information. Rather, the query execution plan is involved in feasible and possible execution of the queries as reflected in Fig. (**2**). In any case, if the query plan is confined to the compilation time, then subsequent mapping in the databases may be required to overcome the inconsistencies.

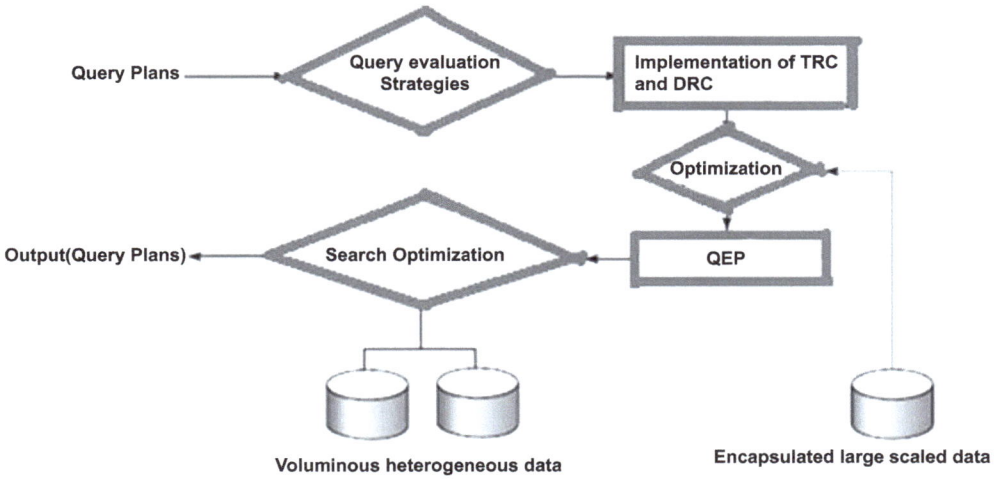

Fig. (1). Strategies of Query Plans associated with voluminous heterogeneous data.

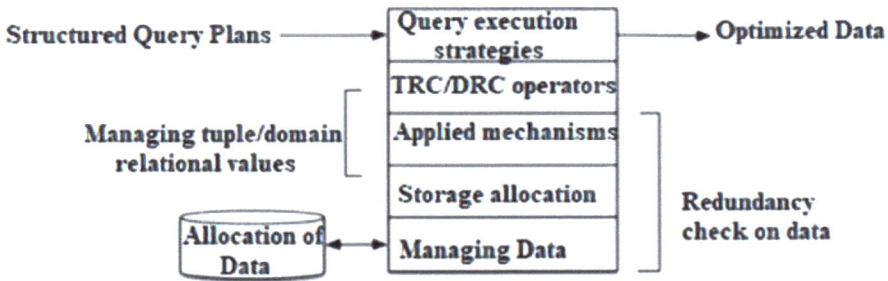

Fig. (2). Implementation structured query plans managing relational values.

ALGORITHM

Step 1: Correlate and match individual index terms of the clustered data in the database db1

for each referenced solution in db1

if db1.query_term in relevancy: obtain the cost factor

else:

Re-generate the db1.query_term and map with clustered data to obtain cost factor

Step 2: Generate the random variables expecting the populated chromosomes, query plans

Step 3: Obtain the fitness parameters f(query_term) | ∨ (query_term) | query_term€ query plans

Step 4: Initialize individual query plan to have q number of random query terms selected from the set of clustered data

Step 5: for i=1 to Q

for every chromosome i

Assign the clustered data to database db1 Recalculate q query terms linked to query plans of db1 Obtain the fitness parameter of query plans

Regenerate the query plans implementing selection, crossover and mutation process Step 6: Determine the fitness parameter of each and individual query plan

fitness (i) =2* (q_i - 1)/Q

Step 7: Obtain the subpopulation and count the ith individual query terms

While linking the databases (db_i) provisioned with clustered data, it is necessary to modify the input and output classifications toward the application of query plans. In fact, the clustered data accumulated in each db_i can be able to map each other based on the entity integrity as well as key values. Accordingly, the values associated with similar keys can be grouped focusing on the solution of individuality.

EXPERIMENTAL ANALYSIS

Generally, the data sets linked with different applications may be provisioned with specific representations and semantics. In fact, the attributes in such situations can be defined through the metadata accomplished with structured and application specific to ensure effectiveness. The main objective is to define the structure of the data along with its uniqueness during the representation. In a normal situation, the semantic approach can be implemented to map the key parameters to accommodate the predictive data and enable standardization of the mechanism.

As reflected in Fig. (3), the processing abilities of the queries depend on the size of the database servers. Somehow, the semantics linked with the situation permits the tool to enable the linkages and preserve the dependencies. The simulation in this case is being performed using MATLAB-13B. The expertise linked to the present situation is focused on the structure of the data sets as well as the linked patterns. Sometimes, the actual streamed data may vary because of range factors, data fusion, etc. So dealing with the large scaled clustered data along with the semantic representation can be a great challenge as cited in Table (**1**). In general, the optimization process of queries specifically in the distributed databases can be provisioned both in the global as well as local level. The queries in the database system are generally input into the controlling site. After the check parameters and validation of the queries, the optimization process can be initiated at global level. In fact, the mapping mechanism of global queries can be realized based on the external fragmentation of global queries. Of course the accumulation of the local data can only be confined to the local databases.

The control mechanism in this situation should be allowed to use the global data dictionary for the accumulation of information and reconstruction of global schema. The global optimizer is responsible to execute the queries at the sites where the fragments are stored. It generates the distributed execution plans for uniform transformation of data. It will help the process to be executed smoothly and in transferring intermediate results. Accordingly, the local queries can be optimized by the local database servers and the local query results can be merged together through union operation in case of horizontal fragments and join operation for vertical fragments (Table **1**).

Table 1. Size of database servers with the cost of query terms.

S. No.	Size of Database Servers	Cost of Query terms (m.sec.)
1	11	0.29
2	22	0.34
3	33	0.55
4	44	0.71

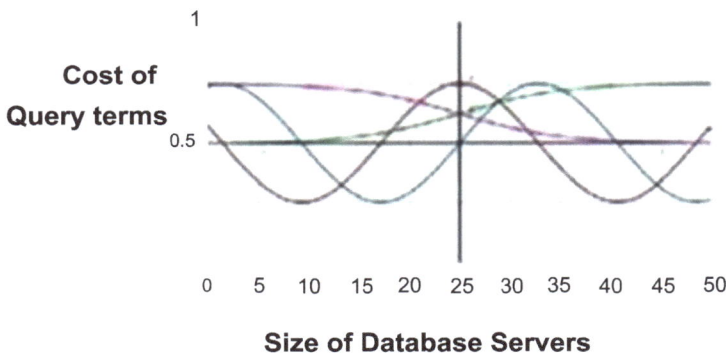

Fig. (3). Size of database servers with the accumulated cost of query terms.

Specifically, the requirements on actual computation are not consistent specifically dealing with large-scale data. In such a situation, it is required to focus on the usability of resources and to prioritize accumulation of resources to manage the complexities linked with the system. While focusing on the query evaluation mechanisms through large-scale processing elements, it is required to think of multithreading concepts and prioritization of large-scale data. As shown in Fig. (**4**), the cost of query plans depends on the size of the databases especially with the normalized data. It is understood that the implementation of normalization is to make the databases simpler and develop the interlink facilities within them. Also, it helps to minimize the redundancies within the databases as reflected in Table (**2**). As observed in many database systems, the query embedded with any programming language can be optimized during the compilation of the program. In such a situation, the optimizer considers the program variables as constant in the query. Of course, the optimality of the desired query evaluation plan depends on the situation linked to the actual execution of the query plans. In case of the non-execution of the query plans within the stipulated time period, the re-optimization is essential to avoid inconsistencies (Table **2**).

Table 2. Size of Database linked with normalized data with the cost of query plans.

Sl.No.	Databases linked with normalized data	Cost of query plans(m.sec.)
1	29	0.41
2	47	0.71
3	55	0.83
4	77	0.92

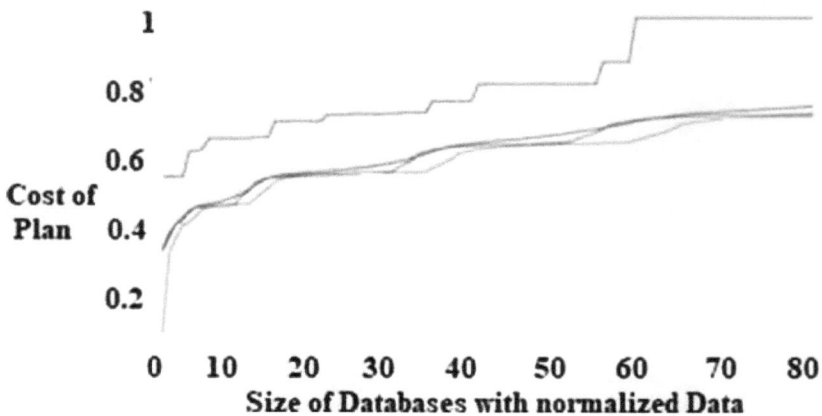

Fig. (4). Size of Database linked with normalized data with the cost of query plans.

DISCUSSION AND FUTURE DIRECTION

Typically while being associated with the clustered data and specifically implementing simulation, it is observed that the classification of these data sets makes the system robust and computationally efficient with certain adaptive systems. As compared with the statistical analysis, it is clear that the obstructions linked to tuning associated with high scaled large heterogeneous clustered data can affect the throughput as well as the operations within the processes. Therefore to eradicate these complexities, it is again required to focus on the hidden patterns and apply association rules on query terms to enhance the efficiency of the system. Sometimes, the distributed patterns obtained can be prioritized on specified groups and can be regenerated from the desired clustered data sets. In fact, this mechanism may work in a much better way while moving the parameterized data from one cluster to another.

CONCLUSION

In general, the technique linked with clustering is intended to obtain the patterns from the associated datasets. Focusing on the learning mechanism as well as behavioral aspects, it is understood that the datasets with similar instances can be provisioned with similar groups based on the specified criteria. Of course, it will be easier to obtain associated similar patterns retrieved from the linked clustered datasets. As the groups are associated with some portion of large-scale data, in such a situation, the computational methods can be adopted to obtain the optimal or near-optimal solution. Accordingly, the search process can be initiated randomly to explore the proficiency with solution achieving optimality.

CONSENT FOR PUBLICATION

Not applicable.

CONFLICT OF INTEREST

The authors declare no conflict of interest, financial or otherwise.

ACKNOWLEDGEMENT

Declared none.

REFERENCES

[1]   C. Reiss, J. Wilkes, and J.L. Hellerstein, *"Google cluster-usage traces: format+ schema,"* *Google Inc.* ICPPW, 2011, pp. 1-14.

[2]   D. Zhang, P. Coddington, and A.L. Wendelborn, "Improving data transfer performance of web service workflows in the cloud environment", *Int. J. Comput. Sci. Eng.,* vol. 8, no. 3, pp. 198-209, 2013.

[3]   Z. Liu, and S. Cho, "Characterizing machines and workloads on a Google cluster", *Parallel Processing Workshops (ICPPW)*, 2012pp. 397-403
[http://dx.doi.org/10.1109/ICPPW.2012.57]

[4]   C. Reiss, A. Tumanov, G.R. Ganger, R.H. Katz, and M.A. Kozuch, "Heterogeneity and dynamicity of clouds at scale: Google trace analysis", *Proceedings of the Third ACM Symposium on Cloud Computing,* 2012p. 7
[http://dx.doi.org/10.1145/2391229.2391236]

[5]   S. Yousif, and A. Al-Dulaimy, "Clustering cloud workload traces to improve the performance of cloud data centers",

[6]   C. Reiss, A. Tumanov, G.R. Ganger, R.H. Katz, and M.A. Kozuch, *Towards understanding heterogeneous clouds at scale: Google trace analysis*, 2012.

[7]   A. Kirby, Al-Dulaimy , W. Itani, R. Zantout, and A. Zekri, "Type-Aware Virtual Machine Management for Energy Efficient Cloud Data Centers," Sustainable Computing: Informatics and Systems",

[8]   S. Tayal, "Tasks scheduling optimization for the cloud computing systems", *Int. J. Adv. Eng. Sci. Technol.,* vol. 5, pp. 111-115, 2011.

[9]   C. Evangelinos, and C. Hill, "Cloud Computing for parallel Scientific HPC Applications: Feasibility of Running Coupled Atmosphere-Ocean Climate Models on Amazon's EC2", *The First Workshop on Cloud Computing and its Applications (CCA'08),* 2008 Chicago.

[10]   I. Raicu, Y. Zhao, I. Foster, and A. Szalay,

[11]   D. Agrawal, S. Chawla, B. Contreras-Rojas, A. Elmagarmid, Y. Idris, Z. Kaoudi, S. Kruse, J. Lucas, E. Mansour, M. Ouzzani, P. Papotti, J.A. Quiané-Ruiz, N. Tang, S. Thirumuruganathan, and A. Troudi, "RHEEM: enabling cross-platform data processing", *Proceedings VLDB Endowment---,* vol. 11, no. 11, pp. 1414-1427, 2018.
[http://dx.doi.org/10.14778/3236187.3236195]

[12]   D. Agrawal, M.L. Ba, L. Berti-Equille, S. Chawla, A.K. Elmagarmid, ´.H. Hammady, Y. Idris, Z. Kaoudi, Z. Khayyat, S. Kruse, M. Ouzzani, P. Papotti, J. Quiane-Ruiz, N. Tang, and M.J. Zaki,

[13]   X. Lin, *Query Optimization Strategies and Implementation Based on Distributed Database.* IEEE, 2009.

[14]   V. Lakshmi, and D.V.K. Vatsavayi, "Query Optimization using Clustering and Genetic Algorithm for Distributed Databases", *International Conference on Computer Communication and Informatics (ICCCI),* 2016.
[http://dx.doi.org/10.1109/ICCCI.2016.7479934]

[15]   P. Bouros, and N. Mamoulis, *Interval Count SemiJoins.* vol. Vol. 10. Open Proceedings, 2018.

[16]   S. Padia, S. Khulge, A. Gupta, and P. Khadilikar, "Query Optimization Strategies in Distributed Databases International Journal of Computer Science and Information Technologies",

[17]   S.K. Samaddar, and S. Pujari, *A Survey on Query Optimization for Databases.* vol. Vol. 9. IJITKM, 2015.

[18]   S.A. Mohsin, S.M. Darwish, and A. Younes, "Dynamic Cost Ant Colony Algorithm for Optimize Distributed Database Query", *Proceedings of the Artificial Intelligence and Computer Vision (AICV2020),* 2020 Cairo, Egypt.
[http://dx.doi.org/10.1007/978-3-030-44289-7_17]

[19]   M.S. Rana, K.S. Mohammad, and A. Shohel, "Distributed Database Problems, Ap-proaches and Solutions—A Study", *Int. J. Mach. Learn. Comput.,* vol. 8, pp. 472-476, 2018.

[20] J. Adriana, and M. Holanda, NoSQL2: SQL to NoSQL databases.*Trends and advances in information systems and technologies. WorldCIST'18. Advances in intelligent systems and computing.,* Á. Rocha, H. Adeli, L. Reis, S. Costanzo, Eds., vol. Vol. 746. Springer, 2018.

CHAPTER 3

Secure Communication Over In-Vehicle Network Using Message Authentication

Manjunath Managuli[1,*], Sudha Slake[2], Pankaja S. Kadalgi[2] and Gouri C. Khadabadi[2]

[1] *Department of ECE, KLS Gogte Institute of Technology, Belagavi, India*

[2] *Department of CSE, KLS Gogte Institute of Technolgy, Belagavi, India*

Abstract: This chapter describes the initial working plan and the project carried out, along with their respective analyses. The project focused on implementing a cryptographic solution in the embedded system to ensure the authentication and integrity of CAN messages. With the rise of the autonomous driving concept in the automotive industry, there is a growing need for digital data processing and communication both within the vehicle and with the external world, creating a significant challenge to protect the data from cyber-attacks during communication. Hence, cybersecurity has become an important topic in the automotive industry. This project was carried out to ensure the security of data during communication on the vehicle Controller Area Network (CAN) using message authentication. The chapter concludes by highlighting the current technology's drawbacks and discussing potential future improvements.

Keywords: Automotive industry, Cyber-attacks, CAN, Cybersecurity, MAC, Message authentication, Secure communication.

INTRODUCTION

The latest key trends in the automotive industry involve transforming vehicles, especially cars, into computers on wheels, which requires the integration of numerous digital features into the vehicle system. These trends include autonomous driving, which grants greater control to the electronic system, as well as connectivity and digitization, electric vehicles, and shared mobility. However, these advancements also create new challenges as they make vehicles more vulnerable to cyber-attacks [1], thereby increasing the opportunities for attacks, broadening the threat landscape, and increasing the potential for attacks to occur.

---

* **Corresponding author Manjunath Managuli:** Department of ECE, KLS Gogte Institute of Technology, Belagavi, India; E-mail: manjunathm16@gmail.com

Brojo Kishore Mishra (Ed.)

Background for Vehicle Security

The latest trend in the automotive industry involves increasing the connectivity between vehicles, which is achieved by providing more connection ports to the external world, mainly through wireless communication technologies such as cloud connection to access the Internet [2]. As a result, communication between vehicles and other external entities, such as infrastructure, is becoming more common, known as Vehicle-to-Vehicle (V2V) and Vehicle-to-External (V2X) communication. However, this increased connectivity also brings with it an increase in threats to customer safety, security, and privacy, as depicted in Fig. (**1**).

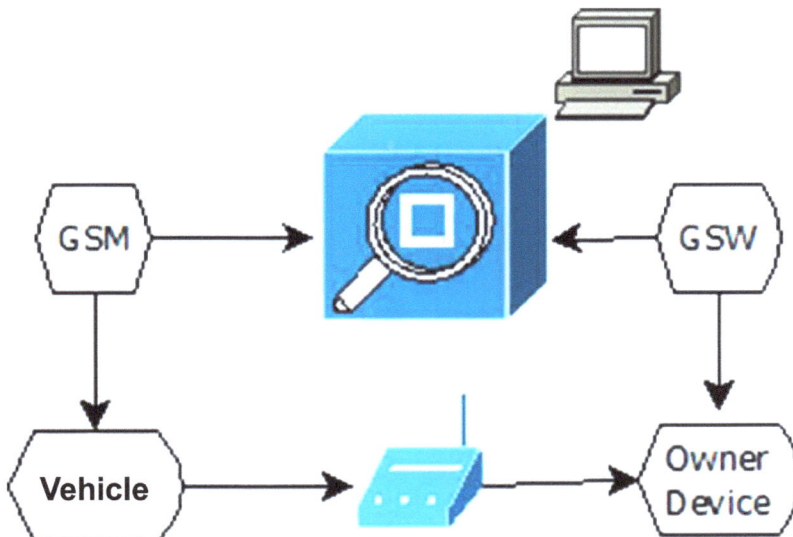

Fig. (1). Overview of connected car concept.

Hacking Incidents on Vehicles

The automotive industry is facing an increasing number of cyber-attacks, with hackers targeting vehicles that are loaded with new technologies [3]. These attacks involve stealing important data, which can later be used to demand money from either the vehicle owner or the manufacturer. The first instance of research on vehicle hacking began in 2010 to analyze the security of modern automobiles. In 2012, incidents of BMW and VW hacks were reported, where the immobilizer and OBD-II ports were used for hacking purposes. A Jeep hacking incident in 2015 became famous, as a researcher was able to hack into the infotainment system and take control of critical assets of the Jeep, leading to the recall of millions of Jeep vehicles [4]. Another incident in 2015 involved a Tesla vehicle being hacked, with the attacker gaining control over the vehicle's doors and windows remotely. The infotainment system, which has wireless connections with the external world through Wi-Fi, Bluetooth, cellphones, and infrared, is often the first target for cyber-attacks on vehicles. Figs. (**2** & **3**) provide an overview of the most interesting and popular hacking incidents of recent years [5].

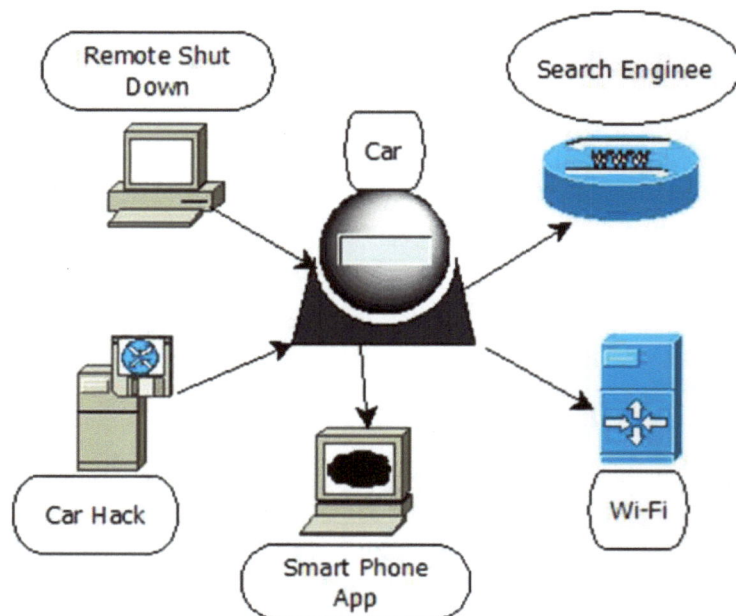

Fig. (2). Overview of connected car concept.

Economic Value at Risk Due to Poor Security Investments

In case of a vehicle hacking incident caused by inadequate security measures, the costs involved in recovering from the incident can be substantial and can have a negative impact on the brand name of the vehicle manufacturer. Naturally, implementing security measures in vehicles requires significant financial investment from both the vehicle manufacturer and product suppliers. The investment required for security implementation is compared to the consequences of vehicle hacking incidents in the Costs vs. Investments graph.

Security Goals

The major components of the cyber security goal are listed as Confidentiality, Integrity & Authentication and Availability in Fig. (**4**).

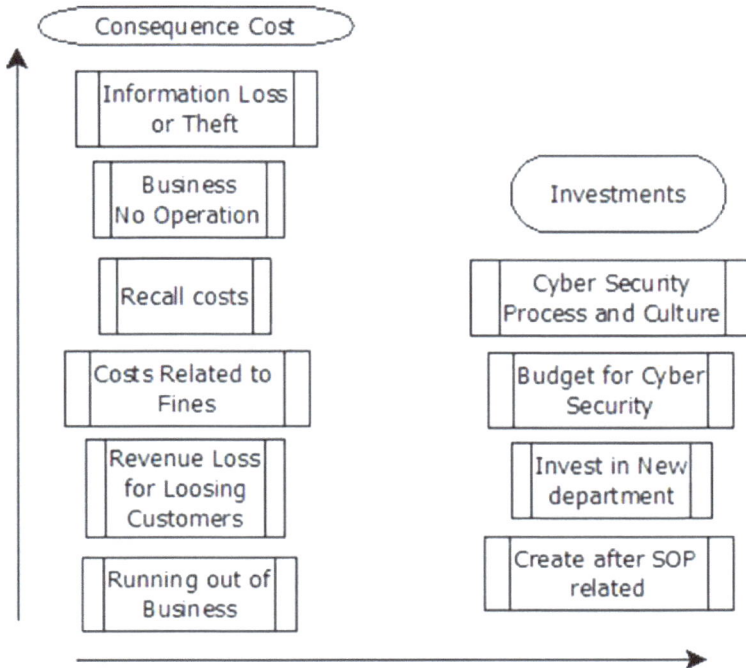

Fig. (3). Security consequences *vs* investments.

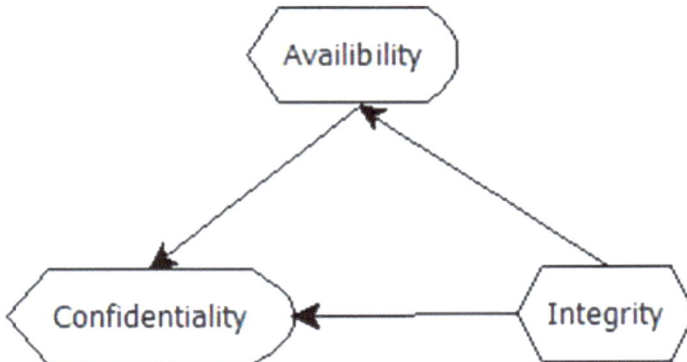

Fig. (4). Security Goals – CIA.

Confidentiality: This indicates that it's important to safeguard information from unauthorized access in terms of both reading and writing [6]. Essentially, people who are not authorized to view the information should not be able to see it in its original form.

Integrity and Authentication: This implies that information must be secured against unauthorized alteration. Authentication is the process of ensuring that the originator of the information and the recipient of the information are mutually recognized.

Availability: This signifies that a service or information should be accessible to an authorized entity at all times when needed. However, there is a risk of unavailability due to network problems such as congestion or deliberate attacks [7]. To ensure that the information is always accessible to the intended party, the aim is to mitigate the factors that may cause non-availability.

Security Attacks

Security attacks pose a risk to security objectives. In the automotive industry, a security attack could have severe consequences, such as endangering the driver or passengers' safety if the safety features fail to function as intended. Consequently, Fig. (5) must prioritize vehicle security considerations during the design and development of safety-related components in the automotive industry.

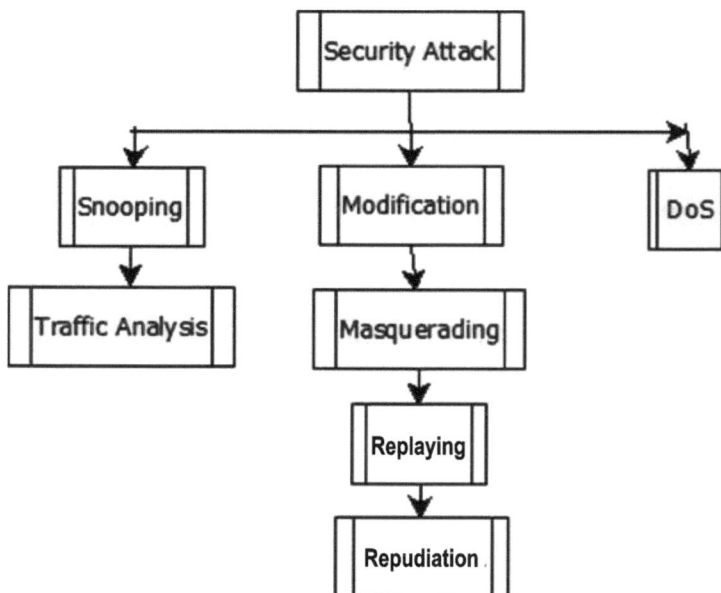

Fig. (5). An overview of different Security Attack types.

Snooping: This pertains to the unauthorized access of information, where an unauthorized individual or entity could potentially steal the information during transmission and use it for their own purposes. To prevent this type of attack, the information should be transformed into a non-decipherable format using encryption methods before transmission. Only an authorized person or entity would possess the ability to decrypt such information, and not an attacker [8].

Analysis of the Traffic: By utilizing encipherment or encryption methods, it is feasible to render the information unintelligible during transmission. However, attackers may still be able to deduce the sender and receiver information by examining the transmission request and response.

Modification: After an attacker has accessed or read the information, it becomes relatively effortless to manipulate it for their own gain, whether by deleting portions of the information, adding supplementary data, or altering the content entirely. In some cases, attackers may simply delay the transmission of the message to disrupt the system's regular functioning [9].

Masquerading: This indicates that an attacker has the ability to impersonate another individual. The attacker can masquerade as either the sender or the receiver to obtain crucial information from others.

Replaying: This refers to a type of attack where the attacker reads and stores the actual message content, and later retransmits the same message for their own benefit. To safeguard against this type of attack, an anti-reply counter can be utilized. This counter increments by one after each successful transmission, ensuring that duplicate messages are not accepted.

Repudiation: Initially the sender will transmit the message to the receiver with some information. And later sender will not agree the request comes from the same sender. Similarly, on the receiver side, the receiver does not agree that the message is received by the same receiver. To avoid such situations, a trusted third party can be used as proof for any communication process.

Denial of Service: In brief, a system may experience DoS (Denial of Service) where the offered service is slowed down or disrupted completely by an attacker, often due to excessive load. Attackers can create such situations by various means, such as flooding the network with false messages to increase the load, or deleting response messages from the receiver so that the sender does not receive any acknowledgement, causing them to send multiple requests continuously, which will further increase the network load.

Techniques to Implement Security Mechanisms

Cryptography and Steganography are the main two security mechanisms used today [10].

Cryptography: Cryptography refers to the practice of concealing information in a secret manner. It is an art form that helps protect information from possible attacks by transferring it into a secure format. Currently, there are three distinct security mechanisms available: Symmetric Key, Asymmetric Key, and Hashing. Symmetric Key involves using a single secret key for both the sender and receiver to encipher the message. Asymmetric Key, on the other hand, requires two different keys (public and private) for encipherment. Lastly, Hashing involves creating a small message digest that is added to the message and used for encipherment [11]. Cryptography techniques are commonly used in secured communication procedures.

Steganography: This refers to the act of concealing information within something else. The original message containing the information is hidden by something else, such as an audio or video clip, other text, or picture. This type of security mechanism is used to pass important additional data along with the original information.

Network Security Model

The fundamental network security model outlines the essential measures required to ensure the security of information transmitted through an insecure communication channel, along with shared secret information at both the sender and receiver ends, as depicted in Fig. (**6**).

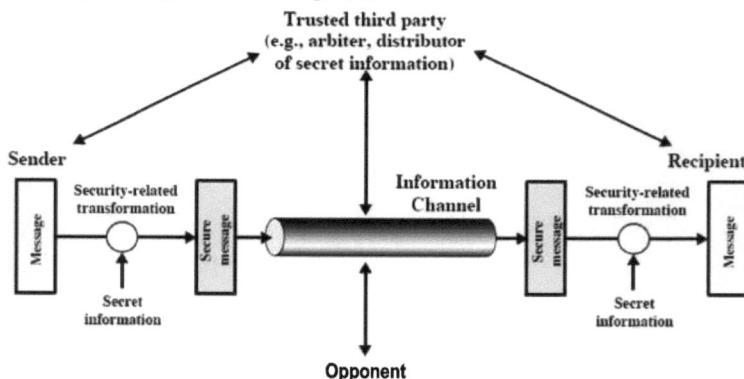

Fig. (6). General network security model.

There are 4 mandatory tasks that need to be considered in designing the network security model:

1. Algorithm design to perform security transformation function.

2. Secret information creation which is used with the algorithm.

3. A proper method needs to be developed for secret information distribution and sharing.

4. The protocol should be specified between communication parties to provide security service.

Security by Design

Security by design refers to the practice of considering all necessary measures to achieve security in the vehicle during every phase of the product life cycle, from requirement specification to hardware and software development, and to verification and validation. In order for a successful attack to occur, there needs to be an attack surface available. To develop a secure product, security must be taken into account from the beginning of the product development lifecycle. The first step is to define the vehicle level [13] and perform a TARA (Threat Analysis and Risk Assessment) to establish security goals and requirements. To identify the attack surface at both the vehicle and product levels, security analysis methods such as FMEA (Fault Mode Effective Analysis) or ATA (Attack Tree Analysis) must be conducted. Cybersecurity concepts should be developed at the vehicle level, including all necessary security mechanism descriptions. The next step is to develop technical security concepts, technical requirements, and security architecture at the vehicle and product levels. At the vehicle level, ECUs that communicate with the external world, such as the Infotainment system, may have several possible attack surfaces, such as Wi-Fi, Bluetooth, Cellular connections, GPS, and USB ports. It is important to design and implement the necessary security mechanisms in such devices to protect other assets of the vehicle [12].

Cybersecurity Concept for Connected Car

To enhance security in vehicles and prevent successful attacks, it is essential to implement a multi-layered architecture and prioritize security as a crucial task. This involves performing an attack tree analysis to identify any potential unauthorized access points in the vehicle and implementing necessary security mechanisms to detect and counteract any successful attacks.

In order to achieve a thorough level of security, a comprehensive strategy must be developed and applied to every Electronic Control Unit (ECU) in the vehicle. It is crucial to separate the ECUs that communicate with the outside world from other safety ECUs. This can be achieved through the implementation of a central gateway in the in-vehicle network, along with security measures to protect this gateway unit. It is important to note that security issues can disrupt safety mechanisms, therefore, better safety standards require better security measures (Fig. **7**).

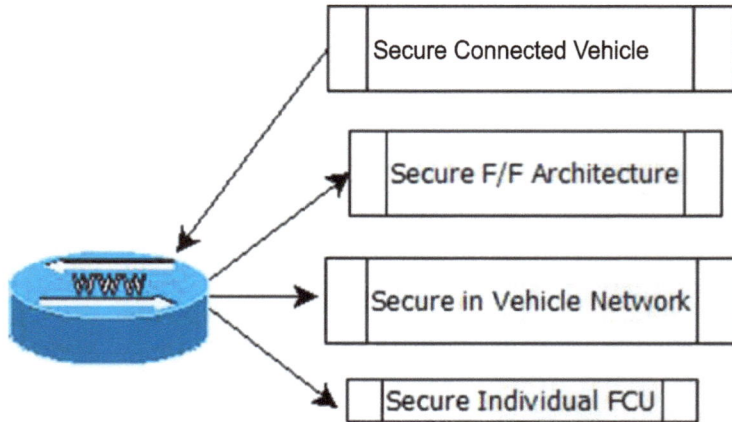

Fig. (7). Four Layer security in vehicle.

Key trend of the current automotive industry is V2V (vehicle to another vehicle) and V2X (vehicle to environment or infrastructure) needs secure communication with external entities. The advanced features like OTA (Over the Air) for software updates,

1. It is crucial to ensure secure interfaces between external devices and systems such as OBD (On Board Diagnostics), Bluetooth, Navigation Systems, Telematics, *etc.* to prevent security attacks that exploit these interfaces. To achieve this, security measures such as firewalls and standard security interfaces can be implemented.

2. When designing a security strategy for vehicles, it is crucial to prioritize and focus on creating a secure architecture that covers the entire system. This means protecting information from the vehicle level all the way to the production level of each Electronic Control Unit (ECU). In cases where external communication is necessary, secure communication should be implemented in both the client and server model. To achieve comprehensive security, the architecture should isolate the safety ECUs from the Infotainment system in the vehicle network by utilizing a secure central gateway unit.

1. Using cryptographic functions to establish secure communication within an In-Vehicle network helps to maintain the authenticity and integrity of transmitted data. This ensures that the information sent over the network remains protected.

2. The Hardware Security Module (HSM) offers a robust, trustworthy platform for implementing security features with fast execution. It operates independently and provides support for rapid software implementation of various security features

such as secure boot, key generation, memory protection, secure update, and key storage.

Designing Secure Automotive Systems

The subject of security in the Automotive industry is relatively new and a popular topic. Therefore, existing technologies and knowledge related to security from other industries such as computer network security are being adapted for use in the Automotive industry. To provide quick security solutions, vehicle designers and product developers utilize security-related processes and technologies from other domains. Automotive safety and cyber security are closely related since security vulnerabilities can impact safety mechanisms. While safety always requires security, the opposite may not be true. Cyber security aims to prevent financial, operational, privacy, and information losses, making it essential to safe vehicle development. During the design phase, privacy, reliability, safety, and security must be considered. For security design, a threat analysis must be conducted at the vehicle level to identify various types of threats due to potential attacks, and mitigation actions should be taken. Multiple layers of security, including external communication security, End-to-End security, In-Vehicle communication security, and individual security, should be implemented at different levels.

ECU level security is also needed [14]. The security architect of the vehicle should consider all these aspects and should list the necessary security tools used for every phase of the product development. Due to the standardization of technology, most of the chip and operating systems specifications are easily available on the Internet. Hackers will also get these details and they will be experts in these domains. Therefore, security designs for vehicles and for every ECU are very much needed to protect the system from vulnerabilities. Lessons learned and best practices from computer networks may be helpful in security design. Also get the idea from other industries like avionics, defence, and industrial automation. Users also need to be educated about the secure usage of the facilities and systems provided in the vehicle to avoid future possible security threats in Fig. (**8**).

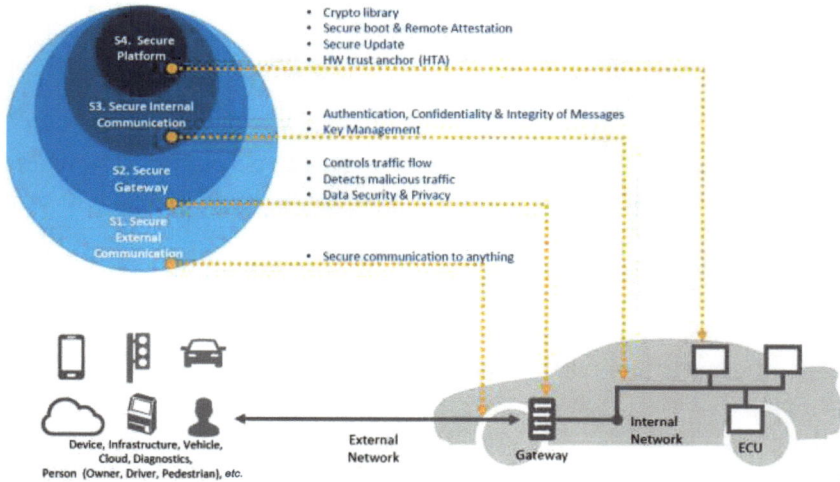

Fig. (8). Designing Secure Vehicle Systems.

Security by Design across CAR Development Lifecycle

Security aspects need to be considered in every phase of the product life cycle starting from requirement specifications to verification & validation. Security concepts and security mechanisms should be addressed at the beginning. Hardware security and Software security requirements should be derived. Software security architecture and secure coding guidelines will enhance and ensure strong security practices. The security strategy of the top-down approach is shown below and covers all different phases in Fig. (**9**).

Fig. (9). Security in vehicle development life cycle.

The best security by design strategy should cover the below points:

1. Organization-level security culture, and security development methods by repeatedly conducting the risk assessments for critical systems or components used in vehicles.

2. Secure project management at the organizational level as well as on the project level.

3. Verification and validation for security (*e.g.*, vulnerability scanning, Fuzz testing, Penetration testing and static code analysis).

4. Security by design can be achieved by reusing and adapting already existing security lifecycle frameworks.

Vehicle Communication Buses

Communication buses are used inside vehicles for data or information transmission like CAN (Controller Area Network), Ethernet, Flex ray, and LIN (Local Interconnect Network). CAN is a very famous and mostly used bus in the automotive industry. In the olden days, vehicle features were limited, and vehicles were not connected with the external world. Because of this vehicle designers in the olden days have not considered the security goals like the CIA. But nowadays a lot of vehicle features are used in vehicles and demand is still more for the autonomous driving concept. This requires the vehicle to be connected to the Internet and requires V2V and V2X communication.

CAN supports multi-master and broadcast types of message transmission. In CAN, lower priority messages will always win arbitration due to the dominance of zero bits. A classical CAN message can carry a maximum of 8 bytes of data, while the newer CAN-FD can carry at least 64 bytes of data. CAN uses message-based addressing rather than node-based addressing like Ethernet, and 11-bit or 29-bit addressing is available.

In the past, all ECUs in a vehicle network could communicate on the same CAN bus, which posed a security risk. If one ECU was compromised, it could monitor and pass the data of other ECUs, leading to security threats. Furthermore, sudden shifts in the communication network were not possible since all ECU development was done using CAN. To improve security, safety and functional ECUs can be separated from ECUs that communicate with the external world, such as Infotainment ECUs, using a central gateway ECU that handles security.

Encryption and decryption methods can be used to achieve the security goal of confidentiality. Authentication and integrity can be achieved using a CMAC-based message authentication method. This method appends part of the generated MAC to the message, and the receiver generates a MAC using the same method to verify the data's integrity. The secret key ensures the message's originator, and MAC verification ensures integrity. The secret key needs to be shared securely between the sender and receiver, and Secure Hardware Extension (SHE)-based Key Management can be used for this purpose.

Key Management is the standard procedure for maintaining multiple keys required for different operations, such as updating the MAC key or Safe Key. Before releasing the product to the vehicle manufacturer, secret keys are updated using the Key Management procedure, which is only known to the OEM. The SHE functional specification outlines the standard steps for updating secret keys using three messages sent in a diagnostic routine request from the Central Gateway ECU or Tester tool. There are a total of 5 messages, with 3 being request messages (M1, M2, M3) and 2 being response messages (M4, M5), as shown in Fig. (**10**).

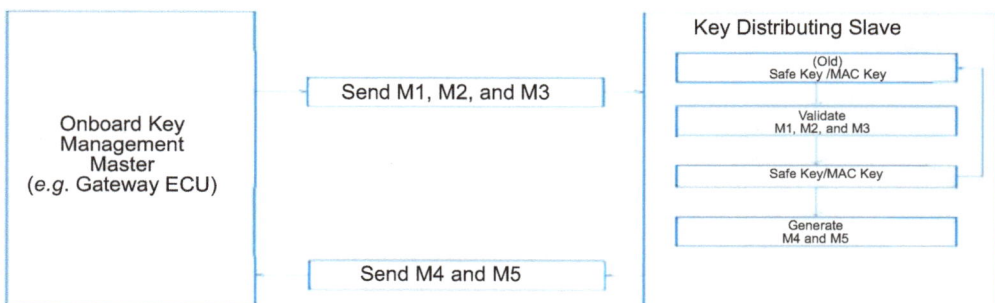

Fig. (10). Key Management Overview.

Format of Request and Response Messages

1) M1 gives information of the destination where the key is programmed

120 bit-UID	4 bit-ID	4 bit-Auto ID

- UID: Unique ID value configured for each ECU unit.
- ID: Information about the key which will be updated in the ECU (0x01 for Safe Key update, 0x04 for MAC key update)
- Auth ID: Information about the key which will be used for generation of internal keys K1 & K2 (0x01 for Safe Key, 0x04 for MAC key).

2) M2 has encrypted key which will be updated

28 bit-Cnt	WP	BP	DP	KU	DWG	0..0	Key (Master Key or MAC Key)

- CNT: Counter for Safe Key Update (When ID of M1 is 0x01) or Counter for MAC Key Update (When the ID of M1 is 0x04)
- WP (Write PROTECTION): indicates update of the encrypting key can be done or not
- BP(BOOT_PROTECTION): limits usage of the key when secure boot has failed. If 1b is sent, usage of the key will be prohibited when the secure boot has failed.
- DP(DEBUGGER_PROTECTION): limits the usage of the key when the debugger is connected. If 1b is sent, usage of the key will be prohibited when the debugger is connected.
- KU(KEY_USAGE): identifies the usage of the key that is registered. 0b will be sent for Safe Key and 1b will be sent for MAC Key.
- DWU(DISABLE_WILDCARD_USAGE): indicates whether wildcards can be used or not in the UID of M1 during key update.
- KEY: Safe Key (When the ID of M1 is 0x01) or MAC Key (When the ID of M1 is 0x04) which will be updated in the ECU
- BP, DP, KU: these flags are effective only if HSM is used.

3) M3 is the CMAC of M1 and M2 together:

128 bit- CMAC/M1/M2

- Concatenation of M1 and M2 of 128 bits is passed as input to CMAC algorithm which uses AES128 as encryption algorithm along with internal key K2 to generate M3.

4) M4 is encrypted data using Counter for Safe Key or MAC Key

120-bit UID	4 bit- ID	4bit Aut ID	Cnt	1	0...0

- UID: Unique ID value configured for each ECU unit.
- ID: Information about key which will be updated in the ECU (0x01 for Safe Key update, 0x04 for MAC key update)
- Auth ID: Information about key which will be used for generation of internal keys (0x01 for Safe Key, 0x04 for MAC key)
- CNT: Counter for Safe Key Update (When ID of M1 is 0x01) or Counter for MAC Key Update (When ID of M1 is 0x04)

5) M5 is the CMAC of M4:

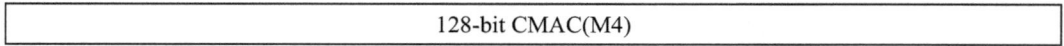

128-bit CMAC(M4)

- M4 of 128 bits is passed as an input to CMAC algorithm which uses AES128 as encryption algorithm along with internal key K4 to generate M5.

Internal Key used for Decryption and Encryption

Messages M2 and M3 contain encrypted input data, which requires the generation of internal keys K2 and K3 to decrypt. Similarly, when responding to a request, the ECU sends encrypted messages M4 and M5, which require the generation of internal keys K3 and K4 for encryption. This process is illustrated in Fig. (**11**).

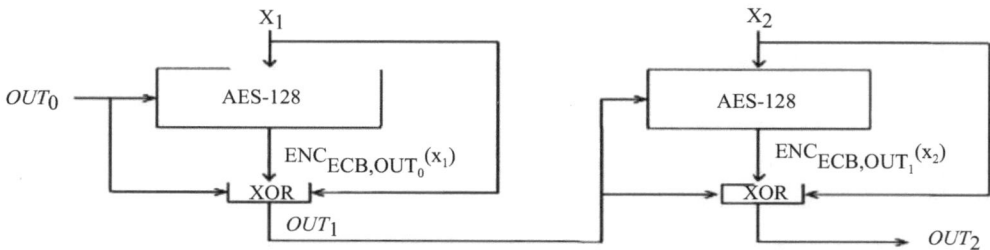

Fig. (11). Miyaguchi Preneel scheme.

Intermediate keys (K1 – K4) are generated using the Miyaguchi Preneel scheme. OUT_0 is the key and X_1 is the input (stored key assigned by AuthID or ID of M1) X_2 is the constant value for encryption or MAC (standard value).

OUT2 will be the key (One of the K1, K2, K3, and K4) derived by AES-MP (Table **1**) .

Table 1. Conditions for calculating keys (Inputs and Outputs for AES MP).

Equation	Use	Input AES-MP		Key o/p
II	Dec of M2	Key assig auth ID	Constant value for encryption	K1
III	Generation of M3	Key assig auth ID	Constant value for MAC	K2
IV	Encryption of M4	Key aut ID	Constant value for encryption	K3
V	Generation of M5	Key auth ID	Constant value for MAC	K4

AES Algorithm

The Secured Hardware Encryption (SHE) defines the Advanced Encryption Standard (AES) algorithm for use in cryptography. To improve security, a 128-bit granularity is employed. In AES, Electronic Code Book (ECB) is the simplest encoding method, which generates cipher output based only on the input and secret key. However, ECB mode has a weakness that allows attackers to perform statistical analysis. To address this weakness, Cipher Block Chaining (CBC), Output/Cipher feedback, and Counter mode were developed as additional cipher modes, as shown in Table **1**.

Sequence of Key Update Procedure

The Onboard Key Management Master sends messages M1, M2, and M3 through Unified Diagnostic Service (UDS) routine requests to update the MAC key or Safe Key for the key distributing slave (EYE). Messages M4 and M5 are the responses from the EYE ECU to confirm whether the key update was successful or failed. These messages are sent when the Onboard Key Management Master requests the routine result *via* UDS, as shown in Fig. (**12**).

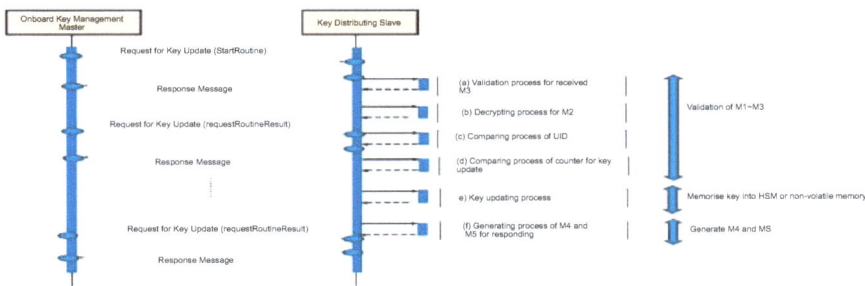

Fig. (12). Key update function.

Routine Control (31 hex) Service

The Routine Control service is one of the Unified Diagnostic Services (UDS). This service is used by the client device for the following reasons:

1. To start the routine,

2. To stop the routine, and

3. To request the routine results.

A routine ID routine Identifier is two bytes in size in Table **2**.

Table 2. Request message definition.

A. Data byte	Parameter Name	Cvt	Hex Value	Mnemonic
#1	Routine Control request service Id	M	31	RC
#2	Sub Function = [routine type]	M	00-FF	LEV_RCTP
#4 #5	Routine identifier Byte#1 MSB Byte #2	M M	00-FF 00-FF	RI_B1 B2
#5 #n	Routine control option record = [routine control option#1 Routine control option #m]	C*/U C/U	00-FF 00-FF	RCEOR_RCO_RCO

1. Sub-function definition for Request message

2. Response message data parameter definition

Steps Involved in Key Update

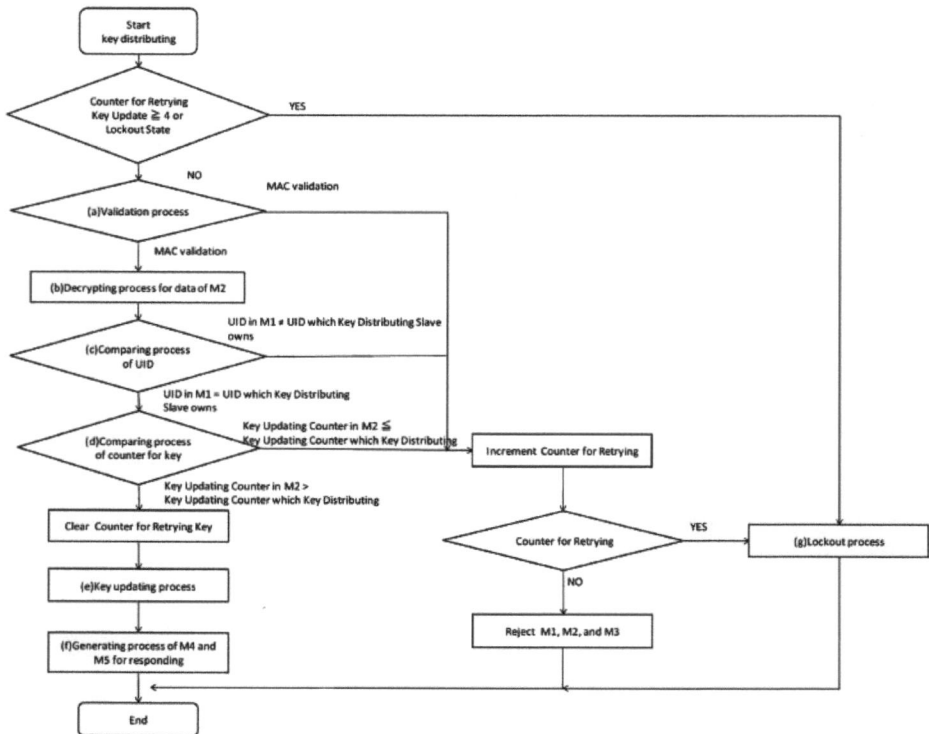

Fig. (13). Flowchart for Key Update.

Step 1:

Validation of received M3: MAC for M3 will be validated by the ECU which received M1, M2, and M3 from Onboard Key Management Master by CAN communication (Diagnostic routine control start request (Fig. **13**).

1. Key distributing slave generates M3 from received M1 and M2 (AES-CMAC algorithm, CBC mode, Key: K2)

2. Compare M3 received from Onboard Key Management Master and generated CMAC from the Key Distributing Slave to validate whether they match or not.

3. In case MAC validation succeeded => Confirm data as legitimate and execute Step-2.

4. In case of MAC validation failed => Increment Counter for Retrying Key Update (If the value of the counter has reached [Key Update Penalty = 4], execute step-7 and respond with a positive response.

5. Counter for Retrying Key Update, the initial value is 0x00

Step 2:

Decryption of M2: Decrypt M2 which Key Distributing Slave had received.

1. AES algorithm, mode: CBC, Key: K1

2. If decryption is successful => execute step 4

3. If decryption fails => Increment Counter for Retrying Key Update (If the value of the counter has reached [Key Update Penalty = 4], execute step-7 and respond by a positive response.

Step 3:

Comparing the process of UID

1. In case UID in received M1 and Key Distributing Slave matched or UID = All "0" in received M1 and value of DWU stored in NVM is "0" => execute step 3

2. In case other than the above condition => Increment Counter for Retrying Key Update (If the value of the counter has reached [Key Update Penalty = 4], execute step-7 and respond by the positive response.

Step 4:

Comparing the process of the counter for key update: compare the counter for the key update in received M2 and the counter for a key update that which Key Distributing Slave owns (stored in NVM).

1. Counter in received M2 > Counter which Key Distributing Slave owns => Confirm data as legitimate and execute step 5.

2. Counter in received M2 ☐ Counter which Key Distributing Slave owns, Increment Counter for Retrying Key Update (If the value of counter reached [Key Update Penalty = 4], execute step-7 and respond by positive response

STEP 5:

Key updating process:

1. Key which will be registered to target ECU can be obtained from decrypting M2, and decrypted key from the process in step-3 should be programmed (should be overwritten) in HSM or non-volatile memory according to information (ID) in M1

2. Safe Key updating or MAC Key updating process will be executed depending on ID.

  a. ID of M1 is 0x01: Execute Safe Key updating process and update Safe Key
  b. ID of M1 is 0x04: Execute MAC Key updating process and update MAC Key

3. Safe key or MAC key programmed in this process should not be able to read by diagnostic communication

Step 6:

Generating process of M4 and M5 for response: Key Distributing Slave will generate M4 & M5.

1. Key Distributing Slave will generate M4 by using the cryptographic system. Part of M4 needs to be encrypted. Algorithm: AES, mode: CBC, key used -K4 (128bit)

2. If the key update has failed, the value of M4 and M5 should be ALL "0". Safe key or MAC key programmed in this process should not be able to read by diagnostic communication

Step 7:

Lockout Process:

1. ECU will become lockout state when Retrying Key Update counter reaches the count 4

2. If ECU received a request for key update (for Safe Key or MAC Key) during lockout state, ECU should respond with negative response

Step 8:

Releasing lockout Process:

1. When IGN become OFF from ON, clear Counter for Retrying Key Update with "0" and release ECU from lockout state

If the Time elapsed since the reception of the start routine is more than threshold value, then stop the key update sequence and increment Counter for Retrying Key Update.

DESIGN AND IMPLEMENTATION

To ensure that critical messages containing important signals or data are genuine, they are sent through the In-Vehicle CAN network between ECUs. This guarantees that the signal or data present in these messages is coming from an authenticated entity. The Configuration ARXML file specific to the ECU specifies the messages that require authentication. Nowadays, the implementation of secured communication is commonly done using the AUTOSAR-based software architecture design.

Overview of the AUTOSAR Standard

The automotive industry uses the AUTOSAR (Automotive Open System Architecture) standard to guide the design and software implementation of Electronic Control Units (ECUs) used in vehicles. This standard provides hardware-independent software solutions and enables parallel development by both vehicle manufacturers and product suppliers. AUTOSAR facilitates the development of reliable and reusable standard modules by defining the architecture, interfaces, and design flow of ECUs. Its availability has encouraged the widespread use of the standard across the automotive industry, leading to the development of many software development tools that help users configure. (software components and generate, integrate, and build software more efficiently. By following the AUTOSAR standard, companies can develop their own software components and integrate them into ECUs. Overall, AUTOSAR standardizes the development process for system and software architecture, software module development, and application development, reducing software development time and costs.

AUTOSAR Architecture Overview

The layered AUTOSAR architecture has mainly three layers:

1. Application: This layer comprises individual software components for application purposes (SWCs). Some of the examples of application SWCs are Traffic Jam Assistance (TJA), Line Keep Assist (LKA), FAN, and Heating Control, among others. The current practice involves developing the application model first and then generating the code from this model, which can be integrated into the Base software. SWCs are the fundamental unit of this layer, and they cannot be further subdivided. They are executed on a single ECU in the vehicle.

2. Run-time Environment (RTE): The RTE layer facilitates communication between various Software Components (SWCs) as well as between SWCs and Basic Software (BSW). A standard interface is provided by the RTE, enabling well-defined abstraction. Various types of RTE ports can be established, such as Client-Server ports and Sender-Receiver ports.

3. Basic Software (BSW): Each sub-layer of BSW provides different services

  i. **Services**: The Service Layer in BSW provides fundamental functionalities to other BSW modules, the RTE layer, and the application layer above RTE. It offers services related to the operating system, communication and memory management, as well as state management. The layer also includes security modules such as Cryptographic Service Manager (CSM) and Secured Onboard Communication (Seok).
 ii. **ECU Abstraction**: The ECU Abstraction Layer services are utilized by the Application Layer functions to communicate with microcontroller-related drivers. Despite the software running on the same hardware board, the ECU Abstraction Layer isolates the higher Application Layer from the actual hardware. It provides an application programming interface (API) for any device, regardless of whether it is an internal or external microcontroller device.
iii. **Microcontroller Abstraction**: The abstraction layer contains drivers that allow direct access to the microcontroller, such as the ADC driver, NVM memory driver, DMA access code, and CAN driver. This layer helps to separate the upper layers from the microcontroller dependency.

iv. **Complex Drivers**: This layer enables the integration of non-AUTOSAR-based components, such as drivers, into the framework, and provides direct interfaces for microcontroller access.

AUTOSAR Software Architecture and Features for Security

The software architecture of the AUTOSAR standard incorporates security mechanisms that are utilized by various software modules and application software components. The architecture provides interface descriptions and procedures to ensure secure communication over the vehicle network. Different security mechanisms are available for implementation, and vehicle manufacturers have the flexibility to develop their security strategies and implement security mechanisms as per their requirements. Fig. (**14**) provides an illustration of the various security mechanisms that can be implemented.

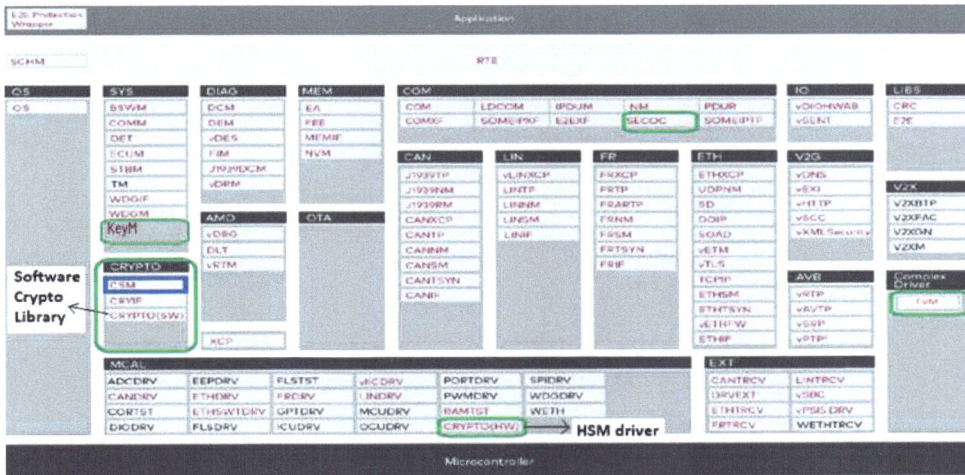

Fig. (14). AUTOSAR 4.3 Architecture Overview.

CSM (Crypto Service Manager): Application software components and basic software uses the standardized interface services provided by the CSM to access the cryptographic algorithms or functions which are present in Crypto (SW) or Crypto (HW).

CRYIF (Crypto Interface): CSM will call the crypto interfaces to pass the service requests from the upper layer to the lower CRYPTO software or hardware drivers. Based on the input Crypto driver will calculate the results using cryptographic functions and the result will pass to the CSM from the crypto interface layer.

CRYPTO(SW): The software-based CRYPTO specification offers a superset of algorithms which can be extended by 'custom algorithms. This is the Software Library for Cryptographic algorithms.

CRYPTO(HW): If the Cryptographic Software Library is replaced by the Hardware Secure Module (HSM), then the Driver used for communication with the HSM module, known as CRYPTO(HW), is necessary. This driver enables communication and configuration of the HSM core features.

Secured On-board Communication: The AUTOSAR SOC module offers a security mechanism that verifies and authenticates the I-PDUs using the Freshness Value Manager (FVM). At the PDU level, the SOC software module guarantees authentication mechanisms for all critical data. It adds a MAC to the message before transmitting it and sends the entire message content to PDUR. When receiving a message, it verifies the MAC and passes the protected data and counter information to upper application SWCs if verification is successful, as shown in Fig. (**15**).

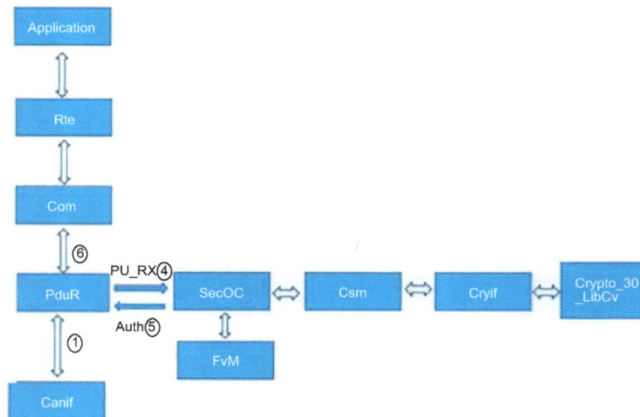

Fig. (15). Design flow within security software modules.

Design Flow within AUTOSAR Security Software Modules

SOC: Rx MAC verification and Tx MAC generation jobs are triggered by Secured On-board Communication module after getting the freshness value from FVM.

FVM: Freshness Value Manager (FVM) stores the reset counter, message counter values which are required for MAC calculation

Csm, Cry If, Crypto_30_LibCv: The crypto stack where the MAC generation and MAC verification takes place.

Implementation of in-vehicle Message Authentication

The design of in-vehicle Message Authentication should prioritize enhancing code efficiency, security, readability, and debug capabilities for improved performance. The data and control flow of message authentication implementation can be seen in detail in Figs. (**16** and **17**), which are illustrated in the two sequence diagrams provided for transmitting and receiving messages, respectively.

Sequence Diagram Authentication during Direct Transmission

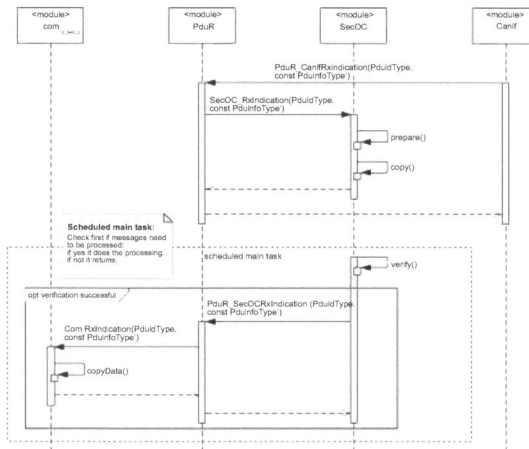

Fig. (16). Sequence Diagram for Authentication during direct transmission.

Sequence Diagram Verification during Direct Reception

The implementation of In-Vehicle Message Authentication in embedded systems can be challenging due to limited bandwidth and resources. Therefore, the design should take into account these constraints and ensure that all global data elements (such as flags, tables, and parameters) required for implementing the specifications are only stored in either Secure RAM or Secure NVRAM, unless otherwise specified. Additionally, software code that does not use these data elements should not have access to them.

Fig. (17). Sequence Diagram for Verification during direct reception.

Introduction to DaVinci Developer tool

The DaVinci Developer tool is utilized for designing the architecture of ECU software application components that adhere to the AUTOSAR standard for software development. This tool facilitates the graphical representation of interface design, linking of software components, and defining the behaviour of runnable tasks. The AUTOSAR is a standardized software architecture developed for automotive Electronic Control Units (ECUs). This architecture comprises user-defined functional software components that are executed on a basic software (BSW) stack with standardized functionality. To ensure that the software components meet the AUTOSAR compliance requirements, the tool provides a consistency check to validate the correctness and completeness of the design, as shown in Fig. (**18**).

Fig. (18). Vector Davinci Developer tool.

Introduction to DaVinci Configurator Pro Tool

The Configurator Pro tool takes an input in the form of an arm format system description file. Additionally, configuration updates can also be made using existing common network description files. Typically, the database file DBC contains the vehicle network information that serves as input for the Configurator Pro tool. During the configuration process, the tool verifies the validity of each parameter or attribute, as well as their interrelationships. If any configuration errors are detected, the tool displays recommended actions for correction. These features make the configuration of complex systems and the integration of generated files into the framework more straightforward. The tool helps generate software code for RTE and BSW software modules with great efficiency. With many built-in features, the tool supports reduced software development time and implementation costs. There are numerous software checks that can be enabled, and the tool's report supports the development of products in accordance with safety standards. Software developers can select the RTE and various Basic software modules configuration options according to their needs.

Introduction to CANoe Tool Environment

CANoe is a software program that helps create a testing environment for simulating an entire vehicle network or just one ECU. Users can perform simulations using CAPL scripts and create visual displays using PANEL. After verification, the tool provides different graphical and text-based windows with relevant information to analyze the results. It also includes a predefined set of test features that can be automated for faster execution, as shown in Figs. (**19** and **20**).

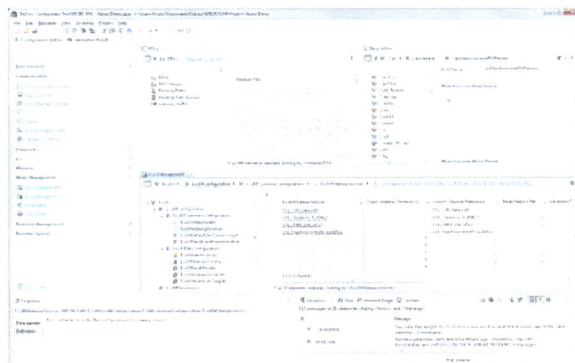

Fig. (19). DaVinci Configurator Pro tool.

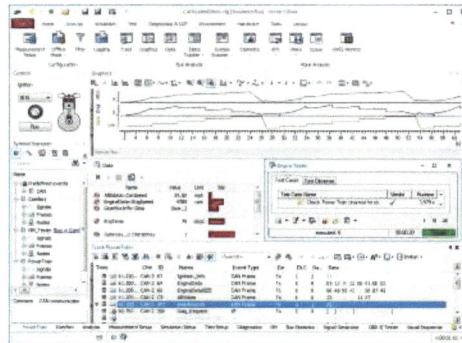

Fig. (20). CANoe user interface.

Outcome information will be recorded in the logging file following the successful completion of the measurement. This logging file can be kept in memory and then used for additional analysis, as seen in Fig. (**21**).

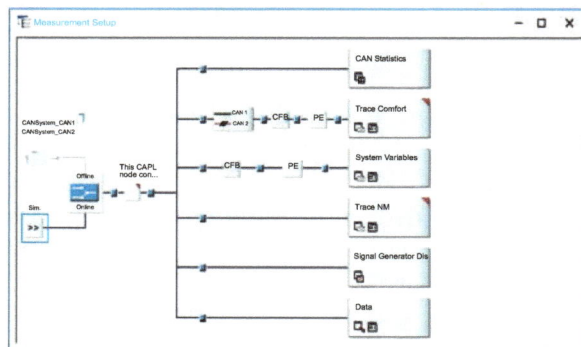

Fig. (21). Measurement Setup in CANoe.

Test Setup and CAN message Data Base for Verification

This chapter provides information about the results obtained by establishing a physical Hardware ECU and a virtual CAN network for transmitting and receiving CAN control messages, including generated MAC. The virtual CAN environment used to simulate the results is shown in the figure below. This environment was created in the CANoe tool, which simulates many CAN nodes using the CAPL programming method. The virtual environment contains multiple ECUs such as Electronic Parking Brake, Electronic Brake system, Engine Management System, Power steering unit, Gateway, and other Units. These ECUs use the CAN protocol to send messages to the main control unit, as shown in Fig. (**22**).

To create the software's database and configuration files, both CANoe and Davinci Developer tools are used. The figures below depict the Content EYE (or Vision) ECU, which displays the MAC and Counter information used by the Control Message. Fig. (**23**) can be used to select the CAN transmit and receive MAC messages for verification from the database.

Software Flashing Method

After configuring all the necessary AUTOSAR software modules to meet the requirements, the code files must be generated from the Davinci Configurator Pro tool and integrated with the base framework. The Tasking compiler can then be used to build the code, resulting in the creation of a .hex file that can be flashed to the Target Hardware board. To perform the flashing process, the Win idea tool and Debugger (Fig. **24**) should be utilized. The Win idea environment for software flashing is illustrated in the following figure.

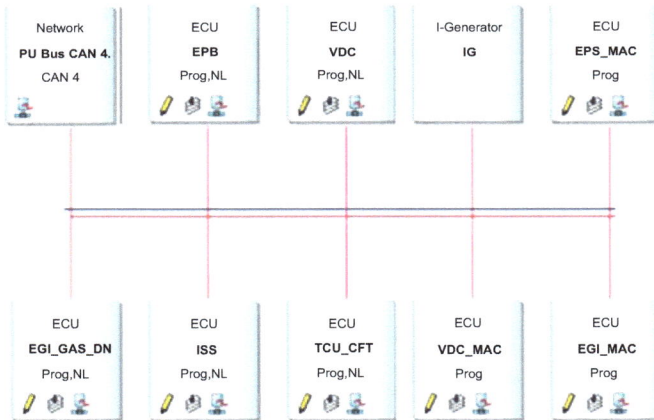

Fig. (22). Network Virtual Simulation Setup.

Fig. (23). Data Base for Vision ECU.

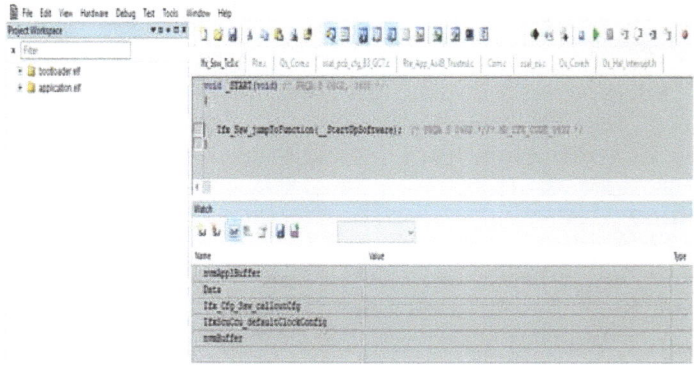

Fig. (24). Win idea tool for software flashing.

After the win idea tool begins the software download process, both the Bootloader and Application software will be flashed to the target hardware board, as depicted in Fig. (**25**). The progress of the download can be monitored as illustrated below.

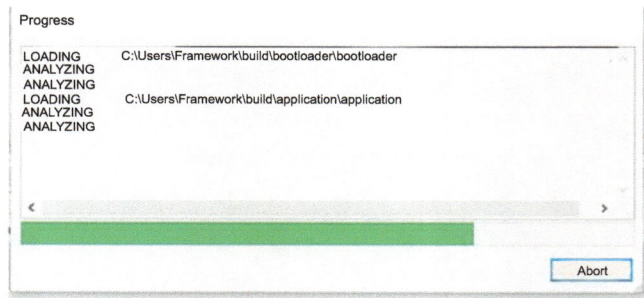

Fig. (25). Software flashing progress.

Secret Key Storage into the Target Hardware Memory

To generate the MAC, a 128-bit key must be input to the CMAC algorithm module along with 128 bits of Authenticated data. The secret Key must be stored in the memory location by using a Key Management tool as shown below. The key management tool will send the UDS command with Service ID ox31 (Routine control service) and follow the Key storage procedure to store the Secret key in the Target Hardware memory. Here the new key of 0xFFFFFFFFFFFFFFFFFFFFFFFFFFFFFFFF is flashing using the Key Management tool. The UDS command sequence is highlighted at the bottom of the tool in Fig. (**26**).

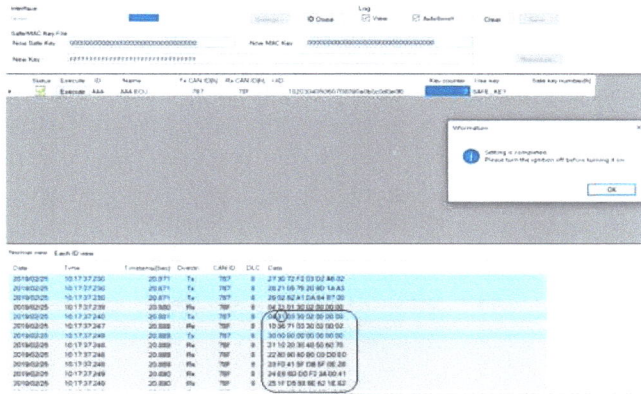

Fig. (26). Key Management tool.

After the Key Management tool successfully stores the Secret Key value in the ECU NVM memory, its correctness can be confirmed during software runtime by using the Win idea debugger watch window with a breakpoint set. It can be observed that the respective NVM memory locations have stored a Secret Key with the same value of 0xFF. For security purposes, some random values are written in the following 8 consecutive memory locations, and then the rest of the Key values are stored, as illustrated in Fig. (27).

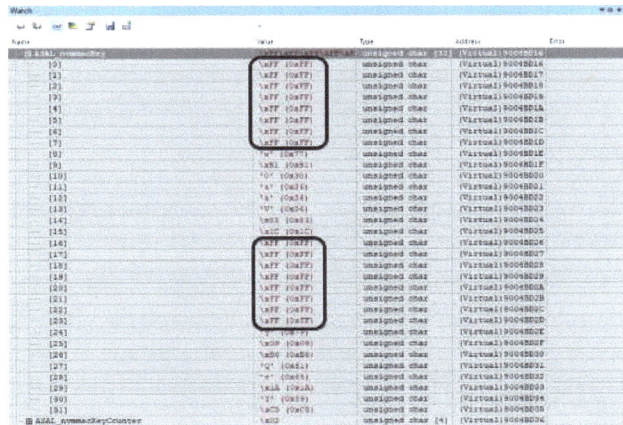

Fig. (27). Secret Key Value on the Debugger Watch window.

Verification Result for Message Authentication

After successfully configuring all security modules, the code files will be generated using the Davinci Configurator Pro tool and integrated into the Framework. The resulting software will be compiled, and the generated Hex file will be flashed to the Target hardware board. Upon software startup, CAN transmit frames with MAC will be visible on the Trace window, as depicted in Fig. **(28)**. Similarly, a CANoe simulation environment can be utilized to send control messages with MAC to the EYE (or vision) ECU. At the EYE ECU side, MAC verification will occur, and if successful, the CAN message data will be extracted and further processed. If verification fails, the entire message will be discarded. The MAC verification result can be observed in the form of a flag named MAC_OK or MAC_NG on another CAN transmit message (ID 0x760), as shown in the figure below. A MAC_OK flag will be set to High for successful MAC verification, whereas a MAC_NG flag will be set to High for MAC verification failures.

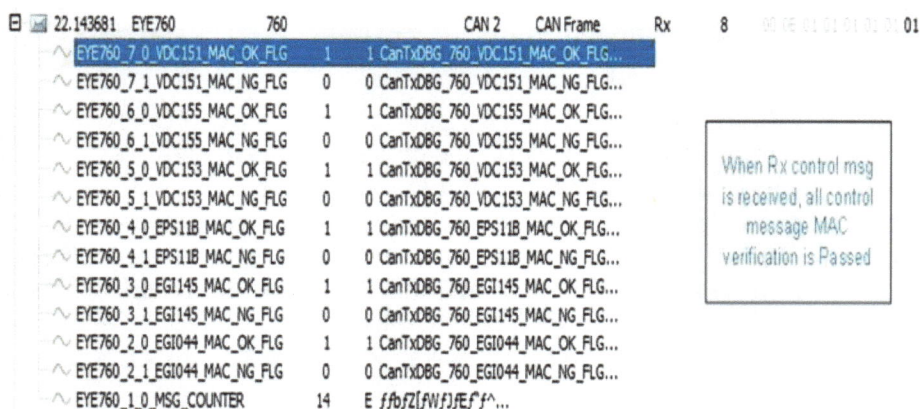

Fig. (28). MAC verification result display for all Receive MAC messages.

MAC Messages

Although the EYE ECU may receive the Rx Control Message accurately, the MAC Verification can still fail if the secret key is entered incorrectly. When this happens, the MAC_NG flag will be raised for all MAC messages. It's important to verify the MAC transmit messages at the receiver's end. One option for doing this is using the CANoe simulation environment, or alternatively, the online CMAC calculator can also be utilized to verify the messages.

Additional Test Methods for Cyber Security Verification and Validation

In addition to verifying the normal functionality based on the specific requirements, extra testing methods must be employed to ensure the validation and verification of cyber security.

1. Vulnerability Scanning: The objective of this test is to identify any weaknesses in the system that could potentially be exploited to compromise its security. The

purpose of the test is to locate security gaps and report any possible vulnerabilities, such as weaknesses in algorithms, in the target system. Organizations typically maintain a database of known security risks that can be used in this type of testing. The vulnerable scan method will use this database to test the object, covering both positive and negative cases to ensure comprehensive testing.

2. Fuzz Testing: Essentially, the purpose of the test is to assess the overall strength of the system. This can be accomplished through manual or automated testing methods, in which systematically malformed input is sent to the system or software in order to evaluate its robustness. The test results are then reported.

3. Penetration Testing: This type of test is designed to simulate an actual attacker's attempt to exploit the target system. Its purpose is to identify weaknesses, potential errors, or vulnerabilities in the system.

CONCLUSION

The automotive industry is currently facing both opportunities and challenges in the domain of cybersecurity. Achieving a fully autonomous level for vehicles is a difficult task and presents numerous technical and business-related obstacles. As a result, it has become a compelling topic of interest for vehicle manufacturers and Tier-N product developers alike.

In recent years, the industry has started to focus on addressing cybersecurity issues related to vehicles. However, the security issues for connected cars are not yet fully understood, and it may take another 2 to 3 years for security countermeasures to become widely integrated into products.

CONSENT FOR PUBLICATION

Not applicable.

CONFLICT OF INTEREST

The authors declare no conflict of interest, financial or otherwise.

ACKNOWLEDGEMENT

Declared none.

REFERENCES

[1] "Textbook: Cryptography and Network Security by Behrouz A. Frozen",

[2] "Automotive Cyber Security, Threat modeling of the AUTOSAR standard master's thesis in Computer

Systems and Networks by ADI KARAHASANOVIC, Vector: MICROSAR Product Information.pdf",

[3]   "SAE J3061 – Cyber security guidebook for cyber-physical vehicle systems",

[4]   A. Manjunath Managuli, "Deshpande and S. H. Ayatti, "Emergent vehicle tracking system using IR sensor", *2017 International Conference on Electrical, Electronics, Communication, Computer, and Optimization Techniques (ICEECCOT),* pp. 71-74, 2017.Mysuru, India.
[http://dx.doi.org/10.1109/ICEECCOT.2017.8284579]

[5]   M. Managuli, and A. Deshpande, "Description and identification of soil quality measuring development using uav's and e-nose system", *International Journal of Recent Technology and Engineering (IJRTE),* vol. 8, no. 3, pp. 3542-3545, 2019.
[http://dx.doi.org/10.35940/ijrte.C5276.098319]

[6]   "ISO 14229: Road vehicles Unified diagnostic services (UDS)-Specification and requirements Intel Security McAfee Whitepaper. Automotive security best practices. Recommendations for security and privacy in the era of the next-generation car",

[7]   V.J. Pandurangi, M. Managuli, S. Salakhe, S. Bangarshetti, and P.N. Kunchur, "Detection & Classification of Electronic Nose System",
[http://dx.doi.org/10.1109/ICICCS51141.2021.9432248]

[8]   Cybersecurity In Automotive, *How to Stay Ahead of Cyber Threats Can specification from Robert Bosch.*.

[9]   Manjunath Managuli, "A role of Electronic nose system Information gathering with smartphone", *Materials Today, Elsevier,* vol. 43, no. 6, pp. 3404-3408, 2021.

[10]   C. Cossack, R. Otis, and K. Salkowski, *Paradigm change of vehicle cyber security.,* 2012.
http://www.evitaproject.org/index.html

[11]   http://ieeecss.org/general/impact-control-technology

[12]   K.T. Krishnamurthy, and M. Managuli, "R. S, K. R. Niranjan, D. Kumar and S. B. Malipatil, "Development of Overflow Prediction and Wall Supervision System for Flood Forecasting", *2022 International Interdisciplinary Humanitarian Conference for Sustainability (IIHC),* 2022pp. 121-125 Bengaluru, India
[http://dx.doi.org/10.1109/IIHC55949.2022.10060205]

[13]   P. Kunchur, M. Managuli, S. Bangarashettar, U. Deshpande, S. Salake, and S. Potnis, ""Resource Provisioning And Load Evaluating In Cloud Atmosphere Using Optimization Techniques", Tianjin Daxue Xuebao (Ziran Kexue Yu Gongcheng Jishu Ban)", *Tianjin Daxue Xuebao,* vol. 55, no. 1, 2022.
[http://dx.doi.org/10.55582/JTUST.2022.55104]

CHAPTER 4

A Decision Model for Reliability Analysis of Agricultural Sensor Data for Smart Irrigation 4.0

Subhash Mondal[1], Samrat Podder[1] and **Diganta Sengupta[1,*]**

[1] *Department of Computer Science and Engineering, Meghnad Saha Institute of Technology, Kolkata, India*

Abstract: Agriculture is the backbone of an Agro-based Country's Economic System as it employs the majority of the population. Internet-of-Things (IoT)-based intelligent systems help reduce losses and make efficient use of available resources. This paper aims to detect anomaly conditions that might occur in sensor nodes related to day-t--day smart irrigational activities in an agricultural field. IoT-based irrigation systems being prone to unauthorized intrusion can cause damage to smart farms in terms of crop damage and infertility of the soil. In this paper, we propose an intelligent decision-making system that can identify Anomalous Conditions and Suspicious Activities. The model discussed in this paper uses the idea of Gaussian distribution, which calculates the expected probability of a given state of an agricultural field and classifies anomalies based on what previous probabilities of an anomaly state looked like. The approach classifies the anomalies with an accuracy of 80.79%, a precision of 0.81, and a recall of 0.54 under test conditions.

Keywords: Smart Farming, Internet of Things, Anomaly Detection, Sensor Nodes, Smart Irrigation.

INTRODUCTION

Anomaly detection, also known as Outlier Detection, is the technique of identifying events that deviate from a systems' normal behavior [1]. Such anomalous events can indicate situations such as technical glitches, a shift in monitored systems' behavior, fraudulent activities, or Cyber-Attacks. Therefore, it is crucial to detect such events for improvement in existing systems, to detect, and prevent cyber-attacks and fraudulent activities. To date, a huge amount of research has been done on Anomaly Detection, earlier by the Statistical Research communities and lately by computer science researchers. Some of the notable Anomaly Detection applications have been applied in detecting credit-card transaction frauds, malignant tumors, detecting a fault in manufactured

---

* **Corresponding author Diganta Sengupta:** Department of Computer Science and Engineering, Meghnad Saha Institute of Technology, Kolkata, India; Tel: 7044598807; E-mail: sg.diganta@ieee.org,msit.edu.in

components like car engines, and for detecting unusual network traffic in a data center. Automated Irrigation Systems rely solely upon the data received from the Perceptron/Sensing Layer, which is made up of Physical Sensors and Actuators [2]. The data from sensing layer while being communicated to the middleware layer by the network layer is vulnerable. The sensing layer is vulnerable to node capturing, Sleep-Deprivation Attacks, False Data Injection Attack, and many more. The Network Layer is vulnerable to Phishing Attacks, Access attacks, DDoS/DoS attacks, Data Transmit attacks, Routing attacks. While the data is being recorded and sent for analysis, there remains a huge possibility of modification of data intentionally/unintentionally, especially in the case of False Data Injection Attacks. In addition, in some regions, manual damage to the agricultural fields by rival farmers is a possibility. Therefore, a pre-programmed routine Automated Irrigation System is not enough. In such cases, it is important to detect such outlier events and report the event to the System Administrator. The various layers discussed above are shown in Fig. (**1**). This chapter focuses on identifying such nonperforming or intruded nodes, and restricting transmission of altered data. The anomalies are detected based on historical data, and any deviation from the normal performance according to the learning curve of the algorithm using the historical data is cautioned. For analysis of the historical data, learning approach has been used which classifies the reliability in a binary class – True Node or False Node; True/False being the state of the node under attack or manipulation. Gaussian distribution function has been used as the learning algorithm. The results from our experiment are satisfactory and presented in the results section of this chapter.

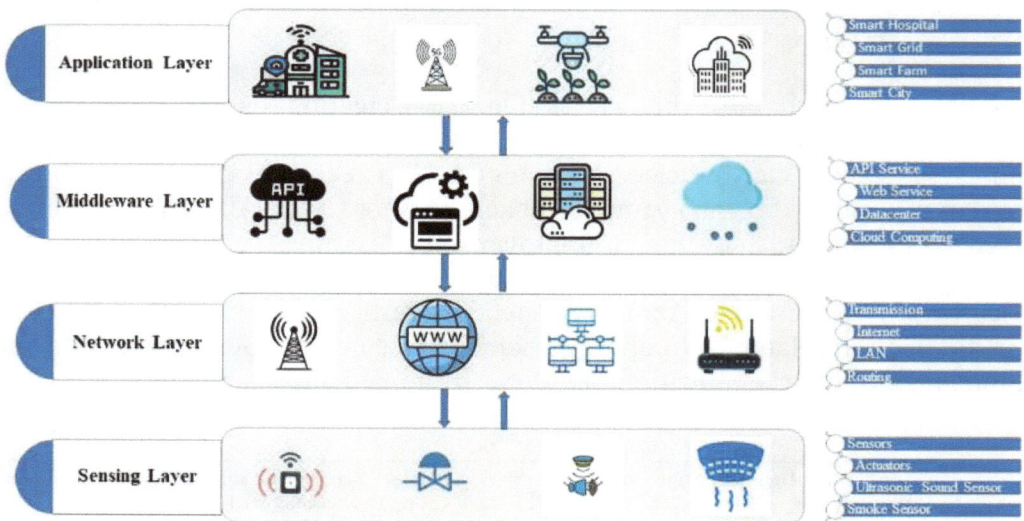

Fig. (1). Layer Structure of IoT.

Some crops are extremely sensitive to minor changes in the environment. In such cases [3], the availability of correct data about environmental conditions is very important for the IoT-based Smart Farming System. For example, if the transmission of soil moisture data is delayed or if False Data is sent to the system, then, it might lead to Over-Irrigation or under-Irrigation. Therefore, it is important for Decision Making Systems in Smart Farms to have an understanding of the data and then decide if the data received is reliable or not. To be applied to Smart Farming, Anomaly Detection Systems need to be lightweight because IoT systems are generally low-powered devices with limited memory and computational capabilities. In this paper, we propose a Lightweight Anomaly Detection Model which can detect and indicate anomalous conditions and give the System an indication of whether the data received by it, is reliable or not.

The rest of the paper is organized as follows. Section 2 presents the Literature Survey followed by the Proposed Methodology in Section 3. Section 4 presents the Results and Analysis of the model with the next section concluding with discussions.

LITERATURE SURVEY

Many academic and industrial researchers are working hard for implementing Secure and Reliable IoT Systems in Smart Farming and addressing open issues in the domain. Readers are directed to Table 2.1 of [4] for the taxonomy on methods for smart farming topics.

Strengthening the security of a system is essential to protect the data and prevent unauthorized access to resources. In this paper [5], a clustering-based algorithm, enhanced DBScan, was used to identify anomaly situations. It was concluded that enhanced DBScan had a higher recognition accuracy and as compared to other algorithms, had a special fast speed.

Agriculture has been one of the most important sectors in India's Economic Growth, yet this sector is lagging behind most of the world because of primitive agricultural methods. IoT and Automation Systems using Artificial Intelligence can handle the problem of crop monitoring and maintenance. An IoT device consisting of multiple sensors was designed [6]. This device ran multiple Artificially Intelligent workflows to ensure that water, fertilizers, and other important components reached the soil, as required.

Smart Farming environments implementing IoT Systems are extremely vulnerable to Cyber Attacks. Such attacks can be very harmful to the country's economy because such dynamic and distributed attacks can cause disruption in Food Supply Chain and limit the supply of raw materials to industries. Such cybersecurity issues and open research questions related to security and data privacy have been discussed in the paper [7].

IoT Systems help monitor and control farm environments from a remote location. When sensor nodes report abnormal data, we cannot know instantly which can cause incorrect decision making. To handle anomalies on time, linear regression was used in this paper [8], to calculate the trends of each sensor in a given time range which can be obtained from slopes of regression lines. To compute the upper and lower bounds, quartile method was used. These upper and lower bounds were used to check if the slopes were exceeding the predetermined threshold. Accordingly, outliers were judged.

Different Automation Practices such as IoT, Machine Learning, and Deep Learning can be implemented in some areas of agriculture such as crop diseases detection, lack of storage management, irrigation management, pesticide control, weed management. Paper [9] proposes an idea of training models in such a way that it identifies plants and flowers accurately and then decides the resources required for the environment of the plant such as the amount of water at a regular interval. Network Architectures such as VGG16, ResNet, Inception, Xception can be used as they are already ready to be implemented *via* python library Keras [10].

A decision support system called the Anomaly hotSpots of Agricultural Production was introduced in the paper [11]. The paper deals with a classification algorithm which gives out warnings by the analysis of rainfall estimates and by the remotely sensed biophysical status of vegetation. Then a summary report is generated for the warnings labelled on the scale of none to four. The administrative units for which the warnings were generated are further reviewed by the on-field experts who inspect for further analysis and help in the process of identification of national level hotspots.

A crop monitoring system with a suitable crop prediction system was proposed in paper [12]. A logistic regression-based model was developed with the help of TensorFlow [13] to predict the chances of proper yield of a certain crop given the current environmental conditions such as Temperature, Soil Moisture and Soil Type. Also, a Support Vector Machine (SVM) was trained using the same environmental data to predict the crop which was most suitable in the given conditions. Also, a web-based application using PHP in the backend was hosted on AWS T2. Micro EC2 [14] instance to help farmers monitor and control on-field machineries. Another android application was developed which showed the current status of the farm and also allowed to configure the field settings.

In the paper [15], few different models were deployed in combination for prediction of historical soil data. The historical soil data include N, P, K, pH, Temperature which were used as input for the ARIMA [16] model, which forecasted the same parameters. The output from the ARIMA model was then fed to the KNN [17] Classifier for Crops that classified values against typical nutrient values of the crops found commonly in the regions. Again, the output from the ARIMA model was then fed to the KNN Classifier for fertilizers which classified the predicted values to the typical nutrient levels obtained by the combination of organic fertilizers. Finally, all the classified data was reported on the website with cultivation guide along with predicted fertilizer for the crop.

PROPOSED METHODOLOGY

The pipeline followed for the proposed methodology has been briefly described in Fig. (**2**), which on the top-level shows 4 stages namely Dataset Acquisition, Preprocessing, Framework and Decision. All the stages have been discussed in subsequent sections. The notations used in this chapter are provided in Table **1**.

Table 1. Notations used in this chapter.

Notations	Meaning
CR	New DeSeasoned Vector
Cr	Data of current year of the features to be de-seasoned
Prev	Data of previous year of the features to be de-seasoned
P(x)	Probability Density Function
m	Number of records in dataset
x_1	Average Air Temperature
x_2	Soil Temperature at 8 inches below ground level
$x\_(3)$	Wind Speed
x_4	Air Pressure
x_5	Soil Moisture
π	Product of expressions

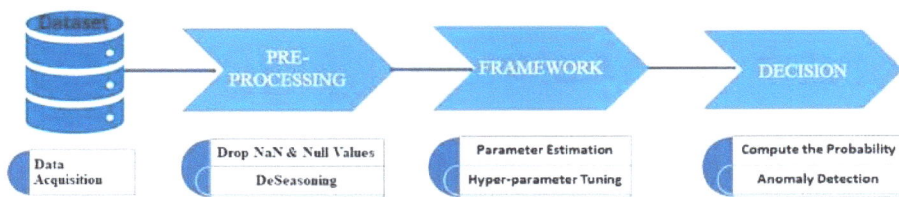

Fig. (2). Proposed Pipeline.

Dataset Acquisition

One of the many challenges of working in an Anomaly Detection System is the limited availability of labeled data for training/validation of models. Often the data tends to contain noise that behaves to be similar to the actual anomalies and therefore it is difficult to make out the difference between the two and remove the noise. The dataset used for the preparation of the model proposed in this paper is collected from the Report Generator 2.0 by the National Water and Climate Centre [18], United States Department of Agriculture. The data reporting sensors are a part of the Soil Climate Analysis Network (SCAN). The key data that the dataset contains are – Precipitation, Air Temperature (Max, Min, and Average) in degC, Soil Moisture in percent, Soil Temperature in degC, Soil Salinity in grams, Solar Radiation in units, Wind Speed in mph, Wind Direction in deg, Relative Humidity in percent, Air Pressure in kPa. According to the Knowledge Base, Soil Moisture is measured using a Dielectric constant measuring device, Soil temperature using an Encapsulated thermistor, precipitation using tipping bucket gauge, air temperature using a shielded thermistor, relative humidity using Thin-film capacitance-type sensor, wind speed/direction using a propeller-type anemometer, solar radiation using pyranometer, barometric pressure using Silicon capacitive pressure sensor. Measurements are at 2", 4", 8", 20", and 40" where possible. All sensor data is reported hourly. Table **2** describes the dataset and Fig. (**3**) presents the feature contributions in the dataset.

Table 2. Dataset Description.

Date (Object)	Air Temperature Average (float)	Soil Moisture – 2 inch (float)	....	Soil Temperature Observed -20inch (float)	Soil Temperature Observed -40 inch (float)
....	....	....	......	....	....

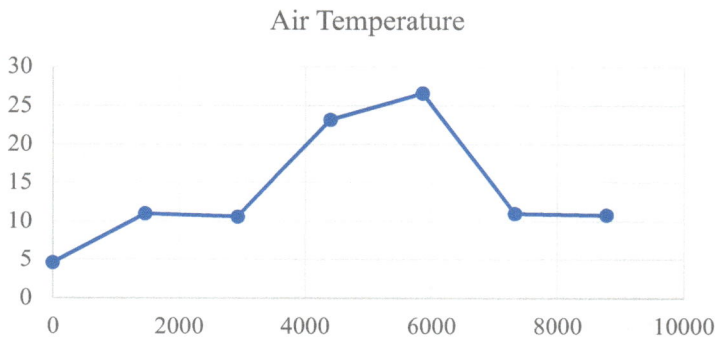

Air Temperature

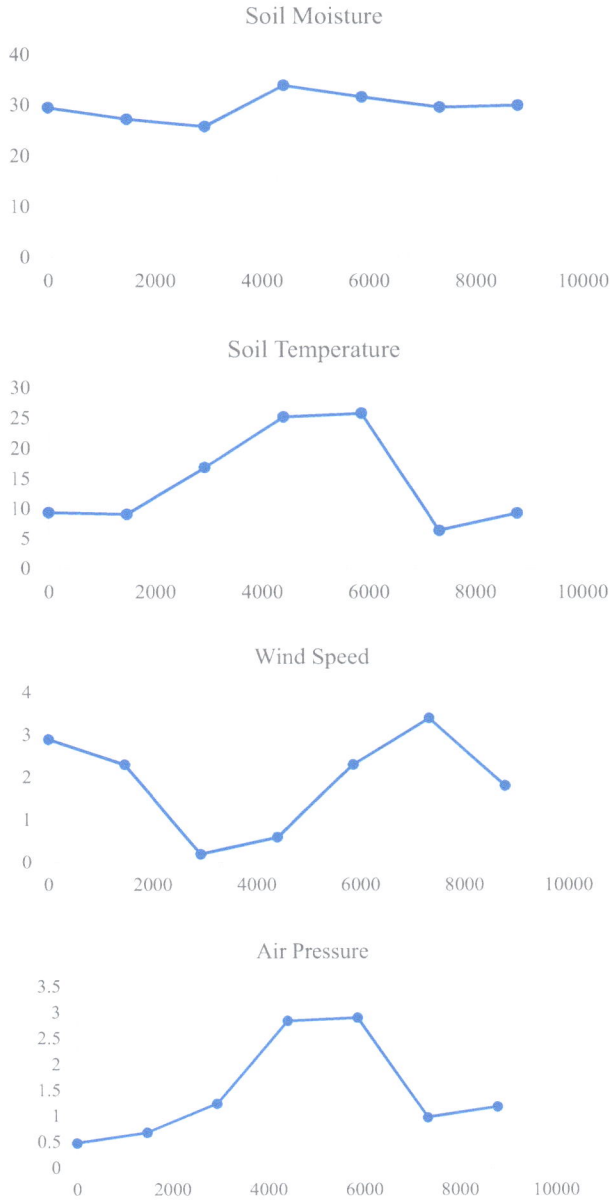

Fig. (3). Feature contributions.

Dataset Pre-Processing

The features used among all the available data were soil temperature, air temperature, air pressure, wind direction/speed, and soil moisture. Though being important, some of the features, such as Relative Humidity, Solar Radiation, Soil Salinity, had to be discarded due to insufficient/erroneous/inconsistent data. The dataset was searched thoroughly for missing data. In case any data was missing, the entire row was removed from the dataset. This removal did not affect the training set much because the number of such rows was less than 0.1% of the entire dataset. Sometimes, it was noticed that some of the fields had -99.9 as their data, which was absurd considering that environmental conditions in an agricultural field are not likely to be such extreme. After careful considerations, some of the rows containing -99.9 in their fields were pushed to the test dataset as these could serve the purpose of imitating actual anomalous conditions. One of the interesting points is that since the dataset is very large gathered from public domain, the data collection had been done from field study; hence, hierarchical clustering [19] could also have been used for data pre-processing. We tend to explore this dimension in the extension of this work.

The hourly reported feature, Air Temperature, showed a seasonal trend repeated every year. Therefore, to eliminate the seasonal component from the data, equation 1 has been employed for de-seasoning the relevant data from the consecutive years, the process is elaborated in [20].

$$CR = \frac{1}{2} \times (Cr - Prev)^2 \qquad (1)$$

Where CR is the new DeSeasoned Vector, Cr is the 1D vector consisting of the data from the current year, Prev is the 1D vector consisting of the data from the previous year.

Framework

The dataset is now cleaned and de-seasoned. Now, the model needs to be trained on the date. In this section, we have discussed the detailed procedure of model training. Section Algorithm is about the Gaussian Distribution which is the core-concept of the proposed model. Next in Section Parameter Estimation, we have discussed how to calculate the parameters, mean μ and variance $\sigma2$. Section Modeling or Training Stage discusses the overall modelling scheme, where the probability of each data point is calculated based on the parameters, mean μ and variance $\sigma2$ which were calculated in the previous section. The calculated probability tells us how likely it is for a given instance to not be an anomaly. Finally, Section Hyper-Parameter Estimation tells us how to calculate the hyper-parameter ε, which will be used to compare and classify a given example as Anomalous or Not-Anomalous. In this regard, it can be noted that since we have used categorical data in this work, it can further be clustered using Silhouette

Coefficient [21], and in places is mixed set of data is present (categorical and, or numerical), then the method used in [22] can be used. Although in our work, the data has been handled using the pre-processing method discussed in the earlier section.

Algorithm

The algorithm is based on Gaussian (Normal) Probability Distribution. In Probability Theory, a Gaussian Distribution is a type of continuous probability distribution for a random variable x. The algorithm is as follows.

Algorithm
1. Load training data and test data from .csv files

2. Select the feature columns which are to be modeled from the data
3. Calculate the probability distribution of the entire dataset with the help of mean and variance which is also Calculated from the entire train dataset.
4. Calculate the range of probabilities and stepsize of hyperparameter vector from which hyperparameter will be chosen
5. Start the model training by traversing possible set of hyperparameter values
for in range min(probability) to max(probability), increment by stepsize:
if eps is our hyperparameter for the current traversal:
then perform classification and get classification report
end if
if current f1 score > previous f1 score:
then update best_Hyperparameter to eps
end if
6. Now with the best_Hyperparameter perform classification on the test data.
7. end

Equation 2 presents the probability density function (PDF) for the distribution.

$$P(x) = \frac{1}{\sigma\sqrt{2\pi}} e^{-\frac{1}{2}\left(\frac{x-\mu}{\sigma}\right)^2} \tag{2}$$

Equation 2 says that, if $x \in \mathbb{R}$, then x is a distributed Gaussian with mean μ, variance σ^2 and standard deviation σ.

Parameter Estimation

The probability $P(x)$ is parameterized by the mean μ and variance σ^2, written as $P(x; \mu, \sigma^2)$.

The parameter mean μ is estimated as follows eq. (3):

$$\mu = \frac{1}{m}\Sigma^m_{i=1}x^i \tag{3}$$

The parameter variance σ^2 is estimated as follows eq. (4):

$$\sigma^2 = \frac{1}{m}\Sigma^m_{i=1}(x^i - \mu)^2 \tag{4}$$

Modeling/Training Stage

We begin with training the model with the training data, as discussed in dataset acquisition. The features selected for modeling are - x_1 = Average Air Temperature, x_2 = Soil Temperature at 8 inches below ground level, x_3 = Wind Speed, x_4 = Air Pressure, x_5 = Soil Moisture. All of the features are distributed Gaussians with parameters respectively (μ_1, σ_1^2), ..., (μ_5, σ_5^2). These features were selected because all of them were indicative of anomalous examples.

After the selection of features, Parameters were estimated for each feature. Now every feature has its own Gaussian model. This model is a Univariate Gaussian Distribution which can be used independently to estimate if a given Gaussian lies in the low probability area indicating an Anomaly specific to the said feature. All the Gaussian models corresponding to the respective features together produce an indicative estimate of a new example of being anomalous or not.

Eq. (5) presents the Probability Density of a given new example x is computed as

$$P(x) = P(x_1; \mu_1, \sigma_1^2) * P(x_2; \mu_2, \sigma_2^2) * P(x_3; \mu_3, \sigma_3^2) * \ldots \ldots * P(x_n; \mu_n, \sigma_n^2)$$

$$= \Pi^n_{j=1}P(x_j; \mu_j, \sigma_j^2) \tag{5}$$

In our case, n = 5, therefore equation 5 represents in Eq. (6)

$$P(x) = \Pi^5_{j=1}P(x_j; \mu_j, \sigma_j^2) \tag{6}$$

In eq. (5), * denotes integer multiplication.

A given example can be flagged as an Anomaly if the computed density of the new example is less than a specific threshold, denoted by the hyper-parameter ε.

The above equation of Px holds an assumption of independent events. In practice, this might not be the case every time but the algorithm still works fine even if events do not occur independently as in the case of air temperature and soil temperature in our dataset as shown in Fig. (4).

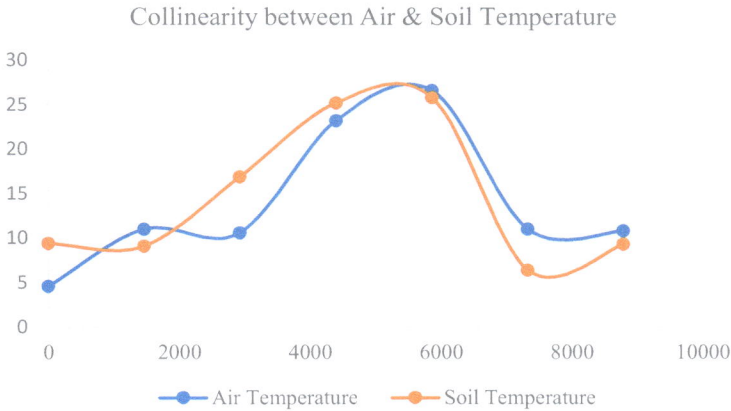

Fig. (4). Collinearity between Air & Soil Temperature.

Hyper-Parameter Tuning

The hyper-parameter ε, was optimized to achieve the highest F1 Score. Initially, the ε was set to the highest probability among all the test cases. Gradually, the ε was brought down in small steps until the best F1 score was found. The ε that gave the best F1 score was used further to classify the remaining test examples.

EXPERIMENTAL RESULT & ANALYSIS

This section discusses Performance Metrics used to evaluate our Anomaly Detection Model. The accuracy of a model is one of the most preferred performance metrics in machine learning. In our case, the dataset was skewed simply because in everyday life we do not encounter anomalies very often. Therefore, to predict "not an anomaly" in every case would yield us a very high accuracy, without actually doing any prediction based on given data. To avoid such misinterpretation, we have used some additional metrics, which are – Precision, Recall and F1 Score.

Precision

Precision is a metric that says how precise/accurate the model is. It tells that out of those predicted positive, how many of them were actually positive. This Metric tells us that out of all the cases, where we predicted the case as an "Anomaly", what fraction was actually "Anomaly". Precision is an important metric when the cost of False Positive is high, as in the case of Email Spam Classification (an important non-spam email could be marked as spam). Precision is calculated as follows in Eq. (7).

$$Precision = \frac{True\ Positive}{Predicted\ Positive} = \frac{TP}{TP+FP} \qquad (7)$$

Recall

The recall is the metric that calculates how many of the Actual Positives were actually captured by the model and marked as positives represented in Eq. (8). This metric tells us that out of all Anomalous cases, what fraction did the model detect as being Anomalous. The recall is an important metric when the cost of False Negative is high. For Instance, if a model classified a cancer patient as a person not having cancer, then it would be very dangerous.

$$Recall = \frac{True\ Positives}{Actual\ Positives} = \frac{TP}{TP+FN} \qquad (8)$$

F1. Score

In some applications it is necessary to control the trade-of between precision and recall. In order to do so, we use a metric called F1 score which helps us to maintain a balance between the precision and recall. This metric is also very useful in cases where the dataset is skewed and a model favouring a certain class in a classification problem will not perform well because F1 score generally tends to take into consideration both the precision and recall at the same time as follows in Eq. (9).

$$F1 - Score = 2 * (PR/(P + R)) \qquad (9)$$

Comparative Analysis

Anomaly Detection being an old and interesting domain holds a collection of advanced and sophisticated algorithms. The Algorithm proposed in this paper has proved to have a precision of 81%, recall of 54%, and an F1 score of 0.64. The results are not record-breaking but it holds a respectable position along with the existing algorithms and at the same time being lightweight, in terms of IoT. Table 3 presents comparative analysis of popular anomaly detection algorithms and also Figs. (5 - 7) present the metrics that the proposed model was tested upon. The AUC Score which indicates our model performance which is derived from the ROC Curve for the proposed model is 0.703.

Table 3. Comparative Analysis.

Algorithm	Accuracy	Precision	Recall	Execution Time (seconds)	Memory Use (in Megabytes)	Entropy
k-means	72.90%	0.78	0.50	2.9	10.05	0.99
Decision Tree	57.60%	0.64	0.55	3.2	10.33	0.41
Naïve Bayes	56.44%	0.72	0.53	5.5	10.31	0.27
Random Forest	79.40%	0.91	0.63	186.5	13.84	0.91
Isolation Forest	85.00%	0.93	0.81	17.9	10.50	0.61
Support Vector Machine	96.60%	0.98	0.79	25.9	10.33	0.23
Proposed Model	80.79%	0.81	0.54	12.1	6.004	0.91

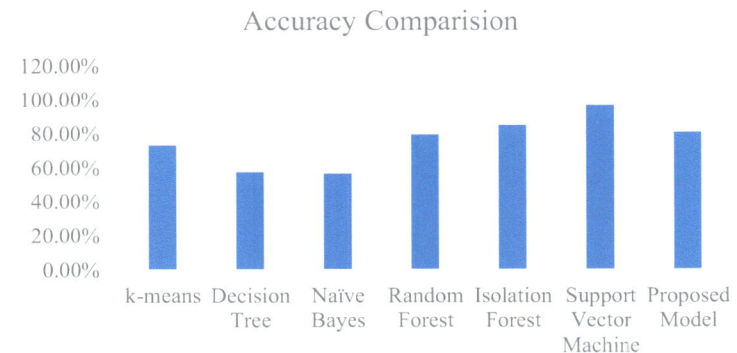

Fig. (5). Accuracy Comparisons.

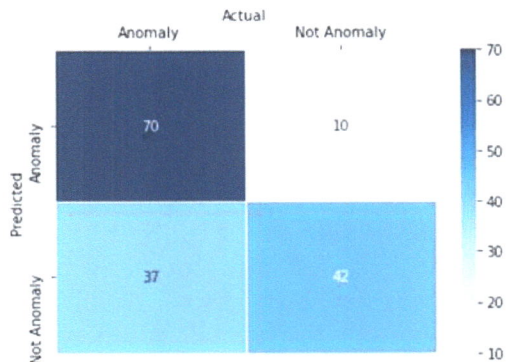

Fig. (6). Confusion Matrix.

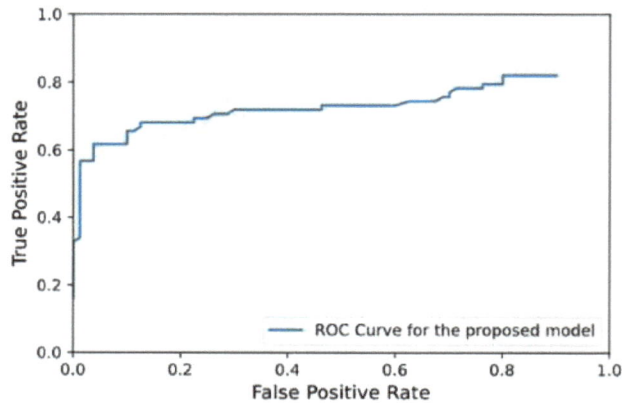

Fig. (7). ROC Curve.

Table **4** presents the standard deviations for the experimental analyses.

Table 4. Standard Deviations.

Algorithm	Accuracy	Precision	Recall
k-means	0.898	1.837	0.001
SVM	0.518	0.111	1.639
Decision Tree	0.518	0.047	1.657
Naïve Bayes	1.202	1.702	2.737
Random Forest	0.094	0.270	2.047
Isolation Forest	0.205	0.269	2.647
Proposed Model	0.100	0.204	2.815

From Table **4**, it can be deduced that the standard deviation for SVM is around 0.518. Moreover since the experiment was binary classification, hence in binary classes, the hyper plane lies in between the two classes. In this regard, SVM takes into account those data-points too which lie close to the other class in the plane. Hence with a standard deviation value of 0.518, SVM properly classifies those values thereby generating the best result in comparison. Moreover, it can be observed from the study that very few numbers of features have been included in classification. In such cases, with few features, SVM reflects the best performance as can also be observed from Table **4**. Moreover, our proposed model fares better with respect to space-time requirements.

Table **5** describes the System Specifications of the Machine in which the Algorithm was run and tested upon. The results presented in this paper are totally derived from the results obtained by running the algorithm on this machine. The table also specifies the Python Libraries that were used in implementing the proposed method.

Table 5. System Information.

System Specifications			
Intel Core i3-7100, 2 core and 4 Threads; Frequency – 3.9GHz, Cache – 3 MB Ram – DDR4 8GB 2400MHz, Non-ECC Python – 3.9 64-bit			
Library	Version	Library	Version
ipykernel	5.5.5	ipython	7.23.1
jupyter-client	6.1.12	jupyter-core	4.7.1
matplotlib-inline	0.1.2	memory-profiler	0.58.0
openpyxl	3.0.7	pandas	1.2.4
scipy	1.6.3	seaborn	0.11.1
ipython-genutils	0.2.0	numpy	1.20.3
matplotlib	3.4.2	scikit-learn	0.24.2

CONCLUSION

With the increasing popularity of modern farming techniques, automation has taken a huge role in reducing human intervention in farming processes hence decreasing labour costs and boosting quality and quantity. Such automated systems depend heavily upon Sensing and Decision-Making Systems in the Network. The main components of smart farming are Observation/Sensing, Analysis/Diagnosis/Prediction, Decision Making, and Action. In such a system, anomaly detection is an important component. Anomaly Detections are extremely useful because they can spot unusual patterns and detect shifting patterns in an agricultural field setting. At times, Faulty Instruments cause decision-making systems to misinterpret a reading and can cause huge damage to the crops. For Example, if a sensor node is not working in the way it is designed, then it can cause the automated irrigation system to overflow the field with water when the field is actually properly irrigated hence causing damage or killing healthy crops. In many parts of the world, stable sources of power are not available but keeping in mind the Concept of IoT Devices and Systems, our proposed model is extremely lightweight and moderately efficient to handle most anomalies while not having any high computation power requirements.

For future improvements to the existing model, we can have a dynamic model where the Gaussian Distribution shifts according to Date, Time, Weather, and other environmental conditions. In addition, it is possible to have multiple model profiles to account for the contextual anomalies concerning the environmental conditions. For our dataset, the data was indeed Gaussian but it might not be the case in every situation and for most cases, it is not. In case of such situations, it is possible to transform the data to Gaussian. Additionally, if transformation is not a feasible option, then we can implement clustering to the dataset and for each cluster centroid, we can build distinct separate Gaussian Models. Then for each new example, we would need to assign the appropriate cluster to the new example and then compute the Probability Density for the given example. After the Probability Density is computed, we can check for the threshold ε and classify it as appropriate. Moreover, as discussed earlier, since the dataset belonged to field studies, hence hierarchical clustering can be used for efficient clustering and pre-processing of the data. Also, we intend to implement the Silhouette Coefficient for data clustering in cases of numerical and categorical data.

CONSENT FOR PUBLICATION

Not applicable.

CONFLICT OF INTEREST

The authors declared no conflict of interest, financial or otherwise.

ACKNOWLEDGEMENT

Declared none.

REFERENCES

[1]   V. Chandola, A. Banerjee, and V. Kumar, "Anomaly detection", *ACM Comput. Surv.,* vol. 41, no. 3, pp. 1-58, 2009.
        [http://dx.doi.org/10.1145/1541880.1541882]

[2]   V. Hassija, V. Chamola, V. Saxena, D. Jain, P. Goyal, and B. Sikdar, "A Survey on IoT Security: Application Areas, Security Threats, and Solution Architectures", *IEEE Access,* vol. 7, pp. 82721-82743, 2019.
        [http://dx.doi.org/10.1109/ACCESS.2019.2924045]

[3]   P.V. Astillo, J. Kim, V. Sharma, and I. You, "SGF-MD: Behavior Rule Specification-Based Distributed Misbehavior Detection of Embedded IoT Devices in a Closed-Loop Smart Greenhouse Farming System", *IEEE Access,* vol. 8, pp. 196235-196252, 2020.
        [http://dx.doi.org/10.1109/ACCESS.2020.3034096]

[4]   A.T. Balafoutis, Smart Farming Technologies – Description, Taxonomy and Economic Impact.*Precision Agriculture: Technology and Economic Perspectives.,* M.A. Oliver, Ed., Springer: Cham, 2017, pp. 21-77.
        [http://dx.doi.org/10.1007/978-3-319-68715-5_2]

[5]   Z. Chen, and Y.F. Li, "Anomaly Detection Based on Enhanced DBScan Algorithm", *Procedia Eng.,* vol. 15, pp. 178-182, 2011.
        [http://dx.doi.org/10.1016/j.proeng.2011.08.036]

[6]   V. Puranik, and A. Sharmila, "Ranjan, and A Kumari, "Automation in Agriculture and IoT", *4th International Conference on Internet of Things: Smart Innovation and Usages (IoT-SIU),* 2019.

[7]   M. Gupta, M. Abdelsalam, S. Khorsandroo, and S. Mittal, "Security and Privacy in Smart Farming: Challenges and Opportunities", *IEEE Access,* vol. 8, pp. 34564-34584, 2020.
[http://dx.doi.org/10.1109/ACCESS.2020.2975142]

[8]   C. Ou, Y. Chen, T. Huang, and N. Huang, "Design and Implementation of Anomaly Condition Detection in Agricultural IoT Platform System", *2020 International Conference on Information Networking (ICOIN),* 2020.
[http://dx.doi.org/10.1109/ICOIN48656.2020.9016618]

[9]   K. Jha, A. Doshi, P. Patel, and M. Shah, "A comprehensive review on automation in agriculture using artificial intelligence", *Artificial Intelligence in Agriculture,* vol. 2, pp. 1-12, 2019.
[http://dx.doi.org/10.1016/j.aiia.2019.05.004]

[10]   "keras-team", keras.

[11]   F. Rembold, "ASAP - Anomaly hot Spots of Agricultural Production, a new early warning decision support system developed by the Joint Research Centre",
[http://dx.doi.org/10.1109/Multi-Temp.2017.8035205]

[12]   R. Varghese, and S. Sharma, "Affordable Smart Farming Using IoT and Machine Learning", *Second International Conference on Intelligent Computing and Control Systems (ICICCS),* 2018.
[http://dx.doi.org/10.1109/ICCONS.2018.8663044]

[13]   https://www.tensorflow.org

[14]   A.W.S. Amazon, https://aws.amazon.com/ec2/instance-types/t2

[15]   S Y Chaganti, P Ainapur, and M Singh, *and S O R, "Prediction Based Smart Farming," in 2nd International Conference of Computer and Informatics Engineering (IC2IE),,* 2019.

[16]   A. Azari, P. Papapetrou, S. Denic, and G. Peters, "Cellular Traffic Prediction and Classification: A Comparative Evaluation of LSTM and ARIMA", *International Conference on Discovery Science,* 2019
[http://dx.doi.org/10.1007/978-3-030-33778-0_11]

[17]   G. Guo, H. Wang, D.A. Bell, Y. Bi, and K. Greer, "KNN Model-Based Approach in Classification". In: Meersman, R., Tari, Z., Schmidt, D.C. (eds) On The Move to Meaningful Internet Systems 2003: CoopIS, DOA, and ODBASE. OTM 2003. Lecture Notes in Computer Science, vol 2888. Springer, Berlin, Heidelberg.
[http://dx.doi.org/10.1007/978-3-540-39964-3_62]

[18]   https://wcc.sc.egov.usda.gov/reportGenerator/

[19]   T. Märzinger, J. Kotík, and C. Pfeifer, "Application of Hierarchical Agglomerative Clustering (HAC) for Systemic Classification of Pop-Up Housing (PUH) Environments", *Appl. Sci. (Basel),* vol. 11, no. 23, p. 11122, 2021.
[http://dx.doi.org/10.3390/app112311122]

[20]   P. Kaushik, P. Yadav, and S. Akhter, De-seasoning-Based Time Series Data Forecasting Method Using Recurrent Neural Network (RNN) and Tensor Flow

[21]   D.T. Dinh, T. Fujinami, and V.N. Huynh, "Estimating the Optimal Number of Clusters in Categorical Data Clustering by Silhouette Coefficient", *International Symposium on Knowledge and Systems Sciences,* 2019pp. 1-17 Da Nang, Vietnam.
[http://dx.doi.org/10.1007/978-981-15-1209-4_1]

[22]   D.T. Dinh, V.N. Huynh, and S. Sriboonchitta, "Clustering mixed numerical and categorical data with missing values", *Inf. Sci.,* vol. 571, pp. 418-442, 2021.
[http://dx.doi.org/10.1016/j.ins.2021.04.076]

Machine Learning based Smart Electricity Monitoring & Fault Detection for Smart City 4.0 Ecosystem

Subhash Mondal[1], Suharta Banerjee[1], Sugata Ghosh[1], Adrija Dasgupta[1] and Diganta Sengupta[1,*]

[1] *Department of Computer Science and Engineering, Meghnad Saha Institute of Technology, Kolkata, India*

Abstract: Growing electricity needs among the vast majority of the population seconded by a voluminous increase in electrical appliances have led to a huge surge in electric power demands. With thediminishing unit price of electric meters and increase of loading, it has been observed that a certain amount of electric meters generate faulty readings after exhaustive usage. This results in erroneous meter readings thereby affecting the billings. We propose a fault detecting learning algorithm that is trained by early meter readings and compares the actual meter reading (AMR) with the predicted meter reading (PMR). The decision matrix generates an alarm if |PMR-AMR|>T; where T equals the threshold limit. T itself is decided by the learning algorithm depending upon the meter variance. Moreover, our system also detects if there is any power theft as such an action would result in a sudden rise in AMR. The learning algorithm deploys six binary classifiers which reflect an accuracy of 98.24% for the detection module and an error rate of 1.26% for the prediction module.

Keywords: Smart Meters, Energy Prediction, Fault Detection, Machine Learning.

INTRODUCTION

Energy be it in any form is the driving force for the development and sustainability of large sectors of the world. The form of energy in which people's livelihood is largely dependent is electricity. It has become an indispensable resource in both commercial as well as residential sectors. Electricity can be transformed into other forms of energy and can be reserved, as well as can be re-transformed into its original form whenever needed [1]. This leads to the fact that it should be used judiciously in order to serve a large sector of people.

---

* **Corresponding author Diganta Sengupta:** Department of Computer Science and Engineering, Meghnad Saha Institute of Technology, Kolkata, India; Tel: 7044598807; E-mail: sg.diganta@ieee.org, msit.edu.in

The growing population has led to a substantial rise in the demand for electricity. As a matter of fact, it has become necessary that we should use this resource wisely. Power consumption prediction can thus help to optimize usage of electricity [2]. Smart meters introduced for electricity management have the ability to increase the reliability and efficiency of power consumption [3, 4]. These meters contain a huge amount of data regarding electricity consumption [5] which allows us to invoke Machine Learning algorithms for future prediction. But these meters can also sometimes provide us with faulty data. Abnormal meter reading can be due to meter failure or a deliberate attempt to manipulating these smart meters. Fault Detection is an important aspect of identifying power theft and other electrical inefficiencies [6]. The researchers have been working from the time immemorial on developing an intelligent system capable of handling such issues.

With increasing technological advancement, to combat the real-world issues, we need more accurate prediction techniques and an enhanced detection mechanism. The introduction of Machine Learning helped researchers in addressing difficulties with the least human interference [7]. In this paper, we proposed an architecture that uses a learning algorithm to predict the meter readings. A fault detection mechanism is then trained and AMR is compared with PMR. The decision module of the architecture generates an alarm when |PMR-AMR| > T, where T is calculated using a gradient descent. The proposed model is capable of generating monthly statistical reports which help in better analysis of each smart meter.With an increase in electric consumption data, it has become possible to design an algorithm for prediction of consumption levels, and detect any anomaly. The machine learning algorithms serve the purpose as they are trained on historical data, and can classify the recent consumption pattern accordingly.

The paper is arranged as follows: related works are discussed in Section 2, our proposed architecture is explained in Section 3, followed by Experimental Results & Analysis in Section 4 and finally the paper concludes in Section 5.

RELATED WORKS

Over the years, many researchers have been addressing the issue of electricity prediction and fault detection. They have used various approaches in order to come up with an efficient solution. In this section we have discussed some of the previous techniques that were made to combat these problems.

In a study [8], Himeur *et al.* reviewed the current trends and also new perspectives of anomaly detection in energy consumption and presented various works that have taken place in this field. They also discussed various problems and challenges that are still needed to be addressed by the researchers. Krzysztof *et al.*

[9], discussed the need for monitoring the rapidly rising electricity prices using smart meters. This model predicts the electrical energy consumption for the next 24 hours using Support Vector Machines and Neural Networks.

Jiang *et al.* proposed a hybrid Machine Learning model consisting of both unsupervised clustering and supervised classification, which has been used [10] to detect the electrical energy usage of consumers based on data relayed by smart meters. Cost-sensitive XGBoost Algorithm has been used for imbalanced data [11] to build a multi-class fault prediction model using Machine Learning Techniques. In another study [12] an LSTM based neural network has been proposed for predicting the electrical energy consumption as well as for detecting anomalous data relayed by the smart grids. This approach focuses on the seasonal and monthly trends in energy consumption and decreases the forecasting error.

Wang *et al.* [13] focused on improved electricity monitoring performance. It is comprised of two modules namely energy consumption habit classifier (ECHC) and an appliance pattern matching classifier (APMC). The clustering algorithms, and other algorithms based on Gaussian Mixture (EM-GMM) can be used to develop energy prediction models as proposed in a study [14]. The uniqueness of our proposed architecture with the existing state of the art architectures is discussed in Table **1**.

Table 1. Other proposed state-of-the-art architectures and their differences with our architecture.

Description	Difference	Refs.
This paper proposes the utilization of Computational Intelligence techniques in various sources of Building Energy Management Systems (BEMS) data to get relevant information.	The model of Building Energy Management Systems (BEMS) operations has been created using modified KNN and fuzzy logic rule extraction techniques while we have used the Machine Learning techniques of Regression and Classification to build our model.	[18]
This study proposes an autoencoder-based ensemble model for smart buildings to detect anomalies in analyzing complex, high-dimensional and large-scale data	Autoencoders are used for inconsistent detection while we are proposing the use of six different classifiers to detect the anomalous readings.	[19]
Atechnique called Symbolic Aggregate approXimation (SAX) has been proposed by Capozzoli *et al.* for efficient electricity management in buildings based on time series data.	The paper uses the SAX process for detecting unexpected patterns in energy values which is different from our anomaly detection layer in which we used the classification algorithms for the process.	[20]

(Table 1) cont.....

Description	Difference	Refs.
The proposed model enables the user to check their real-time power usage for efficient energy management.	This model comprises three layers: acquisition layer, a remote server and an Android application while our model is formed of four layers: data acquisition layer, prediction layer, decision-making layer and analysis layer to predict the energy usage as well as detect anomalies.	[21]
This paper proposed an architecture based on hybrid edge-cloud computing to provide the consumers information regarding their energy usage.	The anomaly detection process is automated and then it is implemented on three different cloud structures while our analysis layer which is responsible for anomaly detection is based on six classification models to compare and contrast their accuracies.	[22]
Deep Learning techniques have been discussed in this paper for forecasting energy consumptions.	Prediction of building energy consumption has been analyzed using three deep learning techniques while we analyze five Regression algorithms in our prediction layer to forecast the energy consumption accurately,	[23]
This paper uses XGBoost for predicting irregular energy consumption. It only focuses on f1 score as a performance metrics.	Our proposed architecture is capable of predicting electric consumption as well as detecting faults using machine learning algorithms. We have benchmarked our performances using different performance metrics to ensure it is free from overfitting.	[24]
The paper mainly focuses on electricity thefts and other previously implemented methods of reducing thefts.	Our architecture is equipped with an electricity prediction module as well as fault detection module. It is able to detect not only electricity thefts but any kind of faults.	[25]
A deep Convolutional Neural Network (CNN) based model is proposed for electricity theft detection.	They have used the CNN component in order to identify the periodicity of normal usage and electricity theft, while our proposed architecture is capable of detecting any sorts of faults.	[26]
The author proposed a hybrid model using CNN and Random Forest for electricity theft detection.	We have used Machine Learning algorithms in our proposed architecture for both prediction and detection	[27]
This paper comes up with a technique which detects meter anomalies and meter tampering. It also detects anomalous meter reading.	In our proposed architecture besides detecting anomalies or faults, we have designed a module which is responsible for predicting electricity consumption.	[28]
The technique aims at reducing the rate of false positive alarms considerably.	In this paper, a new approach called "Monitor" is used which is capable to detect abnormalities by considering the pattern in the past consumption of data.	[29]
This model aims at predicting energy loads using Machine Learning and deep learning techniques of LSTM.	We have designed an architecture using Machine Learning only that is capable of predicting electricity consumption as well as detecting faults in the system.	[30]

In this regard, since the data was basically a field study data collected from a public database, further clustering of the data can be Silhouette Coefficient [15], mixed clustering of different types of categorical, and numerical data [16]. Authors [17] have further proposed a clustering technique which is basically for energy consumption in smart grids.

PROPOSED FRAMEWORK

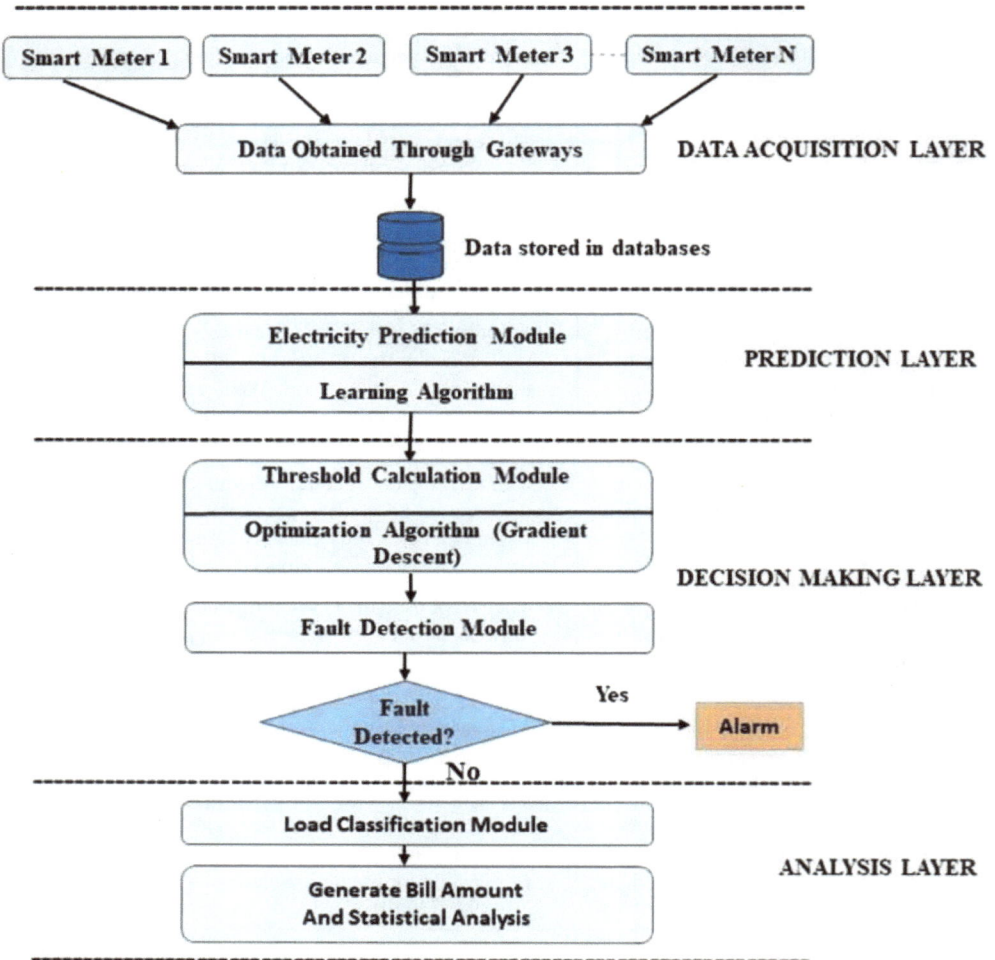

Fig. (1). Proposed Architecture

In our proposed architecture, we have developed an automated system for electricity monitoring using Machine Learning. The architecture is divided into four different layers that perform various independent tasks. Each layer consists of independent modules as shown in Fig. (1). This approach helped us in building a more generalized architecture with enhanced performance. The detailed working of each layer is discussed in the subsequent section.

Electricity Prediction Module

This module is responsible for predicting the electricity consumption using Machine Learning algorithms. In this module, the data that is obtained from the Data Acquisition Layer is fed into our prediction pipeline as shown in Fig. (**2**). The use of prediction pipeline in our proposed architecture helped us in reducing the error probability of our prediction.

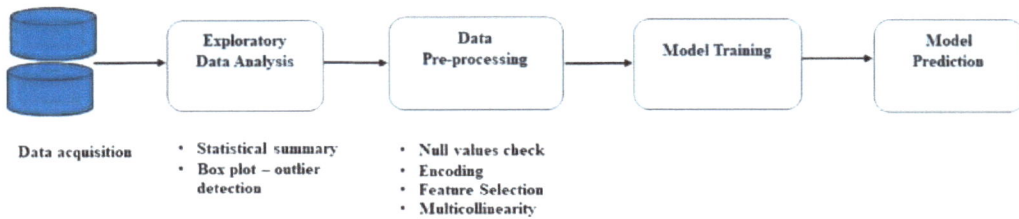

Fig. (2). Prediction Pipeline.

The dataset used for validating our work is Individual Household Electric Power Consumption Dataset [31]. The dataset consists of measurement of electric power consumption of a house with a sampling rate of one minute collected over 47 months. It is a multivalued time series data with 9 attributes and 2075259 set of instances. Since, the data is multivariate, hence in such cases where the data comprises mixed categorical, and numerical data, the proposal shown in referece [16] can be used. The dataset comprised of 1.25% missing values, hence null-value removal had been done in the data pre-processing unit together with encoding, feature selection, and multi-collinearity. Since, the dataset comprised of a huge amount of instances, hence having missing values of 1.25% did not influence the experiment at large.

In the exploratory data analysis phase, the entire dataset was visualized and its statistical summary was studied in order to get meaningful insights from the dataset. The use of boxplot in this step helped us in detecting the presence of outliers in our data. The distribution of original data is shown in Fig. (3). The final diagram for sub-metering-4 was generated to contain the comprehensive consumption of a particular house. Sub-metering-4 data basically contained the summation of the sub-metering-1 through sub-metering-3.

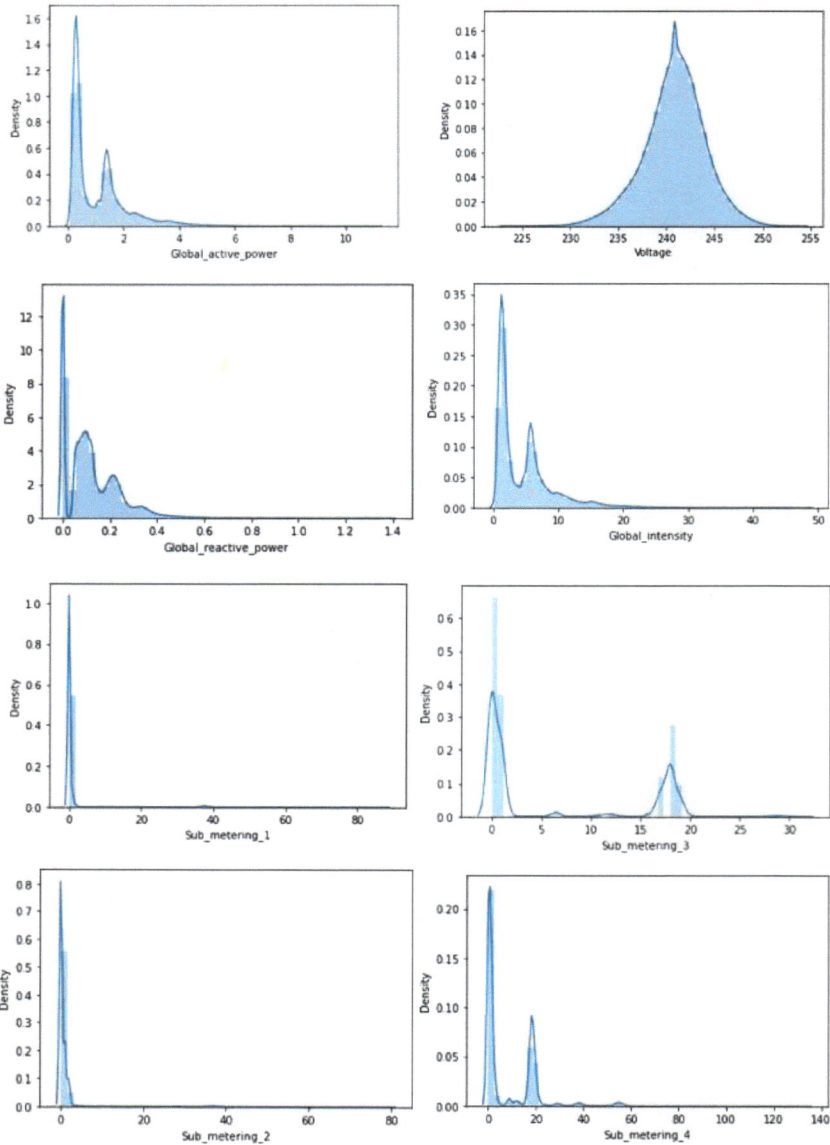

Fig. (3). Distribution of Dataset.

Threshold Calculation Module

The module is responsible for calculating the threshold value required for taking decisions regarding faulty meter reading. The process of threshold calculation has also been automated by making use of a learning algorithm known as gradient descent [32]. It is used to optimize a differentiable function to find the local minimum. The different variants of gradient descent used are discussed below and their corresponding performance is shown in Table **2**.

Table 2. Comparative analysis of different gradient descent algorithms.

Algorithm	Epoch	Learning Rate	Error
Batch Gradient Descent	10	0.01	0.76
	20		0.48
	30		0.38
Mini-Batch Gradient Descent	10	0.01	0.37
	20		0.35
	30		0.24
Stochastic Gradient Descent	10	0.01	0.32
	20		0.15
	30		0.12

i. Batch Gradient Descent - This algorithm finds out the errors of each element in the dataset and then updates the entire model after evaluating the entire dataset. Such an approach increases the efficiency of the algorithm.

ii. Mini-Batch Gradient Descent - This algorithm is a combination of Batch Gradient Descent and Stochastic Gradient Descent. It divides the training data into various batches and further updates them separately.

iii. Stochastic Gradient Descent - This algorithm updates the parameters of each element in the dataset one by one instead of evaluating the observations. It is faster than the other algorithms but might produce a large difference between the error rates.

Fault Detection Module

This module in the decision-making layer of our proposed architecture is solely responsible for detecting whether a fault has occurred in our prediction or not. The threshold value calculated from the previous module is used to classify the meter readings using machine learning algorithms. As soon as it detects a fault, it generates an alarm.

EXPERIMENTAL RESULT & ANALYSIS

In our proposed architecture, we have used different Machine Learning algorithms in both prediction modules as well as in decision making layers. The performance of these algorithms was evaluated using performance metrics that ensured our model was not suffering from overfitting and helped us in building a generalized and robust pipeline. In the electricity prediction layer, we employed five different machine learning algorithms namely Linear Regression, Support Vector Machine (SVM), K-Nearest Neighbor (KNN) Regressor, Decision Tree Regressor and Random Forest. The performance of each algorithm was evaluated using mean squared error, root mean squared error, r squared score and adjusted r square score. The comparative study is shown in Table **3**, Fig. (**4**), and Fig. (**5**). respectively.

Table 3. Performance Comparison of Prediction Layer.

ALGORITHM	MEAN ABSOLUTE ERROR	ROOT MEAN SQUARED ERROR	R SQUARED SCORE	ADJUSTED R SQUARED SCORE
Linear Regression	3.3401	4.3256	0.88	0.86
SVM	3.4578	5.9862	0.93	0.89
KNN	3.5663	5.7698	0.90	0.94
Decision Tree	2.4532	2.5645	0.95	0.93
Random Forest	1.2561	1.1237	0.97	0.98

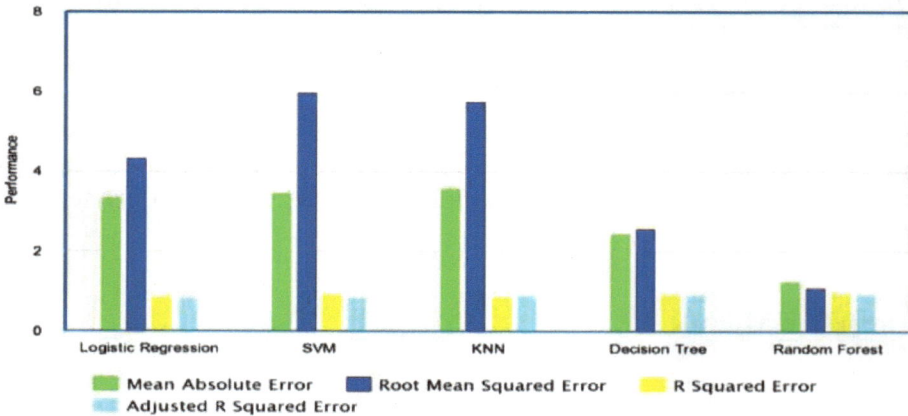

Fig. (4). Performance analysis of electricity prediction module.

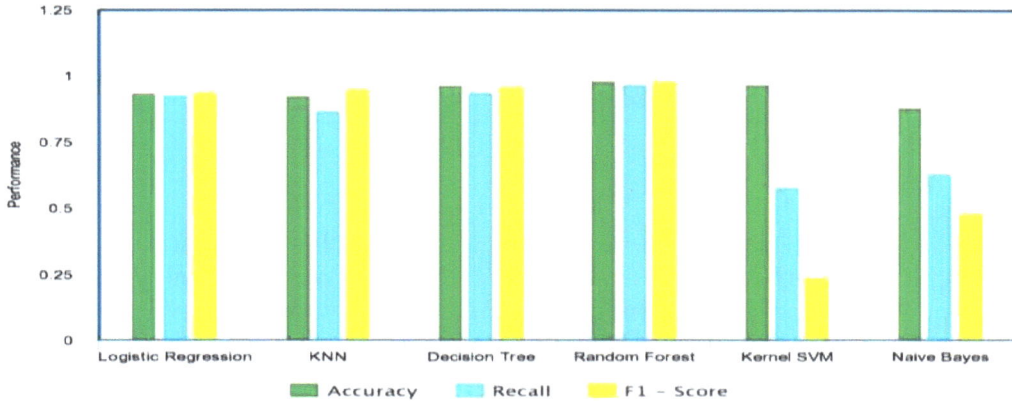

Fig. (5). Performance analysis of fault detection module.

In the decision-making layer, six different classification algorithms were used which helped in achieving a better accuracy in terms of detecting the fault. The main objective was to reduce the false negative; as a matter of fact we focused on achieving a higher value of recall along with accuracy to optimize the performance of the fault detection module. The performance metrics are presented in Table (**4**). The comparative study is shown in Table (**5**).

Table 4. Performance Comparison of Decision-Making Layer.

Algorithm	Accuracy	Recall	F1- Score	Entropy
Logistic Regression	93.41	0.93	0.94	0.67
KNN	92.76	0.87	0.95	0.62
Decision Tree	96.32	0.94	0.96	0.95
Random Forest	98.24	0.97	0.98	0.97
Kernel SVM	96.84	0.58	0.25	0.82
Naive Bayes	88.39	0.63	0.48	0.75

Table 5. Comparison Table with different approaches.

Proposal	Energy Prediction	Fault Detection	Multicollinearity Check	K-fold Cross Validation
[11]	X	✓	X	X
[12]	✓	✓	X	X
[14]	✓	X	X	X
[33]	✓	X	X	X

(Table 5) cont.....

Proposal	Energy Prediction	Fault Detection	Multicollinearity Check	K-fold Cross Validation
[34]	✓	✓	✗	✗
[35]	✓	✗	✗	✗
Proposed	✓	✓	✓	✓

CONCLUSION

We have proposed an AI enabled architecture which is capable of predicting electricity consumption as well as fault detection. We have analyzed various Machine Learning algorithms in order to achieve our task. We have used various performance metrics for benchmarking the performance of our proposed architecture. The decision module reflects an accuracy of 98.24% while the prediction module has an error rate of 1.26% under test conditions.

CONSENT FOR PUBLICATION

Not applicable.

CONFLICT OF INTEREST

The authors declare no conflict of interest, financial or otherwise.

ACKNOWLEDGEMENT

Declared none.

REFERENCES

[1]   https://www.world-nuclear.org/information-library.aspx

[2]   C. Fan, F. Xiao, and S. Wang, "Development of prediction models for next-day building energy consumption and peak power demand using data mining techniques", *Appl. Energy,* vol. 127, pp. 1-10, 2014.
        [http://dx.doi.org/10.1016/j.apenergy.2014.04.016]

[3]   V.C. Gungor, D. Sahin, T. Kocak, S. Ergut, C. Buccella, C. Cecati, and G.P. Hancke, "Smart grid technologies: Communication technologies and standards", *IEEE Trans. Industr. Inform.,* vol. 7, no. 4, pp. 529-539, 2011.
        [http://dx.doi.org/10.1109/TII.2011.2166794]

[4]   Z. Jiang, R. Lin, F. Yang, and B. Wu, "A fused load curve clustering algorithm based on wavelet transform", *IEEE Trans. Industr. Inform.,* vol. 14, no. 5, pp. 1856-1865, 2018.
        [http://dx.doi.org/10.1109/TII.2017.2769450]

[5]   D. Alahakoon, and X. Yu, "Smart electricity meter data intelligence for future energy systems: A survey", *IEEE Trans. Industr. Inform.,* vol. 12, no. 1, pp. 425-436, 2016.
        [http://dx.doi.org/10.1109/TII.2015.2414355]

[6]   S. McLaughlin, D. Podkuiko, and P. Mcdaniel, "Energy theft in the advanced metering infrastructure. DBLP",

[7]   H. Li, https://www.sas.com/en_us/insights/analytics/machine-learning.html

[8]   Y Himeur, K Ghanem, A Alsalemi, F Bensaali, and A Amira, *Artificial intelligence based anomaly detection of energy consumption in buildings: A review, current trends and new perspectives Applied Energy Volume - 287,,* 2021.
        [http://dx.doi.org/10.1016/j.apenergy.2021.116601]

[9]   K. Gajowniczek, and T. Ząbkowski, "Short term electricity forecasting using individual smart meter data", *Procedia Comput. Sci.,* vol. 35, pp. 589-597, 2014.
        [http://dx.doi.org/10.1016/j.procs.2014.08.140]

[10]   Z. Jiang, R. Lin, and F. Yang, "A Hybrid Machine Learning Model for Electricity Consumer Categorization Using Smart Meter Data", *Energies,* vol. 11, no. 9, p. 2235, 2018.
        [http://dx.doi.org/10.3390/en11092235]

[11]   B. Li, "Smart Meters Fault Prediction Technology Based on Cost-sensitive XGBoost Algorithm for Imbalanced Data", *3rd IEEE International Conference on Robotics and Automation Sciences (ICRAS),* 2019pp. 189-195 Wuhan, China.

[12]   X. Wong, T. Zhao, H. Liu, and R. He, "Power Consumption Predicting and Anomaly Detection Based on Long Short-Term Memory Neural Network",
        [http://dx.doi.org/10.1109/ICCCBDA.2019.8725704]

[13]   X. Wang, I. Yang, and S.H. Ahn, "Sample Efficient Home Power Anomaly Detection in Real Time Using Semi-Supervised Learning", *IEEE Access,* vol. 7, pp. 139712-139725, 2019.
        [http://dx.doi.org/10.1109/ACCESS.2019.2943667]

[14]   M. Haykel Zayani, and A. Ben Hamida,

[15]   D.T. Dinh, T. Fujinami, and V.N. Huynh, "Estimating the Optimal Number of Clusters in Categorical Data Clustering by Silhouette Coefficient", *International Symposium on Knowledge and Systems Sciences,* 2019pp. 1-17 Da Nang, Vietnam.
        [http://dx.doi.org/10.1007/978-981-15-1209-4_1]

[16]   D.T. Dinh, V.N. Huynh, and S. Sriboonchitta, "Clustering mixed numerical and categorical data with missing values", *Inf. Sci.,* vol. 571, pp. 418-442, 2021.
        [http://dx.doi.org/10.1016/j.ins.2021.04.076]

[17]   E.U. Shchetinin, "Cluster-based energy consumption forecasting in smart grids", *VII International Conference Problems of Mathematical Physics and Mathematical Modelling,* 2018p. 012051 Moscow
        [http://dx.doi.org/10.1007/978-3-319-99447-5_38]

[18]   O. Linda, D. Wijayasekara, M. Manic, and C. Rieger, "Computational intelligence based anomaly detection for Building Energy Management Systems", *5th International Symposium on Resilient Control Systems,* 2012pp. 77-82 Salt Lake City, UT, USA
        [http://dx.doi.org/10.1109/ISRCS.2012.6309297]

[19]   C. Fan, F. Xiao, Y. Zhao, and J. Wang, "Analytical investigation of autoencoder-based methods for unsupervised anomaly detection in building energy data", *Appl. Energy,* vol. 211, pp. 1123-1135, 2018.
        [http://dx.doi.org/10.1016/j.apenergy.2017.12.005]

[20]   A. Capozzoli, M.S. Piscitelli, S. Brandi, D. Grassi, and G. Chicco, "Automated load pattern learning and anomaly detection for enhancing energy management in smart buildings", *Energy,* vol. 157, pp. 336-352, 2018.
        [http://dx.doi.org/10.1016/j.energy.2018.05.127]

[21]   P. Visconti, P. Contantini, R. de Fazio, A. Lay-Ekuakille, and L. Patrono, "A sensor-based monitoring system of electrical consumptions and home parameters remotely managed by mobile app for elderly habits' control",
        [http://dx.doi.org/10.1109/IWASI.2019.8791399]

[22] Y. Himeur, A. Alsalemi, F. Bensaali, and A. Amira, The emergence of hybrid edge-cloud computing for energy efficiency in buildings

[23] T Liu, Z Tan, C Xu, H Chen, and Z Li, *Study on deep reinforcement learning techniques for building energy consumption forecasting " Energy and Buildings , VOLUME 208,* 2020.

[24] B. Albiro, Employing gradient boosting and anomaly detection for prediction of frauds in energy consumption.*Anais do XVI Encontro Nacional de Inteligência Artificial e Computacional.* SBC: Porto Alegre, RS, Brasil, 2019, pp. 916-925.
[http://dx.doi.org/10.5753/eniac.2019.9345]

[25] S. Shekara Srenadh Reddy Depuru, L. Wang, and V. Devabhaktuni, *"Support vector machine based data classification for detection of electricity theft,"* in *2011 IEEE/PES Power Systems Conference and Exposition.*, 2011, pp. 1-8.

[26] Z. Zheng, Y. Yang, X. Niu, H.N. Dai, and Y. Zhou, "Wide and deep convolutional neural networks for electricity-theft detection to secure smart grids", *IEEE Trans. Industr. Inform.,* vol. 14, no. 4, pp. 1606-1615, 2018.
[http://dx.doi.org/10.1109/TII.2017.2785963]

[27] S. Li, Y. Han, X. Yao, S. Yingchen, J. Wang, and Q. Zhao, "Electricity theft detection in power grids with deep learning and random forests", *J. Electr. Comput. Eng.,* vol. 2019, pp. 1-12, 2019.
[http://dx.doi.org/10.1155/2019/4136874]

[28] B. Coma-Puig, J. Carmona, R. Gavalda, S. Alcoverro, and V. Martin, "Fraud detection in energy consumption: A supervised approach", *2019 IEEE International Conference on Data Science and Advanced Analytics (DSAA),* 2016pp. 120-129 Montreal, QC, Canada
[http://dx.doi.org/10.1109/DSAA.2016.19]

[29] H. Rashid, and P. Singh, "Monitor: An Abnormality Detection Approach in Buildings Energy Consumption",
[http://dx.doi.org/10.1109/CIC.2018.00-44]

[30] X J Luo, L O Oyedele, A O Ajayi, and O O Akinade, *Comparative study of machine learning-based multi-objective prediction framework for multiple building energy loads "Sustainable Cities and Society , VOLUME 61,,* 2020.

[31] G. Hebrail, http://archive.ics.uci.edu/ml/datasets/Individual+household+electric+power+consumption

[32] N. Donges, https://builtin.com/data-science/gradient-descent

[33] M Keytingan M. Shapi, "Azuana Ramli, and L J Awalin, "Energy consumption prediction by using machine learning for smart building: Case study in Malaysia," Developments in the Built Environment, VOLUME 5,",

[34] M.G. Rabby Shuvo, N. Sultana, L. Motin, and M. Rezaul Islam, "Prediction of Hourly Total Energy in Combined Cycle Power Plant Using Machine Learning Techniques",
[http://dx.doi.org/10.1109/CAIDA51941.2021.9425308]

[35] H. Haque, "A Kumar Chowdhury, M Nasfikur Rahman Khan, and M Abdur Razzak, "Demand Analysis of Energy Consumption in a Residential Apartment using Machine Learning," in *2021 IEEE International IOT",* *Electronics and Mechatronics Conference (IEMTRONICS),* 2021pp. 1-6 Toronto, ON, Canada

CHAPTER 6

Investigating the Effectiveness of Mobile Learning in Higher Education

V. Kalaiarasi[1,*], **D. Alamelu**[2] and **N. Venugopal**[3]

[1] *PSG College of Arts and Science, Coimbatore, Tamil Nadu, India*

[2] *KGiSL Institute of Technology, Coimbatore, Tamil Nadu, India*

[3] *Sri Krishna College of Technology, Coimbatore, Tamil Nadu, India*

Abstract: Technology is a fundamental part of the teaching-learning process which has brought plenty of benefits during the pandemic situation. Covid 19 has adversely affected the education system throughout the world. Due to this abrupt change, mobile learning has occupied a dominant place in helping students to handle this unavoidable crisis. The studies focused on online learning, e-learning and also m-learning. However, this study focuses on the effectiveness of m-learning by understanding the satisfaction and intention of the students towards m-learning. Mixed research method approach is used in this study. Structural Equation Modelling (SEM) is used to validate the proposed model. The findings revealed that the majority of the students are satisfied with m-learning. However, there are also some students who express dissatisfaction with learning practical courses through mobile phones, citing insufficient support from their parents and the institution. Additionally, the satisfaction and intention of students play a crucial role in determining the effectiveness of mobile learning (m-learning). The study presents a comprehensive framework for understanding, explaining, and predicting the factors that influence the effectiveness of mobile learning (m-learning) among higher education students. The study also supports the practitioners and educators with useful guidelines for designing a successful m-learning system, particularly in higher education. This will also enable government to frame its the digitized policies appropriately.

Keywords: Higher education, M-Learning, Technology acceptance, Teaching-learning, Triangulation.

INTRODUCTION

As a response to the global Covid-19 pandemic, numerous precautionary measures have been implemented to address the situation. Foremost among these

---

[*] **Corresponding author V. Kalaiarasi**: PSG College of Arts and Science, Coimbatore, Tamil Nadu, India; E-mail: kalaikavin@gmail.com

Brojo Kishore Mishra (Ed.)

measures is the widespread adoption of online education. However, this sudden and unplanned shift to complete dependence on online learning has raised several concerns, despite the fact that online education was not widely prevalent prior to the pandemic. The adoption of online teaching in education has led to a distinctive revolution from traditional face-to-face learning to online learning. Several online tools are developed for assisting and improving learning to feel like a real classroom. Still, there is a lack, particularly in developing countries like India, where there is a substantial technical constraint related to the suitability of devices and availability of reliable internet connection, which poses a serious challenge [1].

The effectiveness and satisfaction levels of online learning are currently under scrutiny. With various modes available for accessing academic materials in online education, such as desktop computers, laptops, and tablets, many students prefer smartphones due to their ease of use. Over time, students' learning approaches have evolved from traditional techniques to e-learning and now to m-learning, with mobile devices playing a significant role in this shift [2]. Previously, mobile learning was not believed and recognized by many of them, even though it is one of the models of learning in higher education. Developments in technology have helped students to enhance their understanding through m-learning. Mobile learning means, "Any sort of learning that happens when the learner is not at a fixed, predetermined location, or learning that happens when the learner takes advantage of the learning opportunities offered by mobile technologies" (AICTE). M-learning is the up-gradation of e-learning.

In many developed countries, m-learning has become the favorite model of learning, due to the growth and utility of the internet and the World Wide Web. Mobile technology touched almost every aspect of human endeavor, including education. Due to this scenario, the advanced blended learning method also emerged.

Mobile learning provides a variety of benefits for learners especially in the education field. The major advantages of m-learning are portability, social interactivity, context sensitivity and connectivity, however, failures also exist. A large number of people who start m-learning are very enthusiastic at an earlier stage, but later, they lose their interest and ultimately stop using m-learning. Information system research clearly shows that user satisfaction is one of the most important factors in assessing the success of system implementation [3]. In mobile learning setting, numerous elements are involved in user satisfaction. The factors affecting m-learning effectiveness are revealed by previous researchers using various descriptive or analytical studies. These factors can be grouped into three groups: technology acceptance, system success, and environmental factors.

Therefore, understanding of m-learning will be helpful to engage students and to improve their learning outcomes.

The main objective of this study is to examine the influence of learner satisfaction and learner intention towards the effectiveness of m-learning in higher education.

The research design comprises both qualitative and quantitative methods to investigate the effectiveness of m-learning.

In India, education has shifted towards a learner-centered teaching model, and as such, this study aims to highlight the key factors that influence the effectiveness of mobile learning (m-learning), particularly in the context of practical-based subjects. Furthermore, it helps to identify and understand the students' perceptions and intentions toward mobile learning in higher education. It assists educators to frame an appropriate course plan to improve learning effectiveness. Further, it will enable to overcome difficulties and reduces the risk of failure during execution.

MODEL CONSTRUCTION AND DEVELOPMENT OF HYPOTHESIS

Technology Acceptance and Learner Satisfaction

The variables within the Technology Acceptance Model (TAM) have been found to exert a significant influence on learner satisfaction [4, 5]. The presumption is that a large number of learners perceive usefulness, and ease of use for course-delivering media, such as course websites, and file-transmitting software. The more positively influencing attitudes toward m-learning are subsequently improving learning experiences, satisfaction, and increasing intention towards using m-learning [6]. The perceived usefulness and ease of use are critical factors influencing learners' perceived satisfaction [7]. TAM consists of two main components namely; perceived ease of use and perceived usefulness in which, an individual perceives using a particular system that would improve performance. Perceived usefulness has a positive influence on students' satisfaction and retention [8]. It has a positive moderate linear relationship towards perceived e-learner satisfaction [9]. This leads to the hypothesis:

H1. Technology acceptances have a positive influence on Learner's satisfaction

System Success and Learner satisfaction

According to DeLone & McLean [10], a system can be evaluated in terms of information quality, system quality, and service quality. These characteristics affect the subsequent system use or intention to use and user satisfaction.

Information quality and system quality would positively affect students' satisfaction with mobile Learning-systems [11]. According to Uddin [12], information quality has a huge impact on user satisfaction.

Information and system quality positively affects the students' satisfaction with mobile learning systems [11]. According to Muda & Erlina [13], system quality has a significant positive effect on user satisfaction, the higher the value of system quality, the higher the level of user satisfaction. Information quality has an influence on user satisfaction [14]. According to Wijayanto [15], top management support strengthened the effect of system quality on user satisfaction. Information quality is the strongest predictor to measure user satisfaction [16]. Thus:

H2. System success has a positive influence on Learners' satisfaction

Environmental Factors and Learner satisfaction

Environmental factors have a direct and indirect impact on the user's perception, comfort, motivation and concentration in their learning environment. The two major influences are the instructor and social factors. Earlier, studies indicated that the instructor's response had a significant influence on the learner's satisfaction [17]. Learners' interaction with others predicts learner satisfaction [18]. According to Arbaugh and Thurmond [17], the learning satisfaction of students depends on how the instructor responds to students' needs and the instructor's capability towards solving problems. Smeets [19] found that the instructor's attitude toward ICT has a significant effect on learner's satisfaction. This leads to:

H3. Environmental factors have a positive influence on Learner satisfaction.

Technology Acceptance and Learner Intention

Performance expectancy to m-learning environment proposes that students feel m-learning is useful, According to the concept of performance expectancy in the m-learning environment, students perceive m-learning as useful because it offers the convenience of learning at their own pace. It will increase learning efficiency [20]. The performance expectancy of m-learning influences students' behavioral intention to use m-learning [21]. TAM is introduced to understand users' acceptance and usage of information systems. Within the Technology Acceptance Model (TAM), perceived ease of use and perceived usefulness are fundamental constructs that influence users' attitudes, intentions, and actual use of information systems (IS) [22]. Hence, it is proposed:

H4. Technology acceptances have a positive influence on Learner's intention.

System Success and Learner Intention

As per DeLone and McLean, both system quality and information quality influence the learner's intention [23]. Information and system quality jointly or separately influence the learner's intention towards accepting mobile learning technologies [11]. E-learning systems cannot be efficient without attaining system quality [24]. Information and system quality have effects on the continuance of the learners' intention through increasing perceived usefulness [25]. The system quality significantly influences the intention to adopt m-Learning [26]. This leads to the hypothesis:

H5. System successes have a positive influence on Learner's intention.

Environmental Factors and Learner Intention

Timely assistance from the instructor encourages learners to continue their learning [27]. Social influence is defined as "the degree to which an individual perceives others' opinion that is important to believe that he or she should use the new system" [28]. In this context, it relates to the impact of influential persons such as friends or University lecturers, it has an impact on student's propensity to adopt m-learning technologies. The individual's behavioral intention to use new technology is determined by social influence [29]. Course coordinators' influence is a significant construct to encourage students to adapt to new technologies in their learning setting. This leads to conclude that lecturers' influence has a positive effect on behavioral intention to use m-learning [21]. Results revealed that social presence is a significant predictor in learners' satisfaction [30]. Thus, the following hypothesis is proposed:

H6. Environmental factors have a positive influence on Learner's intention.

Learner Satisfaction and M-learning effectiveness

Mobile delivery focuses on three specific outcomes: learner performance, attitudes towards mobile courses, and learner satisfaction. E-learning intention plays a mediating role between e-learning satisfaction and e-learning effectiveness [31]. E-learning mode is positively associated with learning effectiveness [32]. The individuals' motivation and prior experience influence learning effectiveness [33]. Accordingly, it is hypothesized that:

H7. Learners' satisfaction has a positive influence on M-learning effectiveness.

Learner Intention and M-learning effectiveness

Performance expectancy and effort expectancy are crucial factors that significantly impact students' intention to effectively adopt m-learning technology [34]. Performance expectancy and effort expectancy are significant factors that affect behavioral intention to use and achieve m-learning effectiveness [21]. Thus, it is proposed that:

H8. Learners' intention has a positive influence on M-learning effectiveness.

METHODOLOGY

The hypotheses are tested empirically using survey data. The study design consists of an exploratory-based case work as a pre-study and a confirmatory phase as the main survey. M-learning users provided requisite qualitative data, which is used to formulate the research problem. Further, the survey instrument is used in the confirmatory phase.

Operational Design

Case study approaches are deemed appropriate for addressing research questions that seek detailed understanding of phenomena under study, including how and what type of research questions [35]. The case study research method has been employed in various disciplines for many years, and the utilization of qualitative research methods enhances the reliability of the research findings [36, 37]. Quantitative methods have intrinsic limitations with regard to uncovering richer insight into research phenomenon that can be better addressed *via* qualitative research [38].

However, qualitative research also has limitations. Academicians found it difficult to investigate the causality between different research phenomena. Qualitative research often encounters challenges in fully explaining the information obtained from respondents and drawing conclusive findings [39]. Qualitative research is not appropriate to respond to all research questions and researchers need to think carefully about their objectives. The majority of studies in the field have concentrated on assessing the success of information systems, using surveys to test the hypothesized relationships [40].

Qualitative methods in conjunction with quantitative methods would provide an ideal approach to study the phenomenon of interest. The integration of qualitative and quantitative approaches helps to address the limitations of each approach by providing both statistical objectivity and a deeper understating of contexts [41].

The study adopted a mixed research method approach, familiarly known as sequential explanatory design method. Fig. **(1)** shows the framework of operational design of the study. The sequential explanatory design method comprises a qualitative phase followed by a quantitative phase. The qualitative data comprises 60 undergraduate engineering students from different disciplines using a triangulation method. The quantitative data is collected through a questionnaire with a sample size of 180 undergraduate engineering students.

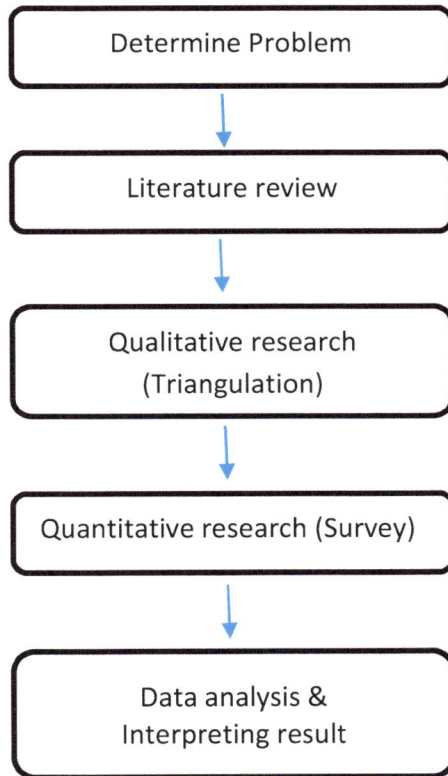

Fig. (1). Framework of Operational Design.

In view of the above, the current research employs a Case Study as a pre-study to formulate research problems and questions. However, the Quantitative research method is applied for evaluating and testing the proposed research model. A descriptive study is carried out in order to determine and describe the characteristics of variables. In this study, the stratified random sampling method was employed, as depicted in Fig. **(2)**, which presents the conceptual model of the research.

The questionnaire shared by Google doc. was randomly distributed among undergraduate students of Universities in Tamil Nadu through social networking sites. A substantial number of students participated in the online survey, with a total of 43 students contacted via online mode for the case study and 180 responses found to be valid for data analysis using the quantitative method.

Data Collection

For the purpose of investigation, interview protocol designed open-ended questions are asked to identify m-learning effectiveness, technology acceptance, system success, social factors, learners' satisfaction and learners' intention. The questionnaires were formulated based on an extensive literature review and expert opinions. The triangulation method is used for data collection. It is a combination of multiple methods to gather data, such as documents, interviews, and observations. According to Yin [35], case study research assured construct validity through triangulation, which includes multiple sources of evidence, a chain of evidence, and member checking. For the main study, the questionnaire is distributed through e-mail to the potential respondents, after getting appropriate acceptance from the respondents. Missing data is always a problem and it can significantly affect the values of the result. In this regard, datasets are pre-processed and missing values are removed in advance. A total of 220 responses were received, out of which 180 were deemed valid and utilized for the analysis.

Instrument Development

The technology acceptance model questionnaire is adopted from Davis [22]. The system success model and learners' satisfaction questionnaire in this study were adopted from DeLone and McLean's [10] Information System Success Model. The environmental factor and learners' intention questionnaire were adopted from Abu-Al-Aish and Jackman [34]. Additionally, the m-learning effectiveness questionnaire utilized in this study was adapted from AL-Fahad's work [42], for this study.

TThe required modifications, wording adjustments, and validation were made to ensure the alignment with the context of mobile learning. To avoid issues that can occur in wordings, measurement and ambiguities, the questionnaire is pre-tested by the English Department Professors. Sekaran & Bougie [43] highlight that such a pre-test is essential, because wording problems significantly influence accuracy [44].

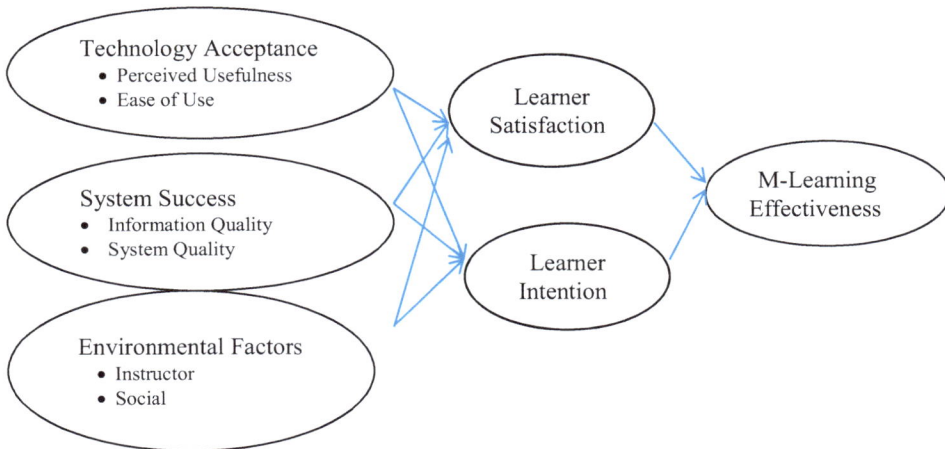

Fig. (2). Conceptual model.

RESULT

Data Analysis and Results – Qualitative Study

Six specific themes that emerged from the qualitative analysis are (a) Technology Acceptance, (b) System Success, (c) Environmental Factors, (d) Learner's Satisfaction, (e) Learner's Intention and (f) M-Learning Effectiveness.

Technology Acceptance

Technology Acceptance encompasses perceived usefulness and ease of use, which are significant advantages for mobile learning users. Students appreciate the convenience of continuous connectivity; however, some have reported difficulties staying connected due to network problems.

The respondents perceive mobile learning as a useful tool for their studies due to its fast delivery method of materials, which makes students more comfortable in their learning process. They believe that m-learning allows them to complete their learning tasks more efficiently. Additionally, a majority of the students reported that learning through mobile devices improved their performance in exams. Furthermore, the respondents expressed positive and confident views about accessing course content through mobile devices.

Students feel like all the data are there in their pockets. All the participants positively viewed the ability to access information through mobile devices. Furthermore, many students mentioned that mobile learning is user-friendly due to its flexible techniques, time-saving nature, ease of use, portability, and the ability to easily clarify doubts. These factors contribute to increased learner satisfaction. However, some students also pointed out that poor network connectivity poses a challenge in fully enjoying the benefits of mobile learning.

System Success

Information and system quality lead to system success in m-learning. Mobile learning system provides content accuracy. It provides information that is relevant to their courses, but some students felt that the relevance of the content is mismatched sometimes.

Mobile learning system provides all information whatever is needed at the right time. The availability of information is the best advantage in mobile learning in the opinion of many students. Additionally, several students expressed that the mobile learning system offers an appropriate level of online assistance and explanations, thanks to its technological advancements and precise explanations that cater to their learning standards. However, some students mentioned that they face challenges in finding exact information or resources within the mobile learning system.

Mobile learning system has a high level of flexibility and students find themselves communicating more, because of mobile devices. However, sometimes they felt that the system quality is the major problem among students. Mobile learning system provides an effective user experience. Finally, students expressed that the quality of the system and information greatly impacts their satisfaction and intention as learners.

Environmental Factors

Students expect a supportive environment from lecturers, parents, career advisors, friends, government *etc.*, for their mobile learning system. Prior to the Covid-19 pandemic, lecturers prohibited the use of mobile devices in class, citing potential distractions. However, now they are encouraging students to bring and use mobile devices for learning. Nevertheless, challenges arise in situations such as presentations, online tests, and practices. Students expressed their willingness to adopt mobile learning if recommended by their lecturers.

Parents generally hold a negative attitude towards the use of mobile phones for learning purposes after class time, as they perceive it as a hindrance to their children's studies. They believe that their children are not attentive in class and often engage in playing games or chatting with friends on their mobile phones.

Most of the career advisors are highly incorporating them to use mobile learning at all levels to increase the success rate. Many of their friends recommend to use mobile learning, but at the same time, they opined that it will lead to a number of health issues. Hence, they recommend laptops /desktops for continuous learning. Finally, they quoted that the Government systems are highly motivating them to use mobile learning, but still, they need to increase technical support especially in network connectivity. Even in urban locations, the network is poor, when they are inside the house. Hence, students often have to go out of their houses or move to the terrace in search of smooth network signals for mobile learning. During examinations, they may have to sit in open spaces of their homes to tackle connectivity issues. The noises from roads, such as bike rides or cars, are seen as distractions during exams. In rural areas, the situation is even more challenging, as students constantly struggle to find a reliable network. Moreover, attending online classes can be interrupted by incoming calls, and the unstable network further compounds the issue. These connectivity issues lead to fatigue, hampering the learning process and resulting in poor performance.

Overall, respondents expressed that there are numerous environmental distractions while using mobile learning. If these issues can be addressed and overcome, it would increase learners' intention and satisfaction with mobile learning.

Learner Satisfaction

The students express satisfaction with the option of attending classes on mobile devices, as the materials provided by the mobile learning system are deemed satisfactory. If given the opportunity, they would be glad to continue using mobile learning even after the pandemic. The majority of respondents feel that their expected learning improvements are indeed achieved through mobile learning.

Mobile computing devices enable increased interactions with course instructors and classmates through mobile learning, which has resulted in high student satisfaction. Students feel that they have ample opportunities and support when using mobile devices for learning, and it effectively caters to their needs. Furthermore, many students report feeling more confident and interested in learning through mobile devices, as it makes learning easy and enjoyable. M-learning also fosters self-motivation among students, leading to increased engagement and higher levels of learning.

Learner Intention

The students mentioned clearly that they planned to use m-learning in their studies during Covid time as well as after that, and they are recommending other students also. Students have suggested providing free Wi-Fi systems, even in rural areas, as an effective means to enhance access to mobile learning.

While some students are enjoying mobile learning (m-learning) systems, they have also expressed that social networking applications are not used for class purposes, as they may potentially distract concentration. They stated that if mobile devices are used for learning, then understanding of subjects will be difficult.

Students said that after the integration of mobile computing devices, the learning environment has changed positively, because education becomes more standard. Information sharing has increased and learning has become easier for everyone through mobile learning (m-learning). However, some students have also mentioned that due to the prevalence of m-learning, interaction with staff has reduced as they are more focused on self-learning. Nevertheless, they find it convenient to respond to text messages and quickly return to their coursework when using mobile devices for learning tasks.

Some students believed that they did not feel distracted while doing mobile learning courses and also recommended others to use m-learning systems out of their experience, as a personal suggestion.

M-Learning Effectiveness

Mobile computing students are happy and stated that mobile learning is an effective method of learning as it gives immediate support for learning anywhere at any time, and it also improved the learning value of the course.

Mobile learning opens up new opportunities for future learning, as students find it highly effective and efficient. IIt enhances convenience and aids in completing study-related tasks more efficiently. Many students quoted that mobile learning is more flexible in accessing the resources used for learning as it can be done anywhere at any time. It is an effective as well as a suitable add-on tool for the timely completion of coursework. It is a faster method of getting feedback, but it is not feasible at times, because of network problem. Students believe that mobile learning is an effective method for both present and future generations to elevate the level of education, which may also create more job opportunities for young learners.

Data Analysis and Results – Quantitative

Demographic data is tested using IBM SPSS. Out of 180 respondents, 111 (62%) are male and 69 (38%) are female. The analysis indicates that 62% of the respondents reside in rural areas, while 38% of the respondents are from urban areas.

SEM in VPLS

The VPLS structural equation modeling technique is used for data analysis. In their study, Straub *et al.* [45] emphasized that for instrument measurements, ensuring reliability and construct validity are essential requirements. Whereas, reliability is a concern of measurement within a construct, construct validity has to do with measurement between constructs. Convergent and discriminant validity are components of construct validity.

Thus, reliability is examined, and convergent and discriminant validity constructs are as follows:

Reliability is used to evaluate internal consistency. Construct CFA analysis of VPLS provides values for Cronbach's alpha for each construct. It can be seen that all the indicators' values are shown to be larger than 0.7. It demonstrates adequate reliability, which can be understood from Table (**1**).

Table 1. Measurement of constructs (with reliability) and Discriminant validity: AVEs versus squared correlation.

Construct	Number of Items	Reliability	AVE	Square root of AVE	Factor Correlations					
					TA	SS	EV	LS	LI	MEF
TA	8	.90	.559	.7476	1.000					
SS	8	.91	.565	.7519	.607	1.000				
EV	8	.76	.327	.5724	.389	.590	1.000			
LS	4	.91	.726	.8523	.608	.608	.286	1.000		
LI	4	.93	.789	.8885	.677	.745	.483	.625	1.000	
MEF	4	.92	.756	.8698	.672	.558	.344	.641	.603	1.000

To check convergent validity, each latent variable's AVE (Average Variance Extracted) is evaluated. It is found that AVE values, except for environmental factors, all others are greater than the acceptable threshold of 0.5. Except Environmental Factors, the convergent validity is confirmed.

To confirm the discriminant validity, Fornell & Laker [46] method is followed. They suggest that the square root of AVE in each latent variable can be used to establish discriminant validity, if the value is larger than other correlation values among latent variables.

Overall, the hypothesized research model is supported. Fig. (**3**) presents the result of SEM VPLS. The total effects on m-learning effectiveness are 0.33 for learner's intention and 0.43 as learner's satisfaction. Furthermore, a total of 47% of variance of m-learning effectiveness is explained by learner's satisfaction and learner's intention; in addition, 63% of variance in learner's intention and 47% of variance in learner's satisfaction are explained by technology acceptance, system success and environmental factors.

Results of Hypothesis Testing

Table (**2**) indicates the acceptance and rejection of hypothesis formed in the study.

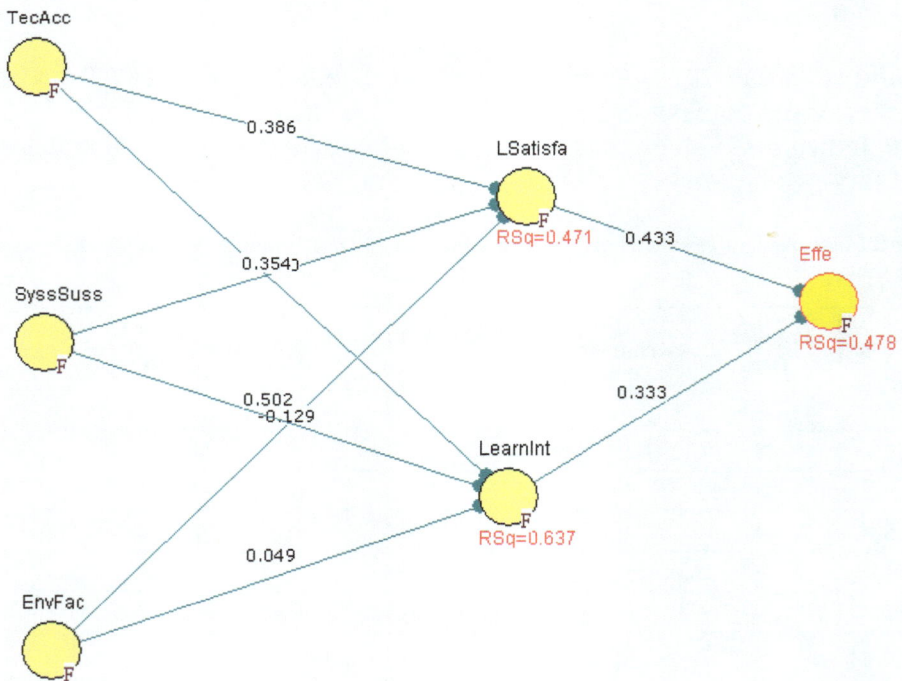

Fig. (3). Structural VPLS model.

Table 2. Summary of results: hypothesis testing.

Hypothesis No.	Hypothesis Statement	Result
H1	Technology acceptance have positive influence on Learner's satisfaction.	Accepted
H2	System success have positive influence on Learner's satisfaction.	Accepted

(Table 2) cont.....

Hypothesis No.	Hypothesis Statement	Result
H3	Environmental factors have positive influence on Learner's satisfaction.	Accepted
H4	Technology acceptance have positive influence on Learner's intention.	Accepted
H5	System success have positive influence on Learner's intention.	Accepted
H6	Environmental factors have a positive influence on Learner's intention.	Rejected
H7	Learner satisfaction have positive influence on M-learning effectiveness.	Accepted
H8	Learner intention have positive influence on M-learning effectiveness.	Accepted

DISCUSSION AND CONCLUSION

The findings from the research adds value to the existing literature on technology acceptance and proposes a framework for understanding, explaining, and predicting the factors influencing mobile learning effectiveness of higher education students. The study provides valuable baseline data for future studies on student's acceptance, learner's satisfaction and intention to use mobile devices as a tool for learning. This research model establishes a framework that administrators and educators can use to evaluate success factors for implementing mobile learning. By understanding the determinants of mobile learning acceptance and effectiveness, the stakeholders can incorporate these factors into the design and implementation phase of mobile learning initiative. Proper planning and suitable strategy are necessary for mobile learning in institutions. The results of the study provide assistance to identify the factors influencing mobile learning effectiveness.

Overall, the results indicated that consistent with previous research, performance expectancy is the strongest predictor of behavioral intentions [20, 28, 47]. Effort expectancy has a positive direct effect on the students' intention to use m-learning technologies. This finding, which supports previous research [28, 29] reiterates that students are more inclined to adopt the new technology, when they know that it has the necessary skills and believe that mobile device and technology are easy to use. Unlike previous research [48], social influence is not found to be a significant determinant of students' intentions to adopt m-learning. However, given the population of educated, independent thinkers, it is quite likely that the students have acquired enough experience to feel comfortable and confident in using the mobile technology. As a result, the opinions of peers have a little effect on their m-learning adoption decisions.

The result confirms that variables technology acceptance, system success and environmental factors influence the satisfaction and intention towards using mobile learning. The learner's satisfaction and intention lead to the m-learning effectiveness in higher education. The success of any m-learning is highly dependent on university educators as well. Therefore, future work will incorporate the acceptance and perceptions of the university lecturers, who are ultimately responsible for the design and delivery of courses.

Online educational systems are facing various problems such as static delivery of material, identification of student's needs and student's interaction. Educational data mining tools play a vital role in improving the effectiveness of m-learning. It assists instructors in understanding about students learning outcomes. Different tools are available in usage like IBM - SPSS Modeler, Weka, EPRules, GISMO, TADAEd, DBMiner, SPINA, ORANGE *etc*. These are used for clustering, classification, predictions, regression, visualizations, association rule and decision tree to improve learning. Data mining helps in the identification of improvement in m-learning. Henceforth, for further research, the impact of data mining on m learning can be included.

The study recommends the instructors and government to support and provide necessary resources to help the students contribute in increasing the standard of education. It is recommended that students seek guidance from their course coordinators when engaging in mobile learning, as this can contribute to improved academic performance. The subject requirements differ from one course to another course; hence, it requires different methods to teach. The best methods are yet to be explored.

ABBREVIATIONS

AICTE	All India Council for Technical Education
AVE	Average Variance Extracted
CFA	Confirmatory Factor Analysis
COVID 19	Coronavirus Disease 2019
e- leaning	Electronic Learning
EV	Environmental Factors
F	Factor
H	Hypothesis
ICT	Information and Communications Technology
IS	Information System
LI	Learner Intention
LS	Learner Satisfaction
MEF	M-Learning Effectiveness
R2	Coefficient of Discrimination
SEM	Structural Equation Modelling

SPSS	Statistical Package for the Social Sciences
SS	System Success
TA	Technology Acceptance
TAM	Technology Acceptance Model
VPLS	Visual Partial Least Squares

REFERENCES

[1]   T. Muthuprasad, S. Aiswarya, K.S. Aditya, and G.K. Jha, "Students' perception and preference for online education in India during COVID -19 pandemic", *Social Sciences & Humanities Open,* vol. 3, no. 1, p. 100101, 2021.
[http://dx.doi.org/10.1016/j.ssaho.2020.100101] [PMID: 34173507]

[2]   S.F.A. Hossain, X. Shan, and M. Nurunnabi, "Is M-Learning a Challenge?", *Int. J. e-Collaboration,* vol. 15, no. 1, pp. 21-37, 2019.
[http://dx.doi.org/10.4018/IJeC.2019010102]

[3]   W.H. DeLone, and E.R. McLean, "E. "Information systems success: The quest for the dependent variable,"", *Inf. Syst. Res.,* vol. 3, no. 1, pp. 60-95, 1992.
[http://dx.doi.org/10.1287/isre.3.1.60]

[4]   J.B. Arbaugh, and R. Duray, "Technological and structural characteristics, student learning and satisfaction with web-based courses: An exploratory study of two on-line MBA programs", *Manag. Learn.,* vol. 33, no. 3, pp. 331-347, 2002.
[http://dx.doi.org/10.1177/1350507602333003]

[5]   K. Wu, Y. Zhao, Q. Zhu, X. Tan, and H. Zheng, "A meta-analysis of the impact of trust on technology acceptance model: Investigation of moderating influence of subject and context type", *Int. J. Inf. Manage.,* vol. 31, no. 6, pp. 572-581, 2011.
[http://dx.doi.org/10.1016/j.ijinfomgt.2011.03.004]

[6]   K.A. Pituch, and Y. Lee, "The influence of system characteristics on e-learning use", *Comput. Educ.,* vol. 47, no. 2, pp. 222-244, 2006.
[http://dx.doi.org/10.1016/j.compedu.2004.10.007]

[7]   P.C. Sun, R.J. Tsai, G. Finger, Y.Y. Chen, and D. Yeh, "What drives a successful e-Learning? An empirical investigation of the critical factors influencing learner satisfaction", *Comput. Educ.,* vol. 50, no. 4, pp. 1183-1202, 2008.
[http://dx.doi.org/10.1016/j.compedu.2006.11.007]

[8]   M.A. Al-hawari, and S. Mouakket, "The influence of technology acceptance model (TAM) factors on students' e-satisfaction and e-retention within the context of UAE e-learning", *Educ. Bus. Soc.,* vol. 3, no. 4, pp. 299-314, 2010.
[http://dx.doi.org/10.1108/17537981011089596]

[9]   N.B. Ibrahim, N.S. Ibrahim, S.M. Zukri, M.S.M.M. Yusof, and N.N. Roslan, "Learners Satisfaction of E-Learning among Public University Students: A Case Study in Kota Bharu", *Journal of Mathematics & Computing Science,* vol. 5, no. 1, pp. 1-7, 2019.

[10]   W.H. Delone, and E.R. McLean, "The DeLone and McLean model of information systems success: a ten-year update", *J. Manage. Inf. Syst.,* vol. 19, no. 4, pp. 9-30, 2003.
[http://dx.doi.org/10.1080/07421222.2003.11045748]

[11]   S. Alharbi, and S. Drew, "Using the technology acceptance model in understanding academics' behavioural intention to use learning management systems", *Int. J. Adv. Comput. Sci. Appl.,* vol. 5, no. 1, pp. 143-155, 2014.
[http://dx.doi.org/10.14569/IJACSA.2014.050120]

[12]   M.M. Uddin, A. Ghosh, and O. Isaac, "Impact of the System, Information, and Service Quality of

Online Learning on User Satisfaction among Public Universities Students in Bangladesh", *International Journal Of Management And Human Science,* vol. 3, no. 2, pp. 1-10, 2019.

[13] I. Muda, and A.A. Erlina, "Influence of human resources to the effect of system quality and information quality on the user satisfaction of accrual-based accounting system", *Contad. Adm.,* vol. 64, no. 2, p. 10, 2019.

[14] G. Sharma, and W. Lijuan, "The effects of online service quality of e-commerce Websites on user satisfaction", *Electron. Libr.,* vol. 33, no. 3, pp. 468-485, 2015.
[http://dx.doi.org/10.1108/EL-10-2013-0193]

[15] H. Wijayanto, T. Haryono, and H. Putri Wikan Estu, "The Influence Of Quality Information Toward User Satisfaction of Enterprise Resource Planning With Top Management Support As Moderating Variable", *Adv. Soc. Sci. Educ. Humanit. Res.,* p. 203, 2019.
[http://dx.doi.org/10.2991/iclick-18.2019.42]

[16] A.I. Alzahrani, I. Mahmud, T. Ramayah, O. Alfarraj, and N. Alalwan, "Modelling digital library success using the DeLone and McLean information system success model", *J. Librarian. Inform. Sci.,* vol. 51, no. 2, pp. 291-306, 2019.
[http://dx.doi.org/10.1177/0961000617726123]

[17] V.A. Thurmond, K. Wambach, H.R. Connors, and B.B. Frey, "Evaluation of student satisfaction: Determining the impact of a web-based environment by controlling for student characteristics", *Am. J. Distance Educ.,* vol. 16, no. 3, pp. 169-190, 2002.
[http://dx.doi.org/10.1207/S15389286AJDE1603_4]

[18] M. Asoodar, S. Vaezi, and B. Izanloo, "Framework to improve e-learner satisfaction and further strengthen e-learning implementation", *Comput. Human Behav.,* vol. 63, no. 1, pp. 704-716, 2016.
[http://dx.doi.org/10.1016/j.chb.2016.05.060]

[19] E. Smeets, "Does ICT contribute to powerful learning environments in primary education?", *Comput. Educ.,* vol. 44, no. 3, pp. 343-355, 2005.
[http://dx.doi.org/10.1016/j.compedu.2004.04.003]

[20] Y.S. Wang, M.C. Wu, and H.Y. Wang, "Investigating the determinants and age and gender differences in the acceptance of mobile learning", *Br. J. Educ. Technol.,* vol. 40, no. 1, pp. 92-118, 2009.
[http://dx.doi.org/10.1111/j.1467-8535.2007.00809.x]

[21] A. Abu-Al-Aish, and S. Love, "Factors influencing students' acceptance of m-learning: An investigation in higher education", *Int. Rev. Res. Open Distance Learn.,* vol. 14, no. 5, pp. 83-107, 2013.
[http://dx.doi.org/10.19173/irrodl.v14i5.1631]

[22] F.D. Davis, "Perceived usefulness, perceived ease of use, and user acceptance of information technology", *Manage. Inf. Syst. Q.,* vol. 13, no. 3, pp. 319-340, 1989.
[http://dx.doi.org/10.2307/249008]

[23] S. W. Chien, and S.M. Tsaur, *Investigating the success of ERP systems: Case studies in three Taiwanese high-tech industries Computers in industry,* vol. 58, no. 8- 9, pp. 783-793, Dec. 2007.

[24] S.A. Salloum, M. Al-Emran, K. Shaalan, and A. Tarhini, "Factors affecting the E-learning acceptance: A case study from UAE", *Educ. Inf. Technol.,* vol. 24, no. 1, pp. 509-530, 2019.
[http://dx.doi.org/10.1007/s10639-018-9786-3]

[25] Q. Ye, Y. Luo, G. Chen, X. Guo, Q. Wei, and S. Tan, "Users Intention for Continuous Usage of Mobile News Apps: the Roles of Quality, Switching Costs, and Personalization", *J. Syst. Sci. Syst. Eng.,* vol. 28, no. 1, pp. 91-109, 2019.
[http://dx.doi.org/10.1007/s11518-019-5405-0]

[26] S.I. Senaratne, S.M. Samarasinghe, and G. Jayewardenepura, "Factors Affecting the Intention to Adopt M-Learning", *Int. Bus. Res.,* vol. 12, no. 2, pp. 150-164, 2019.
[http://dx.doi.org/10.5539/ibr.v12n2p150]

[27]   K.H. Soon, K.I. Sook, C.W. Jung, and K.M. Im, "The effects of Internet-based distance learning in nursing", *Comput. Nurs.,* vol. 18, no. 1, pp. 19-25, 2000.
[PMID: 10673813]

[28]   V. Venkatesh, M.G. Morris, G.B. Davis, and F.D. Davis, "User acceptance of information technology: Toward a unified view", *Manage. Inf. Syst. Q.,* vol. 27, no. 3, pp. 425-478, 2003.
[http://dx.doi.org/10.2307/30036540]

[29]   V. Venkatesh, and F.D. Davis, "A theoretical extension of the technology acceptance model: Four longitudinal field studies", *Manage. Sci.,* vol. 46, no. 2, pp. 186-204, 2000.
[http://dx.doi.org/10.1287/mnsc.46.2.186.11926]

[30]   E. Alsadoon, "The Impact of Social Presence on Learners' Satisfaction in Mobile Learning", *Turk. Online J. Educ. Technol.,* vol. 17, no. 1, pp. 226-233, 2018.

[31]   S.S. Liaw, "Investigating students' perceived satisfaction, behavioral intention, and effectiveness of e-learning: A case study of the Blackboard system", *Comput. Educ.,* vol. 51, no. 2, pp. 864-873, 2008.
[http://dx.doi.org/10.1016/j.compedu.2007.09.005]

[32]   C.L. Ho, and R.J. Dzeng, "Construction safety training via e-Learning: Learning effectiveness and user satisfaction", *Comput. Educ.,* vol. 55, no. 2, pp. 858-867, 2010.
[http://dx.doi.org/10.1016/j.compedu.2010.03.017]

[33]   S.S. Noesgaard, and R. Orngreen, "The Effectiveness of E-Learning: An Explorative and Integrative Review of the Definitions, Methodologies and Factors That Promote e-Learning Effectiveness", *Electron. J. e-Learn.,* vol. 13, no. 4, pp. 278-290, 2015.

[34]   G. Jackman, "Investigating the factors influencing students' acceptance of mobile learning: The Cave Hill campus experience", *Caribbean Educational Research Journal,* vol. 2, no. 2, pp. 14-32, 2014.

[35]   R.K. Yin, *Case Study Research Design and Methods.* 5th ed. Sage: Thousand Oaks, CA, 2014.

[36]   G. Nelson, and S.D. Evans, "Critical community psychology and qualitative research: A conversation", *Qual. Inq.,* vol. 20, no. 2, pp. 158-166, 2014.
[http://dx.doi.org/10.1177/1077800413510873]

[37]   J. Nelson, "Using conceptual depth criteria: addressing the challenge of reaching saturation in qualitative research", *Qual. Res.,* vol. 17, no. 5, pp. 554-570, 2017.
[http://dx.doi.org/10.1177/1468794116679873]

[38]   D.E. Leidner, and T. Kayworth, "A review of culture in information systems research: Toward a theory of information technology culture conflict", *Manage. Inf. Syst. Q.,* vol. 30, no. 2, pp. 357-399, 2006.
[http://dx.doi.org/10.2307/25148735]

[39]   R.S. Barbour, "Checklists for improving rigour in qualitative research: a case of the tail wagging the dog?", *BMJ,* vol. 322, no. 7294, pp. 1115-1117, 2001.
[http://dx.doi.org/10.1136/bmj.322.7294.1115] [PMID: 11337448]

[40]   M.D. Williams, N.P. Rana, and Y.K. Dwivedi, A bibliometric analysis of articles citing the unified theory of acceptance and use of technology.*Information Systems Theory," 37-62.* Springer: New York, 2012.
[http://dx.doi.org/10.1007/978-1-4419-6108-2_3]

[41]   S. Schlauderer, and S. Overhage, "Exploring the customer perspective of agile development: Acceptance factors and on-site customer perceptions in scrum projects", ICIS2013, Proceedings, Project management, 2013.

[42]   F.N. Al-Fahad, "Students' attitudes and perceptions towards the effectiveness of mobile learning in King Saud University, Saudi Arabia", *Turk. Online J. Educ. Technol.,* vol. 8, no. 2, pp. 111-119, 2009.

[43]   U. Sekaran, and R. Bougie, *Theoretical framework in theoretical framework and hypothesis development Research Methods for Business: A Skill Building Approach,* vol. 80, 2010.

[44] W.G. Zikmund, J.C. Carr, and M. Griffin, "Business research methods: CengageBrain. com. It is very important to attract customers and enhance purchasing decision", 2012.

[45] D. Straub, M.C. Boudreau, and D. Gefen, "Validation guidelines for IS positivist research", *Comm. Assoc. Inform. Syst.,* vol. 13, no. 1, p. 24, 2004.

[46] C. Fornell, and D.F. Larcker, "Evaluating structural equation models with unobservable variables and measurement error", *J. Mark. Res.,* vol. 18, no. 1, pp. 39-50, 1981.
[http://dx.doi.org/10.1177/002224378101800104]

[47] B. Kijsanayotin, S. Pannarunothai, and S.M. Speedie, "Factors influencing health information technology adoption in Thailand's community health centers: Applying the UTAUT model", *Int. J. Med. Inform.,* vol. 78, no. 6, pp. 404-416, 2009.
[http://dx.doi.org/10.1016/j.ijmedinf.2008.12.005] [PMID: 19196548]

[48] S.A. Brown, and V. Venkatesh, "Model of adoption of technology in households: A baseline model test and extension incorporating household life cycle", *Manage. Inf. Syst. Q.,* vol. 29, no. 3, pp. 399-426, 2005.
[http://dx.doi.org/10.2307/25148690]

CHAPTER 7

Socio-Economy of Coastal Fishing Community of Southern Coast of Odisha: A Case Study

T. Padmavati[1,*]

[1] *Department of Marine Sciences, Berhampur University, Odisha, India*

Abstract: Many of the country's most important essential zones and urban regions are found on the outskirts of the coastal zone. The activity or processes of socio-economic growth among coastal areas on the usage of coastal resources are essential for understanding the socio-economic state of a region and its long-term management. Sustainable development shows two great notions for the protection of natural resources: (i) environmental protection and (ii) economic development. Development activities are allowed as long as they do not compromise people's quality of life or the viability of the natural systems on which development is based, according to the above two notions. Advanced scientific and technological knowledge is now helping to improve and prevent the unsustainable exploitation of natural resources along the Indian coast. River floods, cyclones, depressions, and, most crucially, coastal erosions are common occurrences in the studied region. This effect can potentially change the socio-economic situations of coastal residents and society. As a result of this background, the author decided to quickly analyze socio-economic conditions and look at the current state and impacts on the study area's socio-economic conditions. Information on the above parameters was gathered to get insight into the research area's socio-economic profile. The current project involves conducting a socio-economic survey on Orissa's southern coast.

Keywords: Fishing Community, Socio-Economy, Southern Coast.

INTRODUCTION

India is a peninsular country in the south Asian subcontinent, with a 7,500 km long coastline. This shoreline comprises more or less fragile ecosystems such as sand dunes, beaches, wetlands, mangroves, and estuaries associated with tidal flats, backwaters, lagoons, and coral reefs. Thus, it is imperative to state that the Indian coastline plays a significant role in the national economy and has a strong imprint on the international economy for its inherent ocean-derived resources.

---

[*] **Corresponding author T. Padmavati:** Department of Marine Sciences, Berhampur University, Odisha, India; E-mail: padmasmart@gmail.com

Being one of the developing countries of Asia, significant parts of the Indian coast are in a state of stress due to the increase of population density, rapid urbanization, and resultant developmental activities like the construction of ports, harbours, jetties, sea walls, and revetment. Many of the critical economic zones and major urban areas are located within the fringes of the coastal zone. As a result, economic and social processes inevitably characterize the coastal systems [1]. Limited coastal land resources and excessive land demand can result in human-earth conflicts. In the urbanization process, land-use changes lead to a series of environmental constraints, especially in developing countries during economic transition or recession [2]. The coastal environment is unable to maintain the flow of goods (*e.g.*, resources for exploitation) and services (*e.g.*, natural defense systems) indefinitely [3]. The coastal areas of India encompass nine states and four Union Territories (UTs). The socio-economic development activity or processes among these major coastal states and UTs are not per capita income, poverty, infrastructure, and socio-economic development. Thus, the study on the utilization of coastal resources is a prerequisite for understanding of the socio-economic status of a region and its sustainable management.

The accessible environmental resources along the fringes of the Indian coastline have been exploited in an unregulated and unsustainable manner with our arena of knowledge. Thus there is an increasing stress over the environmental components. In this context, it is understandable that human and associated environments are vulnerable to natural threats. Before a few decades, coastal environmentalists realized the vulnerability to potential natural hazards if natural resources are consumed uncontrolled. Since then, sustainable development has been challenged in India and worldwide. In the 1980s, the interdependence between economic development, the natural environment, and people was described with the issues on development that meet the national interest without compromising the ability of the future generations to meet their needs and aspirations [4]. In general, sustainable development unveils two admirable concepts for protecting natural resources (i) environmental protection and (ii) economic development. Based on the above two concepts, the development activities are permitted as long as they do not jeopardize people's quality of life or the viability of the natural systems on which development is based.

It has been widely documented that organic and chemical pollution simultaneously puts pressure on fragile coastal ecosystems and that natural resource deterioration is sometimes irreversible [5]. Coastal zones are more vulnerable in different parts of the world, but environmental pollution is higher in developing countries, particularly India. Sustainable development constitutes an integrated and interactive approach that allows understanding the complex relationship between society and nature, simultaneously respecting human rights and assuming that the environment is a vital dimension of the future generation [5]. Moreover, the complex and conflicting interactions of social equity, human security, and environmental sustainability within the social processes of shaping and building development for present and future generations are important issues. Nowadays, advanced scientific and technological knowledge substantially contributes to improving and preventing the unsustainable use of natural resources along the Indian coast. There is a need for research on how societal driving forces (social and demographic, political and institutional, economic and commercial, cultural and technological) influence the nature and distribution of human activities on coastal zones of India as well as the impacts on coastal ecosystems associated with the current and potential alternative patterns of human activity [6].

The coastline of India is 7500 km long, with 3202 marine fishing villages,1332 landing centers, and an Exclusive Economic Zone of 2.02 million Sq. Km, which is set to grow. This is equivalent to 2/3rd of our land area, necessitating significant investment and long-term, balanced growth planning. The marine fisher population in India is about 5 million, of which 3.5 million are currently residents of coastal fishing villages. Most fishermen in coastal fishing settlements lack legal title deeds and adequate houses with basic facilities. Despite several developmental programs providing homes and title deeds, 40% still live in huts and Kutcha houses.

With a 480-kilometer coastline, Odisha has the country's most extensive mineral resource base in terms of iron ore, thermal coal, coking coal, and other essential minerals such as manganese copper and heavy minerals in coastal beach sands. Govt. of Odisha liberalized for the investors (public and private sectors) and provided adequate and additional benefits to Indian and foreign entrepreneurs to establish industries and ports as part of a significant drive for Indian economic growth. Among the five coastal districts of Odisha, Ganjam is one of the most developing districts regarding trading. The extensive stretch of beach bestowed with favorable ecosystem attracts many tourists of the country. The World's most significant nesting beach of olive Ridley sea turtles is adjacent to the Rushikulya Estuary, known as Rushikulya Rookery. The study region experiences multiple recurrent disasters such as river floods, cyclones (notably super cyclone of 1999;Phailin of October 2013;Hudhud of October 2014), depressions, and coastal erosion. On the other hand, Govt. of India has identified Gopalpur as one of the country's Special Economic Zones (SEZs). Govt. of Odisha provided around 2980 acres of land near Chatrapur to Tata Steel Limited (TSL) for their industrial activities (Reference). Indian Rare Earth Ltd (IREL), a sister-wing of the Department of Atomic energy, Govt. of India, is adjacent to Gopalpur Port. The primary activity of this plant is to process the beach sand to acquire the heavy minerals for the multidimensional requirement. Jayasree Chemicals' plant stands for vast scale production of Chloroalkali and caustic soda products a few kilometers away. Port construction activities at Gopalpur are gaining momentum to make it operational as an all-weather port. In addition, to meet the demand for Titanium, a unique Titanium Plant is proposed to establish in this region. Overall, the government and the industrialists closely view this coastal region for further development activities.

In the backdrop of the above developmental activities and resultant future, holistic developmental work of this region with sustainable utilization of natural resources, the present piece on a socio-economic survey on this region is being undertaken very precisely.

INFORMATION AND METHODOLOGY

Various socio-economic parameters were collected from multiple public interface websites, personal interaction with responsible authorities, and local inhabitants during field visits. The information on socio-economic aspects has been compiled from many secondary sources, including government and semi-government offices. The data are collectively presented in this chapter to explain the overall socio-economic condition of the study area.

RESULT AND DISCUSSION

The socio-economic study is an integral part of the Environmental Impact Assessment of a region. There is a massive scope of upcoming projects and port activities. Existing and upcoming projects will have an impact on the environment. The effect may alter the socio-economic conditions of the coastal dwellers and the society. This background prompted the author to conduct a brief analysis of socio-economic conditions and examine the current status and the impacts envisaged by upcoming projects on the socio-economic conditions of the study area. Information on the factors mentioned above has been collected to gain insight into the socio-economic profile of the study area. Before understanding the study area, it's important to represent it regarding Odisha.

Overall population, geography, and literacy of Odisha

Along the east coast of India, Odisha occupies 4.75% of the Indian peninsula's landmass and accounts for 3.74% of the country's population. The state comprises 30 districts, 58 subdivisions, 314 blocks, and 51,048 administrative villages(https://odisha.gov.in/about-us/districts). As per the 2001 census, the population of Odisha is 36.71 million. The literacy rate is 63.61 percent, and the female literacy rate is 50.97%, which is below the national averages of 65.38% and 54.16%, respectively. With a coastline of 480 km along the Bay of Bengal,

Odisha accounts for 8% of the coastline of India. The shoreline of Odisha is shared by six coastal districts, including Ganjam, a prominent coastal region with a 60-kilometer-long coastal line.

Origin, present status, geography, and administrative classification of Ganjam

The name of the Ganjam district derives from the word "Ganj-i-am," which means the Granary of the World. The district is named after the old Township and European fort of Ganjam situated on the northern bank of river Rushikulya, the district's headquarter. The district was isolated from Madras Presidency and formed a part of the newly created state called Odisha, with effect from 1936. The reorganized district consisting of the whole of Ghumusar, Chatrapur, and Baliguda divisions, part of old Berhampur Taluk, Ichapur Taluk, part of Parlakhemundi area, and the whole of Parlakhemundi agency area in the old Chicacola Division.

Table 1. Detail administrative classification of Ganjam district.

Name of District	Name of subdivision	Name of Tahasil	The policestation in the subdivision	Blocks in the subdivision		
				Name	No. of GPs	No. of Villages
Ganjam	Chatrapur	Chatrapur	Chatrapur	Chatrapur	17	80
		Khallikote	Kabisuryanagar	Ganjam	14	11
		Kodala	Khallikote	Hinjilkaut	21	54
		Purushottampur	Kodala	Kabisuryanagar	21	74
		Hinjilkaut	Purushottampur	Khallikote	26	219
			Rambha	Kodala	22	177
			Chamakhandi	Polasara	26	125
			Polasara	Purushottampur	26	95

(Source: National informatics website)

As per the recent reorganized plan for this district by Govt. of Odisha, the seven blocks of the Paralakhemundi subdivision were separated, and the new district of Gajapati came to light. Ganjam district is currently made up of 3 subdivisions, 22 blocks, and 14 Tehsils, with a population of 27.04 lakh (according to the 1991 census) and stretches between 19.4^0 to 20.17^0 N latitude and $84.7.4^0$ to 85.12^0 S longitudes, covering an area of 8070.60 km^2. The study area comprises of Chatrapur division along the Bay of Bengal region. The details of block-wise BPL population distribution and socio-economic conditions of Ganjam are indicated in Tables (**1 & 2**).

Table 2. Detail administrative classification of individual blocks of Ganjam district.

S. No.	Name of the village	G.P	Block	No. of Households	Male	Female	Total Population
1	Venkatraipur	Boxipalli	Rangailunda	259	420	458	878
2	Sano Deegipur	Boxipalli	Rangailunda	120	340	349	689
3	BodoDeegipur	Boxipalli	Rangailunda	252	632	812	1444
4	New Boxipalli	Boxipalli	Rangailunda	396	696	684	1380
5	Ganga Vihar	Boxipalli	Rangailunda	60	180	143	323
6	Old Boxipalli	Boxipalli	Rangailunda	358	751	720	1471
7	New Golabandha	Kamalapur	Rangailunda	508	1410	1430	2840
8	Old Golabandha	Golabandha	Rangailunda	350	917	890	1807
9	Garempeta	Keluapalli	Rangailunda	270	830	850	1680
10	Markandi	Indrakhi	Rangailunda	528	1410	1430	2840
11	Axing	Axing	Chikiti	73	253	260	513
12	Dayanidhipeta	Kotturu	Chikiti	49	236	247	483
13	Ramayapatnam	Kotturu	Chikiti	420	1110	1115	2225
14	Anantaraipur	Sonnapur	Chikiti	126	352	344	696
15	PatiSonnapur	Sonnapur	Chikiti	1180	2977	2895	5872
	15 villages	**8 GPs**	**2 Blocks**	**4,949**	**12,514**	**12,627**	**25,141**

(Source: Report from Aanganwadi Workers (AWW) report, 2011)

Ganjam is the 5th largest district in terms of size. It is the 6th most urbanized district in Odisha, with 17.60% of the population residing in urban areas. In terms of population per sq. km., Ganjam is the 9th most densely populated district in the state. It is nominated as 8th rank in terms of sex ratio in the state. There are only 400 uninhabited villages in the district, whereas 40 villages have a population of more than 5000. Lochapada in Berhampur Sadar P.S. is the district's most populated village (9,240). The economy of the district is mainly dependent upon agriculture. Among 100 workers in the district, 63 are engaged in the agricultural sector. Jarada police station has the highest number of villages (246) in the district, and Gopalpur police station has the lowest number of villages (27) in the district.

Census (Govt. of India) 2011

The government of India carried out the latest census in the year 2011. Categorically the detailed information is provided below.

Ganjam District Population

In 2011, Ganjam population was 3,529,031, among which males and females were 1,779,218 and 1,749,813 respectively. In 2001 census, Ganjam population was 3,160,635; where the population of males was 1,581,986 and the remaining 1,578,649 were females.

Ganjam District Population Growth Rate

There was a change of 11.66% in the population compared to the population as per the 2001 census. In the previous census of India, 2001, Ganjam District recorded an increase of 16.88% to its population compared to 1991.

Ganjam District Density

The provisional data released by the 2011 census of India revealed that the density of the Ganjam district for 2011 is 430 people per sq. km. In 2001, Ganjam district density was about385 people per sq. km. To our knowledge, the Ganjam district administers 8,206 sq. km. of area.

Ganjam Literacy Rate

In terms of Ganjam's literacy rate in 2011, it was reported that it increased from 60.77 in 2001 to 71.09 in 2011. Furthermore, when it comes to gender, male and female literacy rates were 80.99 and 61.13 percent, respectively. The total number of literate people in the Ganjam district was 2,210,050, with 1,262,652 males and 947,398 females.

Ganjam Sex Ratio

The Sex Ratio in Ganjam is 983 per 1000 males compared to the 2001 census figure of 998. The figures mentioned above show that the sex ratio in Ganjam district is declining and has to be improved through a public awareness campaign. The average national sex ratio in India is 940 as per the latest reports of the Census Directorate during 2011. The child sex ratio in the 2011 census was 908 girls per 1000 boys, compared to 939 girls per 1000 boys in the 2001 census.

Ganjam Child Population

Data on children under the age of six were also obtained during the census enumeration in all districts, including Ganjam. There were 420,158 children under the age of six, compared to 475,464 in the 2001 census. Among the 420,158 counts, males and females were 220,159 and 199,999, respectively. Census 2011 found a child sex ratio of 908 compared to 939 in 2001. In 2011, Children under the age of six were 11.91% of the Ganjam district compared to 15.04% of 2001. There was a net change of -3.13% in this, compared to the previous census of India. The detailed information on the Ganjam district is presented in Table **3**.

Table 3. Detail information on Ganjam district as per 2011 census.

Description	2011	2001
Actual Population	**3,529,031**	**3,160,635**
Male	1,779,218	1,581,986
Female	1,749,813	1,578,649
Population Growth	**11.66%**	**16.88%**
Area Sq. Km	8,206	8,206
Density/km^2	**430**	**385**
Proportion to Odish Population	8.41%	8.59%
Sex Ratio (Per 1000)	**983**	**998**
Child Sex Ratio (0-6 Age)	908	939
Average Literacy	**71.09**	**60.77**
Male Literacy	80.99	75.22
Female Literacy	61.13	46.44
Total Child Population (0-6 Age)	**420,158**	**475,464**
Male Population (0-6 Age)	220,159	245,206
Female Population (0-6 Age)	199,999	230,258
Literates	**2,210,050**	**1,631,722**
Male Literates	1,262,652	1,005,585
Female Literates	947,398	626,137
Child Proportion (0-6 Age)	**11.91%**	**15.04%**
Boys Proportion (0-6 Age)	12.37%	15.50%
Girls Proportion (0-6 Age)	11.43%	14.59%

Ganjam District Urban Population

According to the 2011 census of the Ganjam population, 21.78 percent of the population lives in the district's urban areas. In total, 766,563 people live in urban areas, with 396,273 men and 370,290 females. The Sex Ratio in the urban region of Ganjam district was 934 as per the 2011 census. Similarly, the child sex ratio in the Ganjam district was 908 in the 2011 census. There were 72,561 children under the age of six in the urban area, with 38,033 males and 34,528 females, respectively. This entity of the child population of Ganjam district is 9.60% of the total urban population. According to the 2011 literacy census, the average literacy rate in the Ganjam district is 84.24%, with male literacy at 90.02% and female literacy at 78.06%, respectively. A number of 584,608 people are literate in the urban region, among which males and females were 322,504 and 262,104 respectively.

Ganjam District Rural Population

As per the 2011 census, 78.22% population of Ganjam districts lives in rural areas. Totally, 2,753,588 people live in rural regions in the Ganjam district, with males and females numbering 1,381,051 and 1,372,537, respectively. The sex ratio was about 994 females per 1000 males in rural areas. According to Ganjam district data on child sex ratios, there are 897 girls per 1000 boys. In rural areas, there were 325,359 children aged 0 to 6, with males accounting for 171,540 and females accounting for 153,819. The child population constitutes 12.42% of the total rural population of the Ganjam district. The literacy rate in rural areas of the Ganjam district was 68.35% by the 2011 census. Regarding gender, male and female literacy stood at 79.42 and 57.37%, respectively. In total, 1,659,800 people were literate, of which males and females were 960,653 and 699,147 respectively.

Education Facilities

As per the educational concern, the Ganjam district has a good reputation and profile against general educational facilities. Ganjam district has around 3035 primary schools, 680 middle schools, 362 secondary schools, and 65 colleges for higher education. As per higher education concerns, Berhampur University is the only leading university representing south Odisha, particularly in the Ganjam district.

Socio-economic status of the coastal total fishing community of Ganjam

The fishermen's community dominates four blocks of the Ganjam district. Details on fishermen households, fishers population, and fishers engaged in fishing are presented in Tables (**4** & **5**).

Table 4. Fishermen population along Ganjam coast (Source: Census Report, 2001; Assistant Director of Fisheries, Marine, Ganjam).

S. No.	Block	No. of Households	Fishermen Population	Fishermen Engaged in Fishing
1	Ganjam	818	3945	1100
2	Chatrapur	2311	11813	2891
3	Rangeilunda	2472	14088	2550
4	Chikiti	1484	7861	1648

Table 5. Fishermen population along Ganjam coast (Source: Assistant Director of Fisheries, Marine, Ganjam).

No. of Villages	No. of Households	Fishermen population			
		Male	Female	Children	Total
28	7,325	9,709	9,032	18,765	37,506

Fishing Activities

The majority of the inhabitants in the Ganjam district rely on fishing for a living because it is located along the west coast of the Bay of Bengal. The area expanded its fishing operations across 9500 hectares along its 60 kilometers to local market demand. Inland and marine sectors were included in the fishery activity. The scope of this research was limited to the marine industry. The marine fishing community's livelihood operations included catching fish, processing, selling, and related functions [7].

Assets of the Fishermen

As per the BPL list released by the 2011 census by the state of Odisha, about 60% of fishermen do not have primary capital to invest in fishing activity. Some families share their boats, personnel, and nets with their neighbors to catch more fish. Around 37% of families possessed a single ship, and 12% had two or more homes. Only 5% of households, on the other hand, owned mechanized or motorized boats, such as BLCs and IBM or OBM engines [8].

Fishing Fleets

At the moment, there are no trawlers with fisherfolk for leisure activities along Ganjam's coastal waters. The only boats they were using were wooden and fiber-based. The Ganjam coast is home to various hybrid vessels and gear systems. The Ganjam coast's fishing methods can be divided into mechanized and non-mechanized [8]. Motorized (IBM, OBM, BLC) and non-motorized wooden and fiber boats.

Fishing craft

The fishing crafts utilized in Ganjam's coastal district are divided into two categories: non-mechanized and mechanized. The non-mechanized sector has contributed significantly to Odisha's marine seafood production. By nature, their fishing vessels and gear were mainly indigenous. Catamaran/teppa, bar boat (padhua), and Nava were the non-mechanized vessels used for fishing. FRP Catamarans are the mechanized vessels used, and they are financed mainly by Odisha State Government programmers [8].

Information on the detailed account of fishing boats in operation presented a total number of 1508 boats that were found to be in operation at 16 landing centers of the Ganjam district. Among the landing centers, Nolianuagaon was rich in motorized boats (125) and country crafts (200), with a total number of 325. However, Sanaarjipalli was recorded with the highest number of (170) motorized boats representing improved financial performance compared to other landing centers. Landing centers at Sonapur and Gokharjuda were observed with the lowest number of boats (20) in operation during 2013-14 (Fig. **1**).

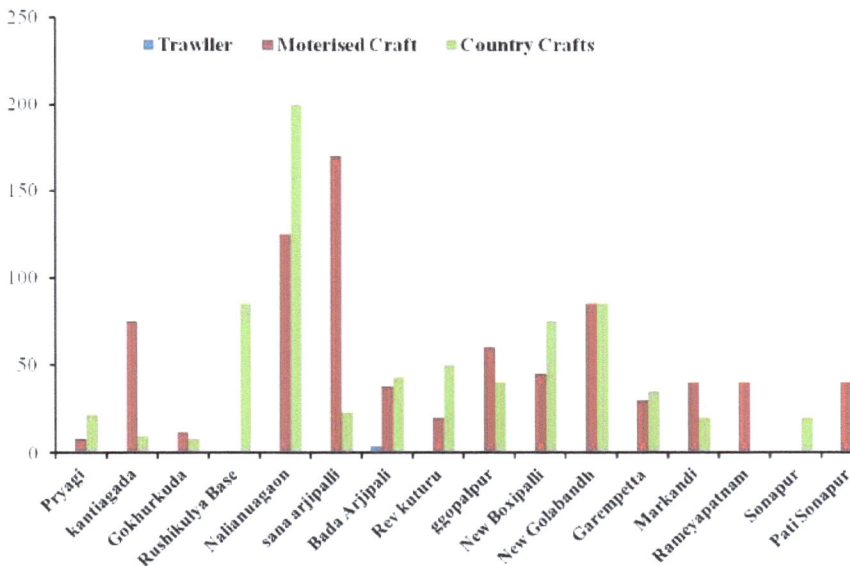

Fig. (1). Information of sea venture means for fishing at major landing centers of the district (Source Asst. Dir. Marine Fisheries, Ganjam as of 31.3.2014).

During the present study, there were 879 numbers of boats (405 numbers motorized and 474 were country crafts found registered and licensed). Up to registration, the total number of boats was 13318, among which 2485 were motorized, and 10833 were country crafts. During the year 2013-14, a total number of 629 boats were found to be renewed, out of which 329 were motorized, and 300 were country crafts (Fig. **2**).

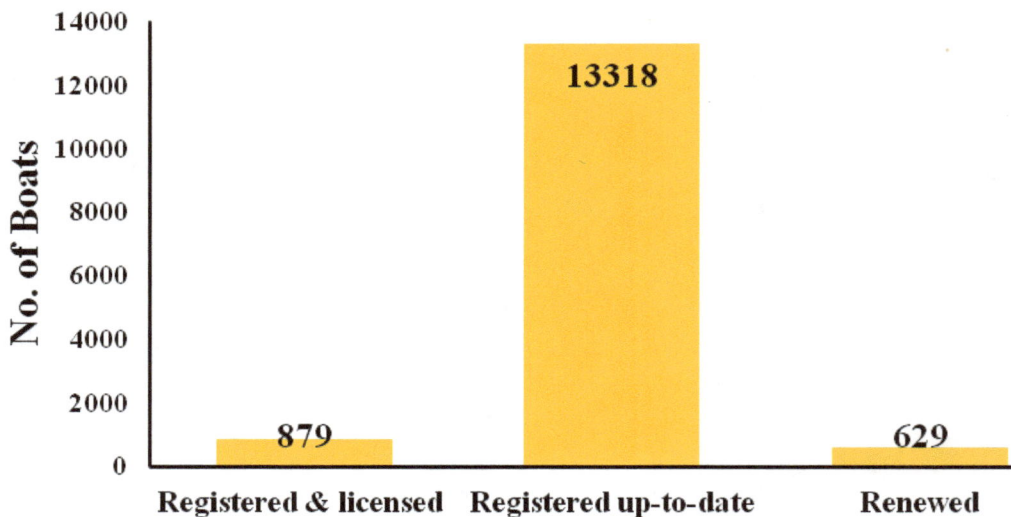

Fig. (2). Total number of boats registered/licensed/renewed during 2013-14 (Source Asst. Dir. Marine Fisheries, Ganjam as on 31.3.2014.

Fishing gear and method

In the past, lift-nets and boat seines were utilized along Ganjam's coast. Depending on the economic conditions of the fishermen, environmental conditions, and the number of species of fish, gill nets and line nets were utilized throughout the shore, namely, Gill-net Bottom drift nets (jagawala), Surface drift nets (kilumala), Encircling nets (Boat seines and Beach seines), Boat and beach seine, Boat seine (irragali), Beach seine (badajalo), Lift-nets Headlines and long lines, Kata, Burdu, SutiKhepajalo, Kata, Burdu, SutiKhepajalo, Kata, Burdu, Sut [8].

Fish Harvest

For 2013-14, the Dept. of Marine Fisheries had targeted an annual harvest of 11000 mt. However, the total catch was 10319 mt. The reduced yield in comparison to the targeted might be attributed to the adverse effect of severe cyclonic storm Phailin on this region, which was the first prey of this natural calamity. During the year 2013-14, the total marine fishery harvest was categorized under fish (9958.90 mt), prawn (354.15 mt), and crab (5.50 mt). Marine fishes dominated the crop during the year 2013-14 (Fig. **3**).

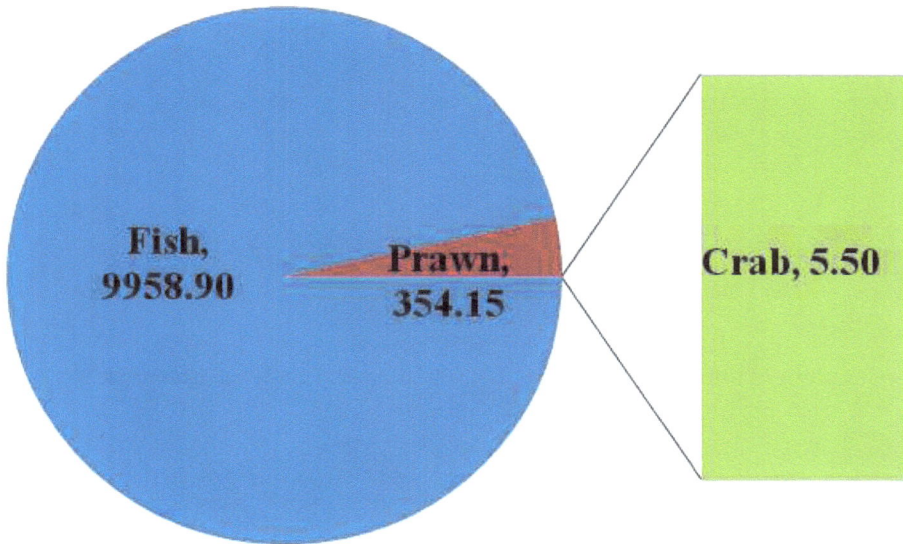

Fig. (3). Fishery harvest (in metric ton) during 2013-14 (Source Asst. Dir. Marine Fisheries, Ganjam as of 31.3.2014).

It was discussed earlier that the numbers of motorized boats were less than country crafts. Due to advantages in stability, first moving, large space, and reduced effort, the use of motorized boats for sea venture for fishing produced significant catch (7963 mt) in comparison to country crafts (2355 mt) during the year 2013-14 (Fig. **4**). Dry fish is an essential residual fishery product in India. It also has significant market values at some particular state and country locations. During 2013-14, 3659 mt dry fish was produced at different landing centers of Ganjam district, which cost about Rs. 1720/- lakhs. Out of 3659 Zmt. Dryfish, 2651 mt., was disposed of in the domestic market and 983 mt in markets outside the state. 5500 fishermen/fisherwomen were involved in dry fish processing during the harvest year 2013-14 (Fig. **5**).

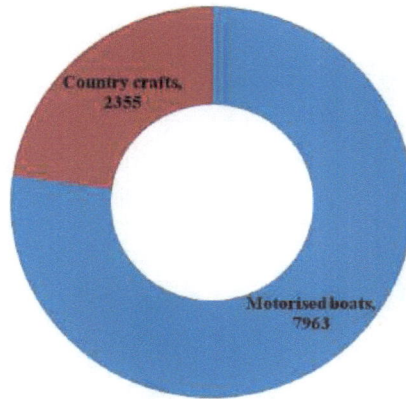

Fig. (4). Quantity of fish landing (in metric ton) by using country crafts and motorizedboats during 2013-14 (Source Asst. Dir. Marine Fisheries, Ganjam as of 31.3.2014).

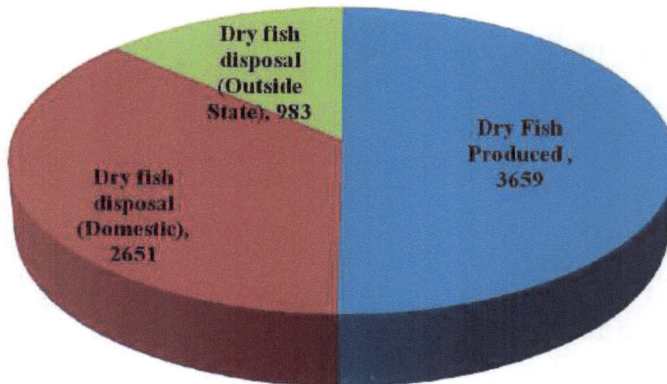

Fig. (5). Dry fish produced and disposal (in metric Ton) during 2013-14 (Source Asst. Dir. Marine Fisheries, Ganjam as of 31.3.2014).

Fish Marketing and Preservation

The research area's fish selling was exceedingly unorganized and challenging. In Ganjam, there were two methods of fish marketing. Direct marketing I and indirect marketing (ii) are two types of marketing. Without an intermediary, fishing resources were sold straight to the buyer through direct marketing. On the other hand, in indirect marketing, Fish was traded through an intermediary known as a broker. Fish were traded in landing hubs and neighboring vending zones such as Gopalpur, Karapalli, and Berhampur in Ganjam's coastline area. For local marketing, fish were shipped to Paradeep, Bhubaneswar, Visakhapatnam, and Kolkota. Some species of prawn and crabs were also exported to other countries [8].

Problems Encountered in Fish Marketing

Despite the reasonable market price, the fisherman is denied the best possible selling price. It is primarily due to a lack of government oversight of the trade, allowing intermediaries to exploit both fishermen and consumers. Another issue in the fish marketing industry is a lack of infrastructure. Only 14 leading fisherman cooperative groups are recognized in the Ganjam coastal area [8].

Socio-economics

While disseminating satellite-retrieved information on Potential Fishing Grounds among fishermen, observations on the fishermen's socio-economic conditions are made. Many causes have contributed to the fall in the fishermen's socioeconomic conditions in this region. The availability of fishing jetties, cold storage, updated craft, modern gears, structured marketing, finance, and GPS-based motorized boats are the primary factors that influence the fishermen's economic situation. These were areas where the district fell short, and they needed to be addressed. For the district's fishermen, late-sea fishing was not a reliable source of income.

In a typical year, they go fishing for 169 days. They believe that to capture a good catch, they must travel to the deep sea, which necessitates modern technology such as motorized boats, trawlers, crafts, and GPS (GPS). They cannot reach the water because the army training school conducts regular missile tests. In addition, they are frequently unable to go fishing due to waterborne diseases. Bad weather and a ban during turtle mass nesting also played a role in the lack of strong catches.

Other problems, such as Andhra trawlers invading coastal areas, have a negative impact on the fishermen's economic situation. Due to a lack of cash, most fishermen claim that they cannot get the necessary fishing equipment. A non-defaulter fisherman's per-capita spending shows that he spends 28 percent on food, 18 percent on health, 17%on education, and 8% on liquor use. He does, however, set aside 6% of his income to pay off the loan. Similarly, a defaulter fisherman's per capita expenditure shows that they spend 33% on food, 15% on health, 5% on education, and 23% on liquor use [8].

Welfare Schemes

According to the BPL census during 2011, Odisha state has a good rank among the states of India. To resolve these issues, Govt. of India has formulated some public welfare schemes, i.e., Indira Awas Yojana (IAY), that is more or less implemented to better the local community in the Ganjam district of Odisha state. These schemes are of the following types, i.e., Saving-cum-Relief Scheme, Accident Insurance Scheme, Assistance for Mechanization Programme, National Welfare fund for Construction of Low-Cost Houses for fishers [8].

Role of Different Banks in Financing Fishermen

To address the BPL issues that persisted across the Ganjam districts of Odisha, several regional banks such as Rushikulya Gramya Bank and State Bank of India, Chatrapur, presently providing the subsidiary loan for the integrated development of fisherfolk. Despite this, many small to medium regional financing institutions such as Rushikulya Gramya Bank, CARD Bank, B.C.C. Banks have implemented different beneficiary schemes to better the local community. These schemes include the IRDP scheme, Bay of Bengal Programme (BOBP), K.C.C. and STEP, *etc* [8].

Fisheries Co-operatives

The National Co-operative Development Corporation (N.C.D.C) and commercial banks provide loans to the beneficiaries through the Fisheries Cooperative Societies (Table **6**). The marine sector received approximately 8% of overall government loans. The NCDC and NABARD finance term loans and working capital to PMFCS (Primary Marine Fisheries Co-operative Society) and apex societies, which helps to finance primary associations. Under the societies Act 1960, three societies were registered in 1996, including Sonepur, Patisonepur, and Gopalpur [8].

Table 6. N.C.D.C: Loan position as on 31.3.2006.

District	No of BLC Availed	Name of the PFCS	Amount of Loan Availed	Balance Outstanding Principal	Interest	Total (in Lakhs)
Ganjam	6	Gopalpur PMFCS	2,46,792	60.683	1,15,941	1,77,624
Ganjam	3	New Boxipalli	2,14,750	1,22,917	1,54,933	2,77,850
Ganjam	5	Bada-aryapalli	2,36,250	1,45,057	1,83,562	3,28,619
Ganjam	3	Patisonepur	1,41,750	95,097	1,64,464	2,59,561
Ganjam	5	Sana-aryapalli	2,36,250	2,36,250	3,51,179	5,87,129
Ganjam	5	Sana NoliaNuaGaon	2,36,250	2,36,250	3,51,179	5,87,429
Ganjam	5	Bada NoliaNuaGaon	2,36,250	2,36,250	3,51,179	5,87,429
Total	32	-----	13,48,292	9,54808	14,26,221	23,81,029

Source: Assistant Director of Fisheries (marine), Ganjam

In some special schemes, the government has provided low-cost houses for the fishermen's families. To date, 234 houses are allotted, out of which, the work of 231 is already completed. The highest numbers of houses have been allotted to Garempetta fishermen's village and the lowest (10) to Anantaraipur and Gokharahuda. Drinking water facility for the coastal fisher folks is a prime requisite. There are no facilities to supply water, tube-wells are the only alternative to drinking water. Record as of 31.3.2014 has shown that six tube-wells are allotted for fishing villages of Ganjam district, out of which, two are completed. A total amount of Rs. 95.10/- lakh has been sanctioned by the government for the house construction, and tube-well boring purpose, out of which, Rs. 87.85/- lakh have been utilized till date (Fig. **6**). Looking at the drinking water insufficiency in the coastal fishing villages, the government should take immediate measures to bore more tubewells at the earliest.

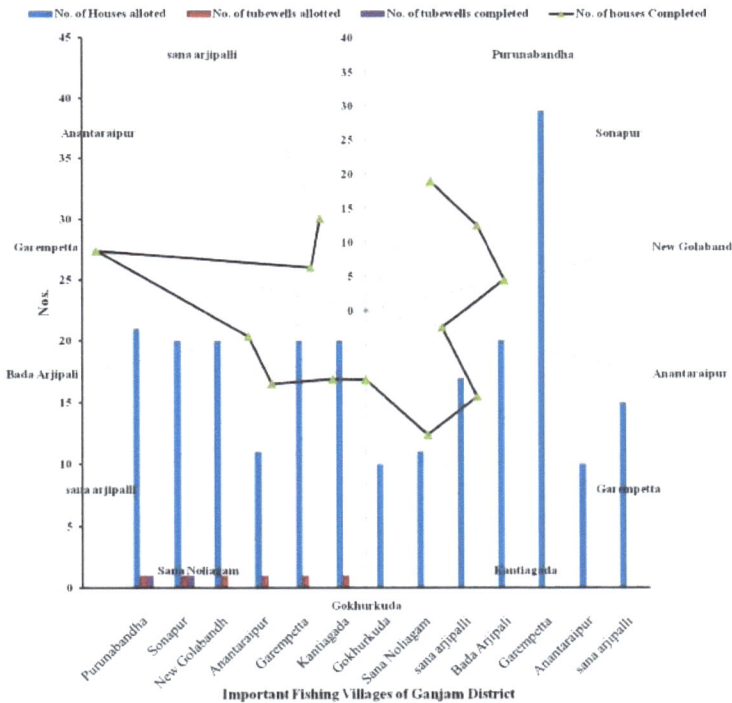

Fig. (6). Physical information on houses and tube wells allotted/completed by govt. since inception (Source Asst. Dir. Marine Fisheries, Ganjam as on 31.3.2014).

Geomorphology

Spatial and Temporal changes in shoreline along the east coast lead to some environmental problems such as beach erosion inundation of seawater towards the coastal area, which resulted in the destruction of many capital resources of fishers. As the longshore sediment transport is northward during pre-monsoon and monsoon time and reverses its direction towards the south during the winter monsoon, a higher rate of northward transport is a cause for continuous northward shifting of the Rushikulya river mouth [8]. The northward movement of this mouth is at present scenario impending the river discharge, which is, on the other hand, creating an excellent flood situation along with the nearby villages. Due to the lack of dredging activity in the Gopalpur Harbor navigational channel, most local fishermen face severe problems for their recreational and fishing trade [8].

Potential Fishing Zone (PFZ) Advisories using Remote Sensing Technology for Reduction of Fuel Consumption and Search Time and Improvement of Catch

Because the fish stock is dynamic and travels further offshore when the vessel approaches it, it is currently difficult for fishermen to pinpoint the exact location and catch the fish school. As a result, the search time, cost, and effort increase. Advanced technologies such as remote sensing to identify possible fishing areas yields outstanding results for fishermen, saving search time, fuel consumption, and manpower while increasing catch. India has demonstrated a promising position in utilizing satellite data for societal purposes. Since 2002, India has had a National Program for the Dissemination of PFZ Alerts (INCOIS); Hyderabad distributes advisories to around 587 nodes across the country's coastline. Fax, telephone, e-mail, electronic display board, newspaper, and radio have all been used to spread information about the possible fishing zone. Increased fish productivity and empowerment of fishermen resulted in considerable socio-economic changes [7, 9].

It is generally established that crucial physical, chemical, and biological elements influence fish adaption in the marine environment. Many pelagic fish species congregate around current borders, mainly where considerable horizontal temperature gradients. Physical, chemical, and biological characteristics must be monitored in space and time, which is time demanding and expensive. Ample synoptic coverage in a short amount of time is an additional benefit of using satellite technology for PFZ forecasting.

SST and Chlorophyll across the Arabian Sea and Bay of Bengal were collected from the NOAA-thermal AVHRR's infrared channels and IRS-optical P4's bands. Potential Fishing Zones are identified using OCM / MODIS Aqua data along the Indian coastline and island regions. INCOIS generates the multi-lingual PFZ Advisories every day, including Sundays, to about 100,000 fishermen at 587 fish landing centers/ fishing villages covering the entire coastline of India under 12 sectors *viz.* Gujarat, Maharashtra, Karnataka & Goa, Kerala, South Tamilnadu,

North Tamilnadu, South Andhra Pradesh, North Andhra Pradesh, Odisha & West Bengal, Lakshadweep Islands, Andaman Islands, and the Nicobar Islands.

During the non-ban and non-monsoon periods, multilingual IPFZ advisories are generated and disseminated to the entire fishermen community located along India's coast and islands via various modes of dissemination, such as telephone, fax, e-mail, website, Doordarshan, radio, news media, and so on. Advancements in information and communication technology have improved coverage and penetration. INCOIS built and implemented Electronic Display Boards (EDB) at key fishing harbours, which have substantially impacted the supply chain, using state-of-the-art cutting-edge technologies accessible at capacity building in the Indian context. About 100,000 beneficiaries/users regularly utilize these services to harvest marine fishery resources effectively. PFZ advisories generated from satellite retrieved SST and Chlorophyll were found more beneficial and effective to artisanal, motorized. Small mechanized sector fishermen engaged in pelagic fishing activities such as ring seining, gill netting, *etc*., thereby reducing the searching time and saving valuable fuel oil and human effort. A validation experiment in Kerala reported a reduction in searching time to be 60-70% for oil sardine shoals in-ring seining with a 30-40% reduction reported for mackerel, anchovy, tuna, and carangid shoals in-ring seining operations [10].

During the non-ban and non-monsoon periods, multilingual IPFZ advisories are generated and disseminated to the entire fishermen community located along India's coast and islands via various modes of dissemination, such as telephone, fax, e-mail, website, Doordarshan, radio, news media, and so on. Advancements in information and communication technology have improved coverage and penetration. INCOIS built and implemented Electronic Display Boards (EDB) at key fishing harbours, which have substantially impacted the supply chain, using state-of-the-art cutting-edge technologies accessible at capacity building in the Indian context. The coastal fisherfolk community is an underprivileged one in our country. Their livelihood can be enhanced if they get exposure to a good catch by adopting less effort and search time. The satellite retrieved information provides the prospective fishing grounds. This study attempted to validate the satellite-based PFZ advisories by engaging boats in PFZ and non-PFZ areas. The study unveiled that CPUE is more in boats operated in PFZ areas than non-PFZ areas in all the sectors of the Ganjam coast. The fishermen took more time to search the fish school without following the PFZ advisories (Figs. **7** & **8**). The hour of fishing is followed by little catch for boats operated in the Non-PFZ area [9]. So it is recommended to use these PFZ advisories for improvement of socio-economy by getting higher fish catch with reduced effort and less time.

Fig. (7). Graphical PFZ forecasts during June and August 2013 for Odisha and West Bengal Coast; red circles notifies forecasting for present study region).

Fig. (8). PFZ forecasts with particular geographic positions through EDBs during June and August 2013 for Odisha and West Bengal Coast; red circles notifies forecasting for present study region).

Socio-economic Situation of Fisherwomen in Ganjam District: A Case Study

Unlike men, women play an active role in the day-to-day survival of the coastal fishing communities, but unfortunately, their contribution to the fishing sector remains unnoticed. Fisherwomen are actively engaged in fish processing and marketing after the fish harvest [11]. They bear the double burden of work for the market and the household. The fisherwomen of Ganjam are illiterate and have no other skill than selling fish. Increasing competition for scarce fish resources makes it difficult for women to procure fish. In the absence of transportation, women are forced to walk 8 to 12 kilometers every day with massive loads of fish on their heads, making fish vending a challenging vocation. . The deficiency in a secondary source of livelihood leads to generate opportunities among the coastal communities, which reduces the opportunity cost of labor to the point where they continue to be employed within the fishery despite minimal returns. Because of their financial inadequacies, fisherwomen in Ganjam borrow money from moneylenders, who then exploit them with usurious credit, keeping them eternally in debt. This occupational convenience forces fish workers to live in a narrow stretch of coastal land. They live in impoverished thatched and mud-walled houses. Transport and communication facilities are good in a few villages like Gopalpur and Arijpalli because of their importance as tourist centers, which are nonetheless inadequate in the proposed villages.

The majority of the women in this area are uneducated, and underage marriage is still common in the fishing community. During the fishing season, fisherwomen devote 9-12 hours each day to fishing operations in addition to their regular household responsibilities. All shore-based post-harvest activities, such as handling, sorting, grading, gutting, drying, and marketing, are done by women. Fresh fish marketing is carried out by more than 70% of the area's fisherwomen.

Significant Problems Associated with the Fisherwomen Community

Lack of Empowerment among Women

Traditional norms and values discriminate against women's family and community decision-making participation. Women in fishing areas have low literacy rates, and the gender divide in the workplace discriminates against them. Women's workloads have increased in fishing towns, forcing many of them to work as farm labourers, construction workers, and other sorts of menial labour on top of their already heavy workloads. Lack of access to government livelihood entitlements *viz.* Public Distribution Systems, Pensions, and other social security systems and poor implementation of government schemes at the grassroots level. Poor women participation in Panchayat Raj System (PRI) and other governance systems.

Inadequate Systems and Techniques to Support Fisher Women Micro-enterprises

Fisherwomen frequently engage in two sorts of fish-related micro-businesses: a) daily fresh fish vending in local markets and b) weekly dry fish processing and selling. These businesses are thriving. However, due to a lack of suitable storage and advanced processing processes, fishermen are obliged to sell fresh and dried fish at a customer-negotiable price. Until today, most fisherwomen were only aware of processing dry fish and any sophisticated techniques. As a result of their traditional methods, a fisherwoman obtains all of the losses in terms of fish. Dry fish processing using solar dryers is one of the many sanitary fish processing procedures available. On the other hand, Fisherwomen could not investigate these available ways to improve their micro-companies in a viable manner due to a lack of awareness and funds. Women who run dry fish businesses must limit themselves to a single market, customarily sold weekly. Due to a lack of marketing support, they never get the opportunity to branch out outside their current market. Other fish-related micro-businesses, such as fish pickling, have yet to be fully explored. Despite the high demand for such products, women did not prioritize this enterprise due to a lack of skills and marketing chances.

Lack of Capacity Building, Skills, and Institution

Many SHGs in coastal fishing communities struggle to access the resources above because they lack a voice, confidence, basic administrative skills, and the capability to negotiate with and obtain support from rural banks, resources, and marketing agencies. Fishery women's organizations are either non-existent or perform at a shallow level. The quality of bookkeeping is said to be below. A significant percentage of impoverished households are not included in the SHG. Due to a lack of capacity-building activities for SHGs and cooperatives in vocational training and micro-enterprise promotion, major SHGs have a low-income level.

Coastal Fishing Community at Gopalpur-on-sea (the Most Important Coastal Site for Fshing and Tourism of Ganjam District): A Particular Case Study

Gopalpur-on-Sea is a town on the Bay of Bengal coast about 15.6 kilometers from Brahmapur in the Ganjam district. It is a modest fishing community where the majority of the residents work in the fishing industry. During the British administration, this settlement was formerly the principal commercial center for the port. This town has one of Odisha's most popular coastal beaches. This beach is quiet and calm, ideal for a relaxing vacation away from the stresses of everyday life. Huge stretches of cocvast trees and cashew nut forest along the coast create a lovely ecology to enjoy. A Light House was built on the beach in 1965 by the Odisha state government to guide the fishermen at night. From the top of the lighthouse, you'll have a bird's eye view of Gopalpur, the sea, and a piece of Chilika Lake. The yearly traditional beach festival at Gopalpur Beach is well-known. On the beach, many local artisans demonstrate their talent by making a variety of handicrafts and sand sculptures. The beach is generally frequented by local fishermen and ladies throughout the year. Local women collect fish caught by fishermen in huge baskets and transport them to local markets to be sold. The ideal time to visit is usually during the winter when many travelers come to enjoy tranquil vacations. Another sea beach, Dhabaleshwar, is near Gopalpur and includes a temple of the same name.

Ongoing Problems and Subsequent Demands of the Coastal Fishing Community of Gopalpur-on-sea

As we are all aware, the livelihood of fishermen shall be well managed if a fishing jetty supports them. As far as a concern to Gopalpur Sea, this region lacks a fishing jetty to convey boats and trawlers to the sea. There is high demand for establishing a fishing jetty near the town. The area's fishermen do not have a place to park their boats. The local fishing community demands a fishing jetty can be established at the connecting point of backwater at Gopalpur with the sea. They do not have a proper drinking water supply facility near the sea beach. While fishing, they find it hard to collect water for the trip. So there is demand for some tube wells near the shore which can be used as drinking water collection points for the fishers. The fishermen of Gopalpur are yet to get any compensatory package from the Indian Army. However, their livelihood is affected by firing anti-aircraft missiles from the Army Air Defence College (ADC), Golabandha. The testing of missiles is conducted for more than 10 days every month. During this period, the fishermen of Gopalpur are asked not to venture into the sea for fishing as a precautionary measure.

In 2014, this region was hit by the severe cyclonic storm Phailin. Specifically, the fishermen were the worst affected. Their boats and nets were destroyed in the cyclonic storm, and they lost their livelihood. According to official records, 2,460 boats were wholly damaged, while 944 were damaged partially. Besides, 2,460 motor engines and 3,404 nets were destroyed in the Phailin. In the absence of fishing equipment, fishermen cannot venture into the sea. At present, there is heavy demand for special assistance by the government to restore their livelihood.

With the help of material gathered from field surveys, existing literature, and many relevant websites, the above-detailed analysis demonstrates that the Ganjam district's socio-economic situation has yet to be improved, despite the government's particular concern. According to the findings of the extensive study [8, 9], there should be a strong fishermen's association to voice their concerns, struggles, and solutions to their issues. The role of intermediaries should be reduced for fishers to sell their catch at a reasonable price and make a profit. Fishermen should be educated about using satellite technology to increase yield and reduce search time regularly through awareness initiatives. Fishermen should be encouraged to use contemporary technologies and Potential Fishing Ground alerts. They should be given low-cost or no-cost global positioning systems to enable them to reach the fish school's potential breeding areas. The Department of Fisheries should hold training and awareness camps in various locations to illustrate the capability and application of PFZ advisories in this regard. The government should develop a proper income strategy for this population during the ban period. During the term of their prohibition, they should be compensated appropriately. Their living conditions will surely improve as a result of this. Opening schools, giving educational kits, encouraging fishermen to support their children's education, and routinely checking current classes are examples of proper education facilities. Throughout the study period, fishermen in Ganjam's coastal region have complained about unlicensed fishing by Andhra trawlers on numerous occasions. To prevent their arrival, the Department of Forest, the Government of Odisha, and the Coast Guard should work together to address this issue. The government should provide basic amenities such as jetty cemented bases at landing centers, roofed large houses for preserving and weighing fish, proper weighing machines, cold storage, transportation facility, and so forth. Loan approval should come with a nominal interest rate and an ancestral perspective. Fishermen should be aware of the many government relief programs established from time to time. The government and non-governmental organizations (NGOs) should play a critical role in empowering them. More fisher welfare-orientated schemes, such as the construction of low-cost houses, coverage of more fishers under plans such as accident insurance, and saving-cum-relief, should be implemented for the overall socio-economic development of fishers. Modernization of existing watercraft is required to safeguard fishermen's safety and increase their earnings.

CONCLUSION

Data on the socio-economic status of coastal residents was also gathered. Any physical or chemical action is bound to disrupt the ecosystem's stability and impact the entire ecosystem, particularly the terrestrial zone. Positive effects on the development of socio-economic factors were discovered in a study on socio-economic factors. The shortcomings of current infrastructure and an examination of aspects such as population, literacy, work possibilities, transit infrastructure, education, and health analysis may be considered. It is suggested that the expansion of industrial sectors be examined because there are abundant resources.

Based on information gathered from field surveys, existing literature, and different relevant websites, the above extensive study collected other reveals that Ganjam district's socio-economic situation has yet to be addressed, despite the government's particular concern. According to the findings of a detailed analysis [8, 9], there should be a strong fishermen's association to voice their concerns, hardships, and answers to their problems. The role of intermediaries should be reduced to allow fishers to sell their catch at a reasonable price and make a profit. Fishermen should be educated about using satellite technology to increase yield and reduce search time regularly through an awareness program. Fishermen should be encouraged to use contemporary technologies and Potential Fishing

Ground alerts. They should be given a low-cost or no-cost global positioning system to reach the potential fish school sites. In this context, the Fisheries Department should hold training and awareness camps in various locations to demonstrate the capability and application of PFZ recommendations. The government should develop a proper income strategy for this population during the ban period. During the term of their prohibition, they should be compensated adequately. This will undoubtedly enhance their living circumstances. Opening schools, giving education kits, encouraging fishermen to enroll their children in school, and routinely monitoring current lessons are examples of proper education facilities. Throughout the study period, fishermen in Ganjam's coastal region have complained about unlicensed fishing by Andhra trawlers on numerous occasions. To prevent their invasion, the department of forest, the government of Odisha, and the coast guard should work together to address this issue. The government should provide basic amenities such as jetty, cemented bases at landing centers, a roofed huge house for keeping and weighing fish, proper weighing equipment, refrigerated storage, a transportation facility, *etc*. Fishermen should be aware of the many government relief programs established from time to time. To empower them, government non-governmental organizations (NGOs) should play a vital role in this regard. More fishermen welfare-orientated plans, such as low-cost housing construction and coverage of more fishermen under schemes such as accident insurance and saving – cum – relief, should be implemented for the overall socio-economic development of fishermen. Modernization of existing watercraft is required to safeguard fishermen's safety and increase their earnings.

CONSENT FOR PUBLICATION

Not applicable.

CONFLICT OF INTEREST

The authors declare no conflict of interest, financial or otherwise.

ACKNOWLEDGEMENTS

The author is thankful to the Head, Dept. of Marine Sciences, Berhampur University, for encouragement for this work. Laboratory facilities of the Indian National Centre for Ocean Information Services (INCOIS) sponsored satellite Coastal and Oceanographic Research (SATCORE) to Berhampur University were availed. The author is thankful to the University Grants Commission, Govt. of India, for providing financial assistance through Rajiv Gandhi National Fellowship (RGNF).

REFERENCES

[1]   "Defining vulnerability': conflicts,Complexities and implications for Coastal Zone Management", *J. Coast. Res.,* vol. 50, no. Special Issue, 2007.

[2]   X. Xu, H. Peng, Q. Xu, H. Xiao, and G. Benoit, "Land Changes and Conflicts Coordination in Coastal Urbanization: A Case Study of the Shandong Peninsula in China", *Coast. Manage.,* vol. 37, no. 1, pp. 54-69, 2009.
[http://dx.doi.org/10.1080/08920750802612788]

[3]   M.D.A. Le Tissier, J.M. Hills, J.A. McGregor, and M. Ireland, "A Training Framework for Understanding Conflict in the Coastal Zone", *Coast. Manage.,* vol. 32, no. 1, pp. 77-88, 2004.
[http://dx.doi.org/10.1080/08920750490247517]

[4]   *Our Common Future.* Oxford University Press: Oxford, 1987.

[5]   N. Laurence, R. Jorge, C. Machado, and L. Rodriguez, An integrated Methodology of biophysical and socioeconomic dimensions to understand land-use change processes in Coastal areas.*Coasting - A Coastal Policy Research Newsletter, 3.* TERI: New Delhi, 2000.

[6]   M. Jorge Rosario, N. Laurence, C.R. Machado, and L. Rodriguez, Measuring,Monitoring and managing sustainability in Indian coastal areas: the socioeconomic dimension. Littoral, 22-26 September. Porto, Portugal (2002).

[7]   K.T. Srinivasa, K.M. Nagaraja, and S. Nayak, "Benefits derived by the fishermen using Potential Fishing Zone (PFZ) Advisories", *Proceedings of SPIE-The International Society for Optical Engineering,* vol. 7150, p. 71500N, 2008.

[8]   K.C. Sahu, S.K. Baliarsingh, S. Srichandan, A. Lotliker, and T.S. Kumar, Socio-Economic conditions of fisherfolk vis-à-vis satellite technology in Coastal District of Ganjam, Odisha". Review of Research. Vol.1Issue.IV/Jan; (a). Pp1-6 (2012).

[9]   K.C. Sahu, S.K. Baliarsingh, S. Srichandan, A. Lotliker, and T.S. Kumar, Validation of PFZ Advisories –A Case Study along Ganjam Coast of Odisha, East Coast of India. Indian Streams ResearchJournal. Vol.1Issue.XII/Jan; (b). pp. 1-6 (2012).

[10]   http://www.incois.gov.in/Incois/advisory_pfz_main.jsp

[11]   L. Nayak, and A.K. Mishra, "Socio-Economic condition of fishermen and its effecton the environment: a case study of Ganjam district, Orissa", *Nature Environment and Pollution Technology,* vol. 7, no. I, pp. 111-116, 2008.

CHAPTER 8

Filtering Techniques for Removing Noise From ECG Signals

K. Manimekalai[1,*] and **A. Kavitha**[2]

[1] *Department of Computer Applications, Sri GVG Visalakshi College for Women, Udumalpet, Tamil Nadu, India*

[2] *Department of Computer Science, Kongunadu Arts and Science College, Coimbatore, Tamil Nadu, India*

Abstract: Electrocardiogram (ECG) records cardiac electrical signal to check for various heart problems. However, it can be impaired by noise. Therefore, ECG signal denoising is a significant pre-processing step that reduces noise and emphasizes the characteristic waves in the ECG data. The frequency range of a simple ECG is usually between 0.5 Hz and 100 Hz. When processing the ECG signal, artifact elimination is the most important resource since artifacts in ECG signal impede the diagnosis of disorders. This work uses MATLAB to reduce noise by applying low pass, high pass, and derivative pass filters. On the PTB database, the performance of these approaches is compared using benchmark measures such as mean-square error (MSE) and signal-to-noise ratio (SNR) to compare various ECG denoising algorithms. The combination of low pass + high pass + derivative pass filters produces low mean-square error (MSE) and signal-to-noise ratio (SNR) values of 0.052 db and 1.185 db when compared to the raw signal.

Keywords: Derivative Pass, ECG Signal, High Pass, Low Pass, MSE, SNR.

INTRODUCTION

Pre-processing techniques assist in the preparation of data for analysis. Before starting primary processing, the data should be pre-processed to remove any detector effects. The most important feature for executing data processing is the pre-processing step.

When data is obtained as a consequence of an experiment, the following step is to model the data so that the required information may be extracted. Globally, the data production will be either too much or too little, or it will be fractured. The

---

* **Corresponding author K. Manimekalai:** Department of Computer Applications, Sri GVG Visalakshi College for Women, Udumalpet, Tamil Nadu, India; E-mail: gvgmanimekalai@gmail.com

term "pre-processing" refers to the act of classifying data into three categories and processing it accordingly. As a result, technologies such as Data Filters, Data Editing, Data Ordering, and Noise Modelling play an important role in any data pre-processing. The Pre-processing of ECG Signals is depicted in Fig. (1).

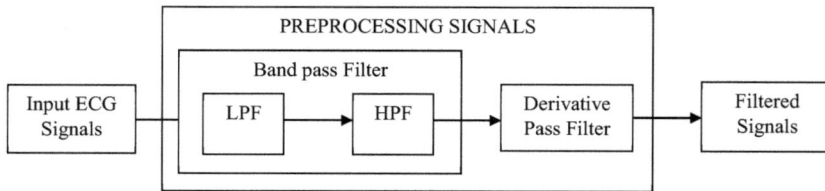

Fig. (1). Pre-processing of ECG Signals.

The signal processing method can be employed in a variety of different ECG analysis and interpretation systems. It is mostly utilised to get a few key characteristic parameters. Consequently, biomedical signal processing is applied to quantitative or primary analyses of physiological systems and is utilised to investigate the phenomena using signal analysis. The sector of biomedical signal analysis or processing methods has progressed to a higher-level characteristic for practical signal processing and pattern analysis approaches that have been proven to be effective. ECG signal processing is a broad topic that covers improving measurement accuracy and reproducibility. The focus of ECG analysis is on ECG interpretation, ambulatory monitoring (also known as Intensive Care Monitoring), and stress testing. Basically, these functions combine to form a basic set of algorithms that condition the data based on various sorts of noise and artifacts, resulting in basic ECG wave amplitude and duration measurements. It can also detect heartbeats and aggregate the information for storage or transmission. The basic ECG is made up of a frequency range ranging from 0.5Hz to 100Hz. As a result, artifact elimination is the most important resource in ECG signal processing. It is considered a critical task for the specialist to diagnose illnesses when artifacts are discovered in the ECG signal. The main contribution is to explore filters such as low pass, high pass, and derivative pass filters. When compared to the raw signal, the combination of Low Pass + High Pass + Derivative pass filters has the lowest MSE and SNR values (Fig. **2**).

ARTIFACTS

The electrocardiograph is a device that measures cardiac potentials on the body's surface, but it has nothing to do with the heart's electrical activity or function. It is critical to keep a focus on these types of artifacts, or else they will lead to unnecessary testing and therapeutic measures.

Monitoring electrodes on the skin surface are used to detect the electrical activity of the heart. It is denoted that the electrical signal is very tiny, often between 0.0001 and 0.003 volts. These signals are estimated in the 0.05 to 100 Hertz (Hz.) or cycles per second frequency range. Other artifact signals with comparable frequency and mostly bigger amplitude are inappropriately diffused across the skin surface and mixed with ECG signals.

An ECG artifact in electrocardiography is not related to the heart. Electrical interference from outside sources, electrical noise produced elsewhere in the body, or inadequate contact and machine malfunction are examples of these. Because artifacts are so ubiquitous, a thorough understanding of them is required to avoid cardiac rhythm misunderstanding.

Types of Artifact in ECG Signal

The goal of the ECG signal technique and signal processing system acquisition is to obtain a noise-free signal. Based on Rahul Kher's *et al.* [1] research, the key sources of noise are listed below.

The terminology and notations used in this study are listed in Table **1**.

Table 1. Terminologies and Notations.

Terminology	Description
ECG	Electrocardiogram
LPF	Low Pass Filter
HPF	High Pass Filter
MSE	Mean Square Error
SNR	Signal to Noise Ratio
DWT	Discrete Wavelet Transform
NI ELVIS	National Instruments Educational Laboratory Virtual Instrumentation Suite
MRA	Multi Resolution Analysis

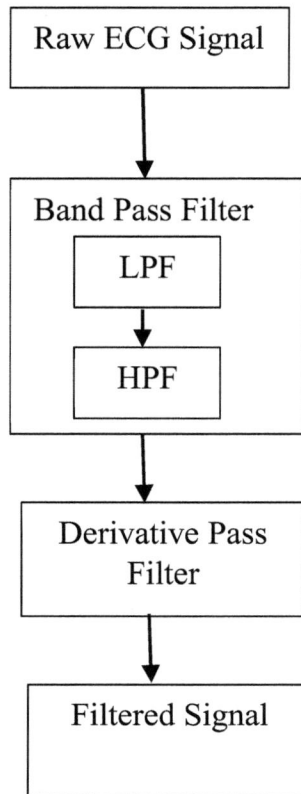

Fig. (2). Flow chart for Proposed Work.

Power Line Interference

Electromagnetic fields produced by a power line, which is a common source of noise in the ECG, can also be observed in any other bioelectrical signal recorded from the body surface. This type of noise is described as 50 or 60 Hz sinusoidal interference with several harmonics.

Because the description of low-amplitude waveforms is incorrect and false waveforms were formed, such a narrowband noise isolates the important analysis and interpretation found in the ECG, which is regarded as a more challenging process. It is critical to minimize power line interference in ECG signals because it's the main cause of the lower frequency ECG waves (P wave and T wave). Fig. (3) depicts how power line interference mostly affects an ECG signal.

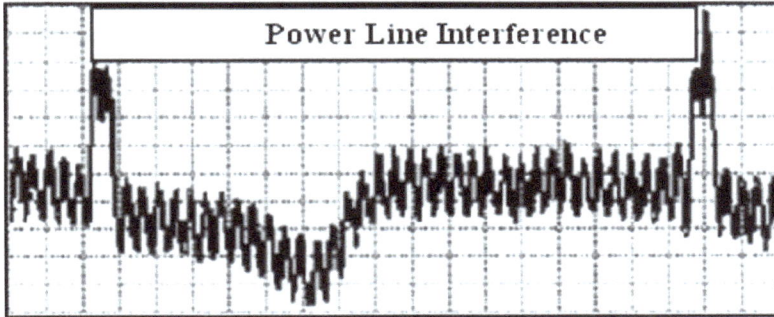

Fig. (3). ECG affected by Power Line (50/ 60 Hz) Interference.

Muscle Contractions

Muscle noise is a key issue in many ECG applications, particularly during workout recordings, where low amplitude waveforms are hidden. Muscle noise, unlike baseline wander and 50/60 Hz interference, is classified as a much more complex filtering challenge since the spectral information recorded regarding muscle activity significantly overlaps that of the PQRST complex. Because the ECG is a repeating signal, advanced approaches, similar to those used in the processing of suggested potentials, can be utilized to reduce muscle noise.

According to Bannerjee *et al.* [2], it is critical to improve signal processing methods that aid in the decrease of muscle noise's impact. Fig. (**4**) shows an ECG signal that has been distorted by muscle noise.

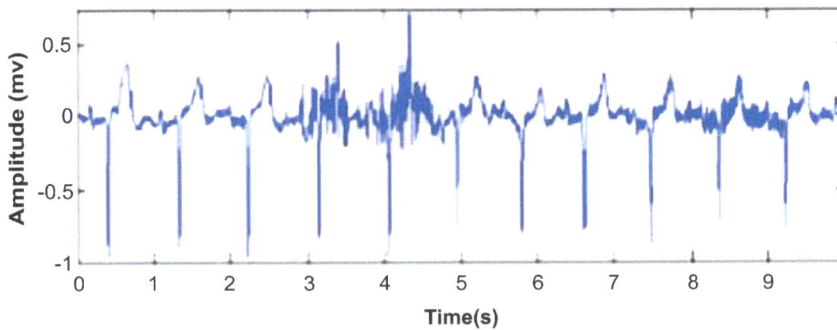

Fig. (4). ECG Signal with Muscle Noise.

Electrode Motion Artifacts

Electrode motion artifacts are mostly caused by skin stretching, which alters the impedance of the electrode-covering skin.

Motion artefacts are signal aspects of baseline wander that are more difficult to counteract since their spectral content is said to overlap extensively with the PQRST complex. They are most common in the frequency range of 1 to 10 Hz. These artefacts are identified in the ECG as large-amplitude waveforms that are frequently mistaken for QRS complexes. An ECG signal is shown in Fig. (**5**) with Electrode Motion Artifacts interfering with it.

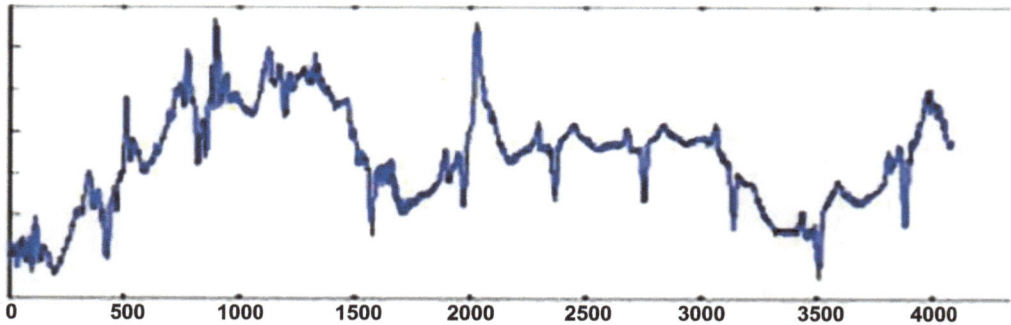

Fig. (5). ECG affected by Electrode Motion Artifacts.

Baseline Wandering

The outcome of baseline wander, also known as baseline drift, is that the signal's x-axis seems to 'wander' or move up and down instead of being straight. As a result, the entire signal shifts away from its normal base. Baseline wander occurs in ECG signals due to improper electrodes, also known as electrode-skin impedance, which is caused by the patient's movement and breathing process (respiration). Fig. (**6**) shows how Baseline Wander affects common ECG signals.

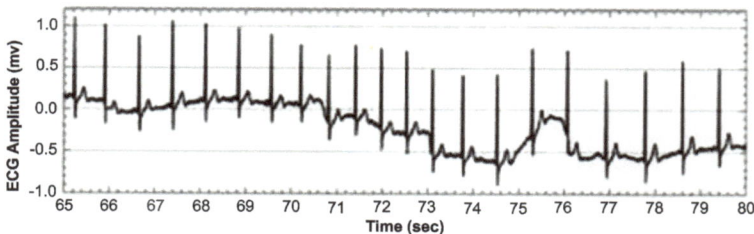

Fig. (6). An ECG Signal with Baseline Wander (Drift).

Reversed Lead

The positioning of the electrodes/leads is regarded as a crucial characteristic.If the red and white lead wires are mistakenly confused, i.e., the white one is placed where the red one should be, and vice versa, an ECG that looks like Fig. (**7**) may follow. It is possible to get a normal sinus rhythm from this ECG by flipping all of the waves upside-down. When this happens, the patient is forced to observe the beat in an entirely different lead. It is also necessary to ensure that the lead wires are connected to the machine. A systole could occur if the patient is talkative. Many machines are intelligent in that they can detect frequent mistakes in this type of environment, which aren't always visible.

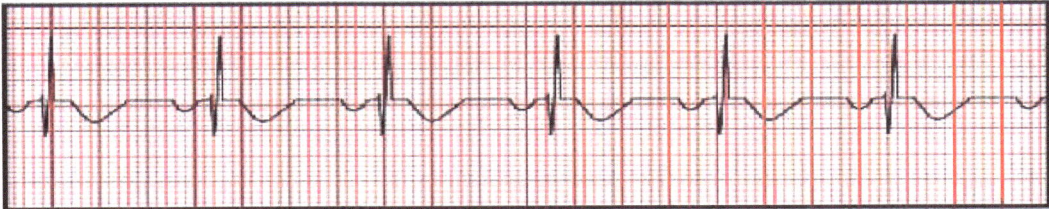

Fig. (7). Wrong placed electrodes in ECG.

There are several approaches for extracting ECG characteristics from a noisy ECG signal. To begin, the ECG signal must be examined to determine whether types of noise mesh with the signal.

ECG RECORDING CONDITIONS

In an air-conditioned, sound-attenuated room with dim lighting, the subjects were tested and assessed. The temperature in the recording room was kept between 20 and 250 degrees Celsius, the humidity between 65 and 75 percent, and the barometric pressure between 650 and 685 millimetres of mercury.

Calibration of the Equipment

The following calibrations were completed each day prior to the calculation.

i. Ambient conditions: As ambient data are used to determine crucial alteration elements for interpreting recorded results, they were monitored on a regular basis. The sensors in the system mechanically recorded the barometric pressure, humidity and temperature.

ii. Volume calibration: Every day, the measurement system containing the Triple V volume sensor was calibrated. For precise flow and volume measurement, a transparent Triple V (digital volume sensor) is required.

iii. Gas calibration: The gas analyzers implied (O_2/CO_2) are combined in the system were calibrated once a day, after the break or warming-up time duration for 30 minutes. The O_2/CO_2 calibration was functioned using the certified gases (BOC,UK) from the calibration gas cylinder (that contains the mixture of 5.2% of CO_2 and Nitrogen) associated to the system. The calibration program runs mechanically and is divided into three major phases:

(a) flushing the tube system (b) determination of delay time and (c) gain settings. At the final process of calibration, the derived parameters were used.

Recording Procedure

Abo Zahhad [3], mentioned the steps used for recordings.

i. Subject data: Before calculating measurements, essential data such as age, gender, height and weight were recorded in the system. The height was calculated by a standard scale denoted with centimeters and the weight was measured with clothing by implying digital weighing.
ii. The breathing mask, that was created to form an airtight cover is used over the subject's nose and the mouth is fixed by straps (mask used for adults with dead space of 70 ml) and care was taken so that the air will not leak out through the sides of the mask.
iii. The Triple V sensor (Plate M1) was associated with the breathing mask at one end and at the other end can find the integrated gas analyzer system used in the compact housing passing through the twin tubes.
iv. A specialized workload protocol was added based on the functions of the recording session and selected to run in the experiment. The recorded data was stored in the hard disc of the PC referred to as (Pentium III).

ECG Signal Filtering

Chang [4] explained the rapid advancement of electronic and communication technologies, as well as new features in computer techniques such as Deep Learning and large data analysis, have led to new approaches to providing healthcare. The bulky medical equipment is being replaced by smaller electronic devices that are connected to computers, laptops, and smartphones. The programmed analysis for a simple understanding of ECG data through modern computer algorithms is one of the primary components present in computerized remote health care systems.

Filtering methods are mostly utilized for signal pre-processing and have been established in a variety of systems that function or are used for ECG analysis. The ECG signal is pre-processed to detect baseline drift, motion artifacts, and other disturbances seen in the original recorded signal. Noise immunity is regarded as a crucial attribute and defined as an advantage in every indicated electronic gadget. The input signals cannot be guaranteed to pass through the actual processing unit while a signal processing method is in use. Before beginning the actual process, a few processing steps must be completed. It is known as "pre-processing." Depending on the demanding requirement, there may be simply one or a large number of pre-processing unit cells. Signals are refined and readied for entry into the real processing through pre-processing, which also includes the process of reducing undesirable noise in the pre-processing units.

The ECG is described as an instrument, which is used to monitor and record the electrical activity of the heart. Electrical signals that are seen in the heart usually lead the normal mechanical function and monitoring these signals will result in clinical significance. ECG is also used in various fields like catheterization laboratories, found in coronary care units, and is mainly used for routine diagnostic implications in cardiology. Cardiologists readily interpret the ECG waveforms in order to classify them into a normal and abnormal pattern which are the basis of ECG signals and are generally denoted as P wave, T wave and QRS complex in Fig. (8). The changes found in these parameters denote the disease found in the heart that is caused due to many reasons. Essential filters were used to obtain the spike-free signal.

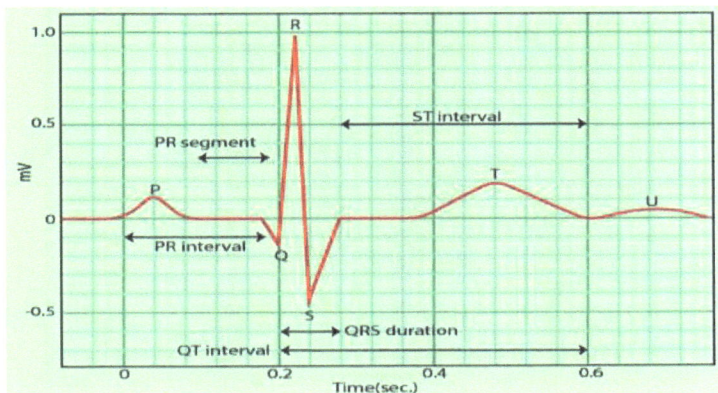

Fig. (8). A standard Scalar ECG Signals.

A filter is a circuit that helps to increase some of the frequencies used for its input while attenuating others. There are four basic types of filters: high pass, which increases frequencies above a particular value, low pass, which increases frequencies below a certain value, and band pass, which increases frequencies within a specific band. An analogue filter and a digital filter are the two most common types of filters. Analog filters necessitate complex mathematical calculations, but digital filters only necessitate basic calculations.

The filtering process of the ECG is contextual and should be functioned only when the required data remains ambiguous. Many researchers have experimented with the reduction of noise found in the ECG signal. Generally, the different types of interference that affect ECG signals may be detected by using bandpass filters; but the restrictions found in bandpass filter is depressing, as they are not capable of producing the best result. At the same time, the filtering methods are implemented only based on the type of noises found in the ECG signal. Martinek *et al.* [5], explained, in some signals, the noise level can be found very high and it is not possible to identify the noise through a single recording, it is essential to have a proper understanding of the noise processes that are implied before one attempt in the filter or in the pre-processing of a signal [4]. The ECG signal is described as very sensitive in nature and even if a small noise that is mixed with the original signal it will result in a change in the characteristics of the signal. Data that are found to be corrupted with noise must either be filtered or totally discarded. Filtering method is one of the major issues for design consideration in the real-time heart monitoring systems. Table **2** shows the description of ECG waves in a clear manner.

Table 2. Description of ECG waves.

Feature	Duration	Description
P wave	<80ms	Depolarization of atria
PR interval	120-200ms	Reflects the time the electrical impulse takes.
QRS complex	80-100ms	Rapid Depolarization of the right and left ventricles.
J point	--	The point at which the QRS complex finishes and the ST segment starts.
ST segment	--	Represents the period when the ventricles are depolarized.
T wave	160ms	Repolarization of the ventricles. It is upright in all leads except a VR and leads V1.
U wave	--	Hypothesized to be caused by the repolarization of the interventricular septum.

Yadav *et al.* [6] developed an amplifier by integrating an instrumentation amplifier AD620 from Analog Devices to get a peak value in the 1v range with a 1000 advance. On the NI ELVIS (National Instruments Educational Laboratory Virtual Instrumentation Suite) board, he used a band pass filter with a cutoff frequency of 0.5Hz-150Hz to gather the ECG signal.

Decomposition

The method of decomposing a given signal into a sum of simpler signals is sometimes referred to as signal decomposition. The multi-resolution decomposition is enabled by obtaining a scale-invariant interpretation of the image. Singh *et al.* [7] explained the only way to decompose a signal into numerous scales with varied time and frequency resolutions is to use the Multi-Resolution Analysis (MRA) technique [Singh *et al.*, 2016]. The Wavelet Transform technique uses several basic functions to break down a signal.

A wavelet function is chosen and then decomposed up to level l in the wavelet decomposition method. The first phase involves applying the Wavelet Transform to the Denoising technique, which aids in the identification of the mother wavelet, which combines as a group of functions, either by compression, stretching, or translation. The breakdown level is the following phase. Wavelet decomposition allows you to adjust the resulting coefficient before applying it to a signal, and signal reconstruction is used to remove the unwanted signal components. Poungponsri *et al.* [8] found the wavelet decomposition of the signals produced at level N using a wavelet function and level N.

There are various methods of decomposition of a signal are list below:

- Discrete Wavelet Transform based Decomposition
- Empirical Mode Decomposition
- Multi Resolution Analysis
- Shift Invariant method

Discrete Wavelet Transform based Decomposition

The DWT functions through a filter bank that helps to decompose the signal in the manner of uninterruptedly coarser approximations and it is described in Fig. (9).

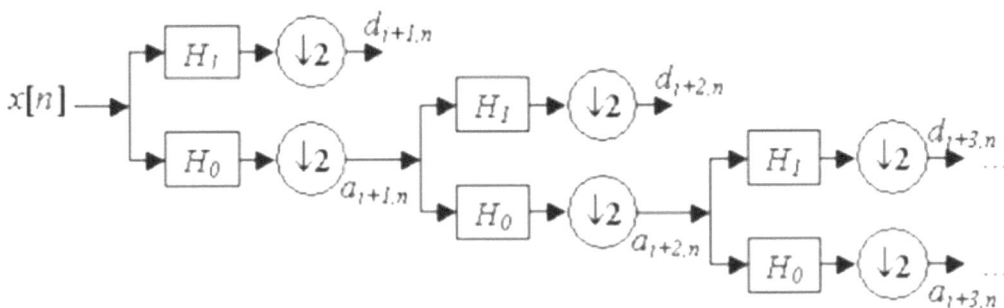

Fig. (9). Filter bank for a 3 level DWT decomposition.

Where H_1 signifies a high-pass complementary filter and H_0 specifies a low-pass complementary filter, $d_{j+k,n}$ are referred to as detail coefficients and $a_{j+k,n}$ are indicated as the approximation coefficients at level $(j + k)$.

ALGORITHM: DWT DECOMPOSITION

Step 1: ECG signal is read and the length is calculated.

Step 2: The Signal is decomposed using wavelet.

Step 3: Coefficients are selected, as most energy of is concentrated in these coefficients.

Step 4: The wave is reconstructed using the detail coefficient. Where $d_{j+k,\,n}$ are referred to as detail coefficients and $a_{j+k,n}$ are indicated as the approximation coefficients at level $(j + k)$.

Step 5: A function d4* (d3+d5)/2n is defined to reduce the oscillatory nature of the signal where d3, d4, d5 are the detail coefficients and n is the level of decomposition.

Step 6: Derivate up to level 5 is made using the transfer function.

Step 7: The output coefficient that is produced by the low pass filter is referred to as the approximation coefficient denoted in equation (1).

$$a_{i+1}[n] = \begin{cases} a_i * \overline{K}[2n], & i < N \\ a_i * \overline{K} - N[n], otherwise \end{cases} \tag{1}$$

Step 8: The output of the high pass filter is referred to as the detailed coefficient which is shown in equation (2):

$$y_{i+1}[n] = \begin{cases} a_i * f[2n], & i < N \\ a_i * \underline{f} - N[n], otherwise \end{cases} \tag{2}$$

Step 9: The approximation coefficient at the next part is divided into two functions detail and approximation coefficients, it is shown below in equation (3):

$$a_i[n]=\begin{cases} a_i * \hat{k}[n] + \breve{y}j + 1 * \hat{f}[2n], & i < N \\ \frac{1}{2}(a_{i+1} * \hat{f}_{i-N}[n] + y_{i+1} * \hat{f}_{i-N}[n]), otherwise \end{cases} \quad (3)$$

Step 10: Then moving on to the next level of the decomposition function, the approximation coefficients that are obtained are again decomposed and the process is continued until it reaches N levels.

For instance, let us assume that the signal is described as S_j. In the synthesis filter, the signal is then decomposed by implying a high pass filter which is described as $H_1(n)$ and a low pass filter which is described as $H_0(n)$. As a result, the efficient detail coefficient and approximation coefficient are obtained. Then moving on to the next level of decomposition function, the approximation coefficients that are obtained are again decomposed and hence the process is continued until it reaches up to N levels as described in Fig. (8) where, N =3 is included in this work. If the expected maximum number of levels up to L have been attained, the signal is declared as fully decomposed. The next step which is implied in decomposition method is to calculate the level of noise intensity that is shown for various levels, denoted in equation (4) and equation (5),

$$\alpha_j = \left(\frac{median(|d_j|)}{0.6745}\right) \quad (4)$$

$$\eta_j = \alpha\sqrt{2\, In(L)} \quad (5)$$

The result of wavelet decomposition is considered as the approximation and the detail coefficients that are derived at every level of the decomposition method. Then the wavelet frequency thresholding that are produced between the detail coefficient and the approximation coefficient is examined in the upcoming sections.

Denoising of ECG Signal

In the wavelet-based denoising process, a threshold value is chosen and implied in the detail coefficients at the level of each decomposition function. Thresholding is the name given to this useful function. It's also known as a basic nonlinear method because it only works on one wavelet coefficient at a time. Thresholding's main goal is to threshold each coefficient produced by comparing it to a set threshold. If the coefficient is smaller than the set threshold, it is set to zero; otherwise, according to Yadav *et al.* [9] it is kept or adjusted.

There are two essential tasks: First is the task about how to select the threshold and how to function the thresholding. But the function of thresholding is merely dependent upon the type of thresholding method it follows and the thresholding rule that are formulated for the given application. Surekha *et al.* [10] mentioned there are two methods of thresholding, such as the hard and the soft methods. Thresholding normally produces a low pass and smoother form for the original noisy signal. The threshold values are useful to smooth out or to eliminate some detailed wavelet coefficients of the original signal. The derived noiseless signal is then restored in the time domain by implying the modified coefficients. Different types of thresholding methods are as follows:

- Hard and Soft Thresholding
- Wavelet Thresholding
- EMD-Thresholding
- Wavelet-based Thresholding
- Wavelet Frequency Thresholding

Hard and Soft Thresholding

Hard thresholding is considered the simplest method to use when compared to the soft thresholding method which consists of complicated mathematical derivations. Hard thresholding is defined as a method in which all the derived coefficients under a fixed threshold T that depends on noise variance are discarded. Soft thresholding is a process in which not only all the coefficients below the threshold are discarded but all the coefficients above a fixed threshold T are shrunk. This shows that soft thresholding is an extension of hard thresholding: first, setting the elements to zero whose absolute values are lower than the threshold and then shrinking the nonzero coefficients towards zero. Generally hard thresholding is essential for the data compression purpose.

The hard threshold methods are described in Fig. (**10**), showing the bigger variance and it is unbalanced, *i.e.* sensitive with even small changes in the signal. Therefore, the soft thresholding method is considered to be much more stable than hard thresholding and it is referred to have a bigger bias because of the reduction of larger wavelet coefficients. Besides, compared to hard thresholding, Soft thresholding ensures no discontinuities in the resulting signal as shown in Fig. (**11**).

Wavelet Thresholding

Wavelet Thresholding method is used for the denoising process. Having an essential and suitable wavelet function, this thresholding method with its effective thresholding rule plays a major role in the process of signal denoising. Thresholding methods that function along with discrete Wavelet Transform based filtering are useful in modifying the derived coefficients.

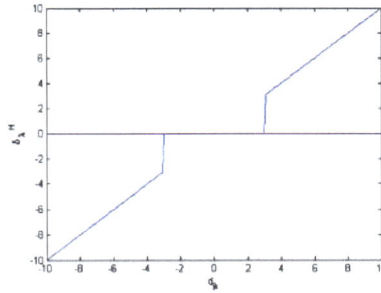

Fig. (10). Hard Thresholding.

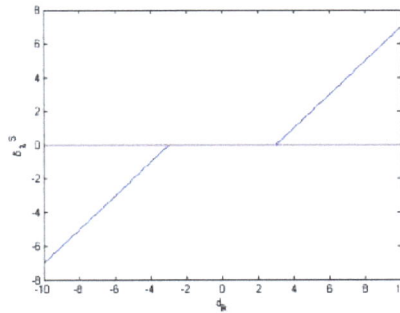

Fig. (11). Soft Thresholding.

The noise in the signals can be easily reduced by using the wavelet thresholding method. Selection of an effective analysis function, as well as the type of thresholding and threshold values, can be done in a number of ways. The universal threshold T, which is proportional to the standard deviation of the noise, is defined in equation (6):

$$T = \sigma\sqrt{2\,InM} \tag{6}$$

Where, M describes the signal size and denotes the noise variance and it is given in equation (7):

$$\sigma^z = \left(\frac{median(|X_i|)}{0.6745}\right) \tag{7}$$

Where, ($|Xi|$) denotes the median value for the absolute values of wavelet coefficients that is Xi. Hard thresholding is denoted in equation (8):

$$x_i = \begin{cases} x_i, |x| \geq 1.414\sigma[In(L)]^{0.5} \\ 0, |x| \leq 1.414\sigma[In(L)]^{0.5} \end{cases} \tag{8}$$

Where, $1.414\sigma[InL]^{0.5}$ is considered as the threshold value. Soft thresholding is described in equation (9):

$$x_i = \begin{cases} \frac{x_i}{|x_i|}, (|x_i| - 1.414\sigma[In(L)]^{0.5}), |x_i| \geq 1.414\sigma[In(L)]^{0.5} \\ 0, \qquad\qquad\qquad\qquad |x| \leq 1.414\sigma[In(L)]^{0.5} \end{cases} \tag{9}$$

EMD-Thresholding

EMD obtains a subband like filtering resulting in fundamentally uncorrelated IMFs. Although the corresponding filter-bank arrangement is by no means pre-determined and fixed as in wavelet decomposition, one can accomplish thresholding in each IMF in order to nearly ignore low energy IMF parts which are expected to be significantly despoiled by noise. The Empirical mode decomposition is an adaptive data-driven technique that is used for the effective decomposition of a noisy signal into its functional components.

Wavelet-based Thresholding

Wavelet-based nonlinear thresholding is an effective and efficient method for noise reduction only to the extent to which the wavelet representation of the noise-free signal is sparse. In this method, the process of obtaining each coefficient from the detail subbands with a thresholding function is applied to obtain the output.

Wavelet Frequency Thresholding

The basic idea of wavelet frequency thresholding is based on the judgment of the extent of their relationship from the similarity to orders of geometric curve shapes. The closer these are, the greater frequency thresholding of the corresponding order exists and vice versa. According to this, the wavelet frequency analysis of the wavelet coefficients according to the relationship among the approximate time sequences can be computed. This method not only can filter most of the noise, but it can also commendably hold signal details. More than that, this technique can very well compromise the problem of remaining signal details and noise suppression as well. For this reason, the signal processed by wavelet frequency thresholding has better smoothness and similarity. And as such, wavelet frequency thresholding is used in this work. Generally, wavelet frequency thresholding is represented by the given equation:

1. Calculate the mappings of the initial values for various sequences, it is denoted in equation (10).

Let

$$Yj' = Yj / yj\ (1) = (yj'(1), yj'(2), \dots \dots \dots \dots \dots, yj'(n)) \tag{10}$$

Where j=0,1,.......M

2. Calculate the difference of the mappings, it is denoted in equation (11).

Let

$$\Omega j = (\Omega j(1), \Omega j(2)., \Omega j(n)) \tag{11}$$

Where $\Omega j\ (g) = |x'0\ (g) - x'j\ (g)|$ and j=0, 1, 2 …N.

3. Calculate the biggest and the smallest difference of $\Omega j\ (g)$,, it is denoted in equation (12).

Let

$$R = \max j \max g \Omega j(g) \text{ and } r = \min j \min g \Omega j(g) \tag{12}$$

4. Calculate the incident coefficients, it is denoted in equation (13).

$$\Omega, \text{ where } \varepsilon\ (0,1): y = 1,2, \dots \dots \dots, n \text{ and } j = 0,1,2, \dots \dots, N \tag{13}$$

5. Calculate the wavelet frequency thresholding, it is denoted in equation (14) and equation (15).

$$\text{So, } \gamma = \frac{1}{n} \sum_{g=1}^{n} y_i(g) \text{ where } j = 0, 1, 2, \dots \dots, N \tag{14}$$

$$\gamma_{0j}(g) = \gamma\left((x_0(g), x_j(g))\right) = \frac{\min_j \min_g |X_0(g) - X_j(g)| + \partial \max_i \max_g |X_0(g) - X_j(g)|}{|X_0(g) - X_j(g)| + \partial \max_i \max_g |X_0 - X_j(g)|} \tag{15}$$

Through this method, the threshold is calculated as, THR = j • γj then sustain the original value when a position Wavelet Transform coefficient value is referred as the larger one while comparing to the threshold, or else it remains the value zero.

6. Calculate the threshold by implying the formula, it is denoted in equation (16)

$$T = S[N]/24 \qquad\qquad (16)$$

where S[n] stands for the original signal. The results that are attained after the wavelet frequency thresholding method are the decomposed and denoised signal. This denoised signal is then moved for the reconstruction function of the original signal.

ECG Signal Filtering Techniques

Low-Pass Filters

Low-pass filters helps to reduce the high-frequency noise found in ECG signals.

The noisy signal stops the smoothed ECG signal by producing high-frequency noise, it is shown in equation (17).

$$f_c = \frac{1}{2\pi\omega_c} \qquad\qquad (17)$$

Where, f_c is the Cut-Off frequency, ω_c is the Low Pass filter Resistance. Since the corresponding impulse response has an infinite length.

High-Pass Filter

High-pass filters help to detect Low-Frequency noise in ECG signals. A straightforward method used in the design of a filter used to select the ideal high-pass filter as a starting point is shown in equation (18).

$$f_c = \frac{1}{2\pi\tau_c} \qquad\qquad (18)$$

Where, f_c is the Cut-Off frequency, τ_c is the High Pass Filter Resistance. Since the corresponding impulse response has an infinite length.

Derivative Base Filters

Derivative filters are commonly functioned with slope calculations. The derivatives of the received signals are used to denote the significant quantities.

Derivative filters result in averaging with a low pass filter, the current derivative minus the past derivative and it prevents the high frequency noise from affecting the calculation of the derivative, which is very sensitive to noise, it is shown in equation (19).

$$f_c = \frac{1}{2\pi} x(n+1) - x(n-1) \qquad (19)$$

where n-1 is the past derivative and n+1 is the future derivative.

EVALUATION CRITERIA FOR DENOISING

This section describes the denoising methods along with terms of SNR and MSE methods of the denoised signal. The performance evaluation was done based on the SNR and MSE is described in the following section.

Signal to Noise Ratio

Generally, Signal to Noise Ratio referred as SNR, comes under the technical term used for the power ratio produced between a signal and noise. It is described in terms of the logarithmic decibel scale. The Signal to Noise Ratio is defined as the ratio that presents the true signal amplitude for the standard deviation of the noise. The measuring unit for SNR is decibels (i.e) dB. The quality of the signal is considered as the Signal to Noise Ratio, which is shown in equation (20).

$$\text{SNR} = 10 \log \frac{S_{original}}{S_{noise}} \qquad (20)$$

Where $S_{original}$: Original signal without noise, S_{noise} :Noisy signal

Mean Square Error

The variation shown between the denoised signal and the original signal is called as the Mean Square Error also referred to as MSE. The measuring unit for MSE is decibels (i.e) dB. Equation (21) calculates the MSE for ECG Signal.

$$MSE = \frac{1}{M} \sum_{j=1}^{M} \left(y(j) - \overline{y(j)} \right)^2 \qquad (21)$$

Where, yj: Original signal, yj: Denoised signal and M: is the length of the signal.

EXPERIMENTAL RESULTS

The performance of the classification method is not only based on the classifier, but it is also based on the features and enhanced ECG signal processing Morphology Filter (MF), a built-the ECG morphology and time domain features.

In this paper, the performance metrics like SNR and MSR were taken into account to denoise the ECG signal. After denoising the Raw ECG Signal, Feature Extraction was carried out to extract the required features, which will show the pathology present in the heart. Fig. (**12**) shows the original ECG signal and Fig. (**13**) shows the denoised image, such that the noise present in the ECG signal was removed. Fig. (**14**) shows the result of the Low pass, High pass and Derivative base filter on Raw ECG signal through SNR and MSR.

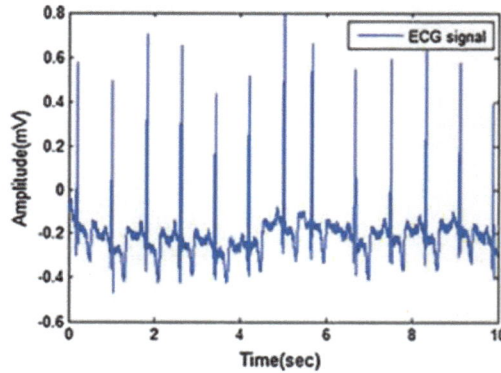

Fig. (12). Original ECG Signal.

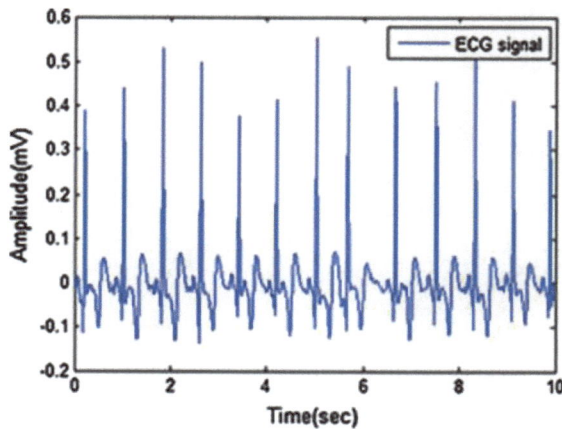

Fig. (13). Denoised ECG Signal.

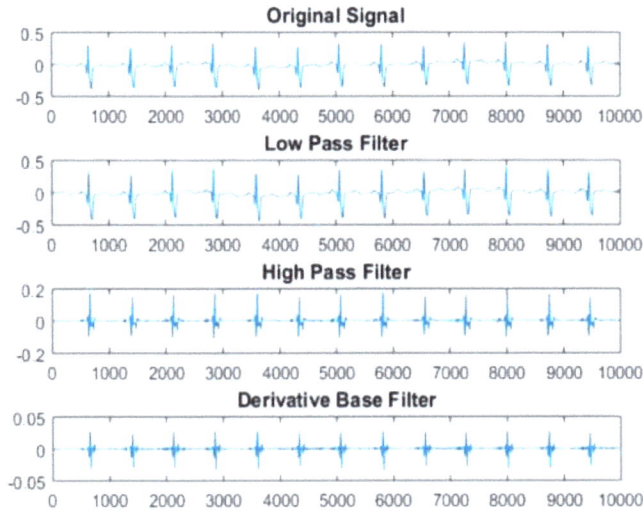

Fig. (14). Comparison of Original Signal and Filtered Signal.

Table 3. Comparison of MSE and SNR values of various filters.

Measures	Raw Signal (dB)	Low Pass (dB)	Low Pass+ High Pass (dB)	Low Pass+ High Pass + Derivative Base (dB)
SNR	0.102	0.096	0.065	0.052
MSE	3.180	2.386	2.096	1.185

Table **3** shows the comparison of various filter techniques adopted for Pre-processing the ECG Signals based on the performance metrics such as Mean Square Error and Signal to Noise ratio. Among the results, the combination of Low Pass + High Pass + Derivative pass filters shows minimum MSE and SNR values when compared with the raw signal. Fig. (**15**) shows the pictorial representation of the comparison of various filter techniques adopted for Pre-processing the ECG Signals based on the performance metrics, Signal to Noise Ratio.

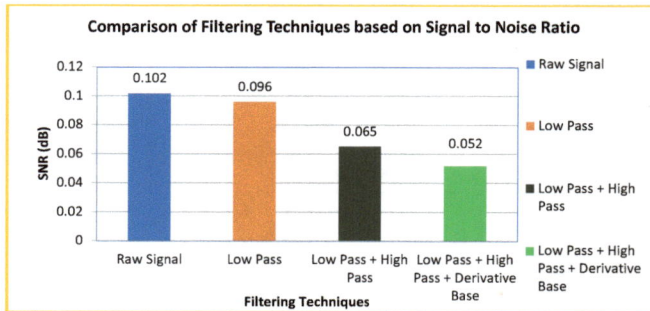

Fig. (15). Comparison of SNR values of various filters.

Fig. (**16**) shows the pictorial representation of the comparison of various filter techniques adopted for Pre-processing the ECG Signals based on the performance metrics, Mean Square Error. Among the results, the combination of Low Pass + High Pass + Derivative pass filters shows minimum MSE and SNR values when compared with the raw signal.

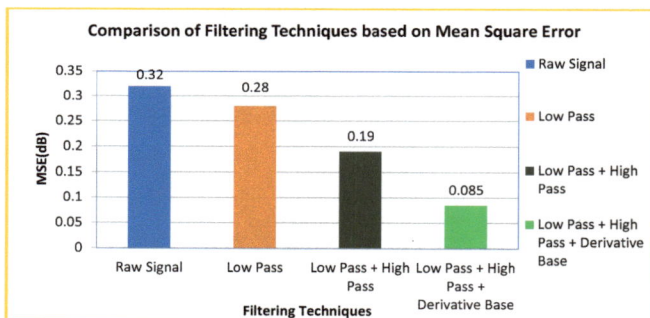

Fig. (16). Comparison of MSE values of various filters.

CONCLUSION

The electrocardiogram (ECG) is a type of biological waveform that gives vital information about the heart and its function. Noise in the ECG is a condition that decreases the accuracy of disease detection. As a result, removing the noise from the ECG signal will make it easier to identify the disease. With the use of Matlab, this study explores filters such as low pass, high pass, and derivative pass filters. When compared to the raw signal, the combination of Low Pass + High Pass + Derivative pass filters shows minimal MSE and SNR values of 0.052db and 1.185db, respectively.

CONSENT FOR PUBLICATION

Not applicable.

CONFLICT OF INTEREST

The authors declare no conflict of interest, financial or otherwise.

ACKNOWLEDGEMENT

Declared none.

REFERENCES

[1]   R. Kher, "Signal Processing Techniques for Removing Noise from ECG Signals", *J. Biomed. Eng.,* vol. 1, pp. 1-9, 2019.

[2]   S. Banerjee, and M. Mitra, "Application of Cross Wavelet Transform for ECG Pattern Analysis and Classification", IEEE Trans InstrumMeas Vol.63, Is. 2, pp: 326, 2013.

[3]   M. Abo-Zahhad, *ECG Signal Compression using Discrete Wavelet Transform.* Discrete Wavelet Transforms-Theory and Applications: InTech, New York, 2011, pp. 143-168.
[http://dx.doi.org/10.5772/16019]

[4]   K.M. Chang, "Arrhythmia ECG Noise Reduction by Ensemble Empirical Mode Decomposition. Sensors", Vol. 10, Is.6, pp: 60–63, 2010.

[5]   R. Martinek, R. Kahankova, J. Jezewski, R. Jaros, J. Mohylova, M. Fajkus, J. Nedoma, P. Janku, and H. Nazeran, "Comparative Effectiveness of ICA and PCA in Extraction of Fetal ECG From Abdominal Signals: Toward Non-invasive Fetal Monitoring", *Front. Physiol.,* vol. 9, p. 648, 2018.
[http://dx.doi.org/10.3389/fphys.2018.00648] [PMID: 29899707]

[6]   S.K. Yadav, R. Sinha, and P.K. Bora, *Electrocardiogram Signal Denoising using Non-Local Wavelet Transform Domain Filtering.,* 2015.
[http://dx.doi.org/10.1049/iet-spr.2014.0005]

[7]   V. Singh, and A. Tiwari, *Optimal Selection of Wavelet Basis Function Applied to ECG Signal Denoising. Digital Signal Processing,* 2006.

[8]   S. Poungponsri, and X.H. Yu, "An adaptive filtering approach for electrocardiogram (ECG) signal noise reduction using neural networks", *Neurocomputing,* vol. 117, pp. 206-213, 2013.
[http://dx.doi.org/10.1016/j.neucom.2013.02.010]

[9]   O.P. Yadav, and S. Ray, "Smoothening and Segmentation of ECG Signals Using Total Variation Denoising –Minimization-Majorization and Bottom-Up Approach", *Procedia Comput. Sci.,* vol. 85, pp. 483-489, 2016.
[http://dx.doi.org/10.1016/j.procs.2016.05.195]

[10]   K Surekha, and B. Patil, *Transform Based Techniques for ECG Signal Compression.Int J ApplEng Res Vol.11,Is.9,,* p. 6139, 2016.

CHAPTER 9

Deep Learning Techniques for Biomedical Research and Significant Gene Identification using Next Generation Sequencing (NGS) Data: - A Review

Debasish Swapnesh Kumar Nayak[1,*], Jayashankar Das[2] and Tripti Swarnkar[3]

[1] *Department of Computer Science & Engineering, Institute of Technical Education and Research, Siksha 'O' Anusandhan Deemed to be University, Bhubaneswar, India*

[2] *Avior Genomics, Mumbai, India*

[3] *Department of Computer Application, Institute of Technical Education and Research, Siksha 'O' Anusandhan Deemed to be University, Bhubaneswar, India*

Abstract: In the biomedical research areas of whole genome sequence (WGS) analysis, disease diagnosis, and medication discovery, Next Generation Sequencing (NGS) data are the most recent and popular trend. The use of NGS data has improved the analysis of infectious diseases, WGS, illness identification, and medication discovery. Although the amount of NGS data is massive, researchers have worked and are continuously working to improve its quality and precision. Modern computational techniques increase the biological value of NGS data processing, making it more accessible to biomedical researchers. Although the complexity of NGS and the required computational power to analyse the data pose a significant threat to researchers, the introduction of various branches of Artificial Intelligence (AI) such as Machine Learning (ML) and Deep Learning (DL) has given analysis, prediction, and diagnosis a new direction. Deep Learning's potential has been demonstrated in a variety of fields, including biomedical research, where it has outperformed traditional methods. The development of deep learning algorithms aids in the analysis of complicated datasets such as NGS by giving a variety of advanced computational methodologies. Different DL approaches are designed to manage enormous datasets and multiple jobs, and the genetic research business could be the next industry to benefit from DL. This paper discusses a variety of DL methods and tools for analysing NGS data in the fields of contagious diseases, WGS analysis, disease diagnosis, and drug design.

---

* **Corresponding author Debasish Swapnesh Kumar Nayak:** Department of Computer Science & Engineering, Institute of Technical Education and Research, Siksha 'O' Anusandhan Deemed to be University, Bhubaneswar, India; Tel: 8249718815; E-mail: swapnesh.nayak@gmail.com

Brojo Kishore Mishra (Ed.)

Keywords: Artificial Intelligence (AI), Deep Learning (DL), Infectious disease, Machine Learning (ML), Next Generation Sequencing (NGS), Whole Genome Sequencing (WGS).

INTRODUCTION

In the recent past, biomedical research has seen a heavy demand for high-throughput sequencing data. High-throughput sequencing in the current scenario is a primary approach for the research of genomics, molecular diagnosis, quantification and classification of metagenomics, genomic feature selection, prediction, and many more. A High-throughput sequence like Next Generation Sequencing (NGS) has a great impact on biomedical research due to its accuracy and time effectiveness [1]. Thousands of sequences can be obtained in very minimal time in the case of NGS. Most importantly, it comes with a very minimal cost compared to the other traditional sequencing techniques. The NGS in the computational view is rather a big omics data for analysis, classification, selection, and prediction; adding to this, the biological significance is a must for all the steps of analysis [2, 3].

The advent of NGS gives the ultimate flexibility to bring transformation in the research areas like bio-computational, biomedical, precision medicine, and biochemistry [4, 5]. It is also found that the huge amount of data in NGS helps to bring changes to the research area of proteomics, epigenetics, transcriptomics, and genomics [6]. In the areas of genomic research, NGS brings revolution by providing a huge amount of data with very less time. The NGS data can be obtained for nucleotides and gene expression, but the major limitation is the accuracy of the huge amount of data generated in a short period. However, it has been found that if the NGS data is processed extremely well before becoming input to any of the analytical phases, it might increase the potential and accuracy of the results [7 - 9].

The gene expression NGS data contains crucial information about different levels of differential activation of the genes which are involved in the evolution and development of any disease. The researchers and physicians have to apply an appropriate tool or technique which can efficiently identify the differentially expressed and significant genes. RNA-Seq is a high-throughput sequencing technique that contains the gene expression data and helps the researcher and physicians to go deeper into the diagnosis and prediction of the disease state of any specific disease especially cancer [10, 11]. The NGS data greatly influenced the research areas of biomedical and bio-computational science from 2010 to 2021. In a survey conducted in 2018, it is said that the global NGS market will grow more than 400 times by 2026 as shown in Fig. (**1**).

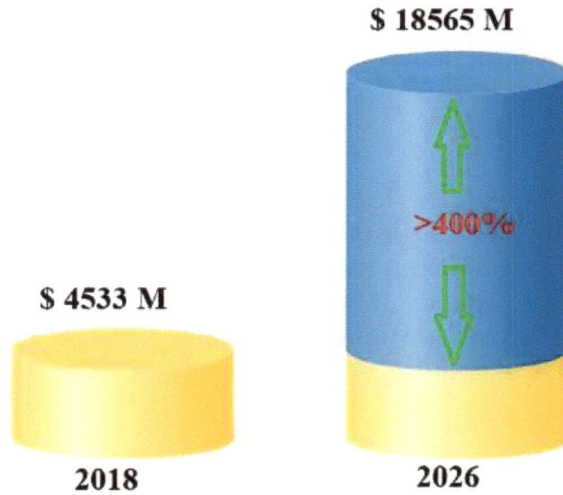

Fig. (1). Global next generation sequencing-market.

Researchers in biomedical, computational biology, and life science fields are nowadays in the search of rapid and accurate computational techniques which can be developed with a very minimal cost and produce more significant results. The advancement of computer science, particularly the newly created computational methods in Artificial Intelligence (AI), makes it possible to handle big data.

At the moment, the trend in infectious disease research is promising. Recently, the study has focused extensively on the infectious disease brought on by the transmission of an infectious agent from an animal or a human to a human. The infectious disease is categorized into four different parts based on the infection agent, Fungi, Viruses, Bacteria, and Parasites. Globally and especially in the Asian continent, infectious diseases like malaria, dengue, typhoid, Tuberculosis (TB), and Hepatitis are major threats. It is also found that there is a rapid growth in infectious diseases in India, and this is due to three major factors *i.e* huge population, lack of medical facilities, and most importantly lack of awareness among the people. The majority of deaths in India are caused by a variety of infectious diseases as shown in Fig. (**2**).

DEATH CAUSED BY FOUR MAJOR INFECTIOUS DISEASES IN INDIA-2020

17200**7163**

52055

256795

- Malaria
- Hepatitis
- Typhoid
- Tuberculosis

Fig. (2). The deaths caused by the four major infectious diseases in India for the year 2020.

Early detection of infectious diseases can assist medical professionals in setting up the necessary facilities for treatment and diagnosis in a reasonable timeframe. There are several studies on prediction related to the spreading ratio of infectious diseases based on the NGS data [3]. Comparable pathogen identification approaches can be used for infectious diseases, but due to a large amount of data, Deep Learning techniques are preferred. Moreover, DL models can handle heterogeneous and complex datasets and get beyond the problems with model dependency and the curse of dimensionality. In addition, DL offers higher model accuracy (prediction/classification) as the dataset size grows.

We have seen the revolutionary advancement of genomic research and infectious disease analyses, as well as the enormous expansion of biomedical data, over the last few decades. The issue has shifted from accumulating biological data to extracting usable knowledge from it. Biomedical data analysis is a demanding new subject that has emerged as a result of the rapid development of biological data analysis tools. The continual development of biological data mining technology, on the other hand, has resulted in a significant number of successful and scalable algorithms [12 - 14]. The advancement to the Artificial Intelligence (AI) techniques like Machine Learning (ML) and Deep Learning (DL) gives a cutting-edge direction to the fields of biomedical and bio-computational research. The increasing research trend in the field of biomedical especially sequencing data analysis is reflected in Fig. **3(a)** and **3(b)**. In Fig. **3(a)**, it is seen that the identification of genetic difference (genotyping) is high in comparison to interpretation, whereas seen in Fig. **3(b)**, the process of determination of the exact sequence of a certain length of DNA (interpretation) is increasing significantly in comparison to genotyping. This change in the relationship between genotyping and its interpretation is being observed in less than a decade.

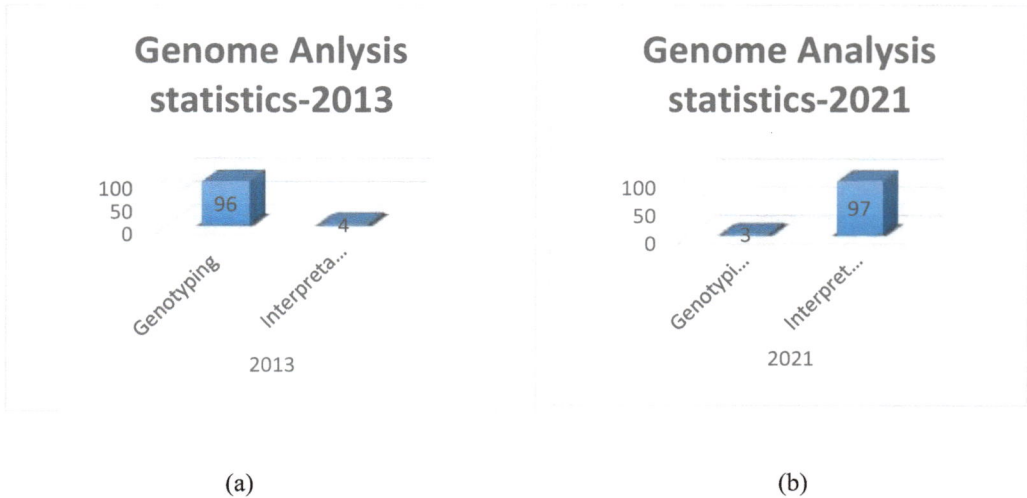

(a)   (b)

Fig. (3). (a) Genomic data analysis statistics in 2013 (b) Genomic data analysis statistics in 2021.

It's worth paying attention to and researching how to construct a bridge between the domains of machine learning and genomics to successfully evaluate biological data. We should look into how to employ data mining for successful biomedical data analysis, as well as highlight certain research questions that could lead to the development of more powerful biological machine-learning algorithms.

We detailed all of the stages involved in the analysis of NGS data and the use of DL approaches in this paper, which aids the researcher in finding an alternate and effective answer to traditional analytic tools.

BACKGROUND

The cell is the fundamental unit of a living organism, in the real world some species exist with a single cell, whereas the human has millions of cells [5]. Sequencing data especially DNA sequencing are the backbone of research areas like whole genome analysis, disease prediction, and drug discovery.

The Sanger sequencer machine shown in Fig. (4) is used for sequencing and is the mostly accepted sequencing technique for biomedical researchers and is treated as the gold standard. It was invented in the year 1977 and since then it is widely used in the biomedical research field for DNA sequence analysis. The process of generating the sequence in terms of time and cost is too high.

Fig. (4). The 3730 Sanger sequencer.

In the recent past, there are research work carried out based on the analysis of various gene expression data, and microarray data are commonly used in various analysis and prediction models. The gene expression microarray data are user-friendly and easy to analysis, but the major drawbacks of microarray data are a large number of gene expression values with a very less number of samples and data redundancy. The NGS data are far ahead of Microarray data with the combination of quality, uniqueness, time, and cost. In disease identification and prediction, it is important to identify the gene and its mutation which is responsible for causing the disease. The selection of the particular (disease creator) gene, gene correlation, and hub gene identification helps in accurate prediction of diseases and thus makes the diagnosis easier [15].

The use of NGS data for biomedical research came into the picture in the year 2009 [16]. The previously used Sanger sequencing is treated as the gold standard but the major limitation to this is the time and computational cost involved to carry out the sequencing process. In the literature, several computational techniques and statistical tools are used for the processing and analysis of various types of NGS data. The NGS data for DNA sequencing, RNA sequencing, and exome sequencing are widely used nowadays because of the improved accuracy of the research results and more biological significance.

The process of sequencing includes the reads and alignment of reads concerning the reference genome as shown in Fig. (5). The three key processes in the NGS data analysis process are primary, secondary, and tertiary data analysis. Some processes are carried out automatically by the sequencing apparatus, while others are carried out after sequencing has been completed.

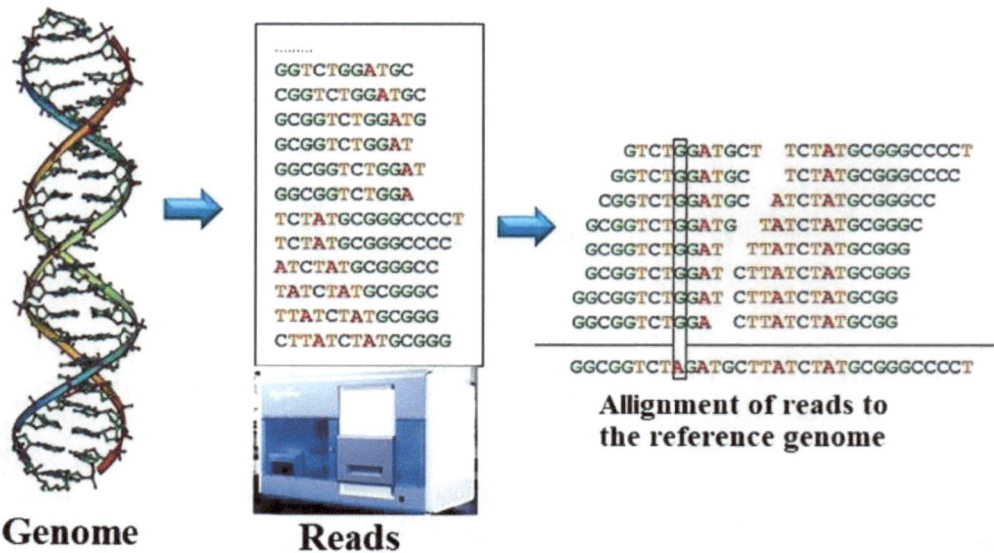

Fig. (5). Short read and alignment of reads with the reference genome.

The conversion of raw instrument signal data into sequence data containing nucleotide base calls (throughout a sequencing reaction, the process of inferring the order of nucleotides in a template), such as FASTQ files, is the first step in the primary analysis. After NGS readings have been translated from raw signals, primary analysis entails pre-processing them.

NGS secondary analysis entails a series of processes, each of which is carried out by a software tool, and which vary by application and add to workflow complexity. Clinical labs require automated and standardized secondary analysis pathways to facilitate NGS assay development and routine clinical testing.

The NGS analysis workflow's third and final stage addresses the critical issue of making meaning of the observed data. Variant annotation is the first stage in the tertiary analysis, and it adds more information to the variants found in the previous processes.

The abbreviations used in this paper are listed in Table **1**.

Table 1. List of abbreviations used in this paper.

Abbreviation	Meaning	Abbreviation	Meaning
AE	Auto-encoders	FO	Feature optimization
AI	Artificial Intelligence	LASSO	Least Absolute Shrinkage and Selection Operator
ANN	Artificial Neural Network	LSTM	Long Short-Term Memory
BAM	Binary Alignment Map	MIL	
BCL	Binary base call	ML	Machine Learning
BDE	Binary Differential Evolution	MLNN	Multi-layer Neural Networks
BLogReg	Bayesian logistic regression	mRMR	Minimum Redundancy Maximum Relevance
CFS	Correlation-based Feature Selection	ONT	Oxford nanopore
DA	Data Augmentation	PCR	Polymer Chain Reaction
DL	Deep Learning	PE	Pair-end
DNN	Deep Neural Network	QC	Quality Control
DNA	Deoxyribonucleic Acid	RF	Random Forest
dNTPs	Deoxynucleotides	RNN	Recurrent Neural Networks
ddNTPs	Di-deoxynucleotides	SMLR	Sparse Multinomial Logistic Regression
E-Net	Elastic net	SLogReg	Sparse logistic regression
FASTA	Fast-all	SU	Symmetrical Uncertainty
FCBF	Fast Correlation-Based Filter	SVM-RFE	Recursive feature disposal for support vector machines
FNN	Feed-forward Neural Network	TL	Transfer-learning
IG	Information Gain	UCSC	University of California, Santa Cruz

DNA SEQUENCING

DNA is a biological macromolecule that is made up of deoxyribonucleic acid. Its primary role is to store data. DNA sequence data is currently growing at an exponential rate due to advances in sequencing technology, which has transformed the study of DNA sequences into the big data era. Sequencing technology has progressed through three stages in the evolution of biological information technology. The first-generation sequencing technology refers to the chain termination method proposed by Sanger and the chain degradation approach proposed by Gibert [17]. Sanger sequencing is still frequently employed in traditional sequencing applications and verification, but the cost of sequencing is quite high, and throughput is poor, limiting its true large-scale applicability.

Sanger Sequencing

The Sanger approach for DNA sequencing is a commercial sequencing method that has been utilized mostly for the past thirty years. Sanger sequencing or chain-termination sequencing is based on the use of 2`-deoxynucleotides (dNTPs) and 2`,3`-dideoxynucleotides (ddNTPs) for synthesis and termination of synthesis of the complementary DNA template, respectively [18].

Next Generation Sequencing (The Rising Trend)

The history of high-throughput NGS sequencing starts in the year 2009, the team lead by Nick McCooke invented next-generation sequencing (NGS) during his work at DNA Electronics company. This is a technology that reads the DNA at an extremely high speed and thus is now very much popular worldwide for research and analysis of genes as well as precision medicine design [19]. Before NGS another sequencing like Sanger can deal with the short DNA sequences, the NGS makes a revolution and gives the researchers the to go for the long sequences (Fig. 6).

Fig. (6). Applications of NGS data in various areas of biomedical research.

When compared to traditional Sanger sequencing, next-generation sequencing (NGS) has revolutionized clinical genetics by allowing researchers to study hundreds of genes at an unparalleled speed and at a cheaper cost. The entire process of generating a high-throughput sequence like next-generation sequencing nowadays is mostly controlled by Illumina [16]. The basic concept behind generating the NGS data is just to put the samples into a cartridge and keep that cartridge in an Illumina sequencer and follow the sequencing procedure to obtain the resultant sequence. The entire process may take several hours but is very minimal compared to the traditional sequencing techniques available in the market.

On the other side, when using the classic sequencing approach to amplify DNS sequences, the polymer chain reaction (PCR) is a huge hurdle because it requires a specific lab and a high level of biological skill to complete. But, the introduction of high-throughput sequencing techniques especially Illumina technology makes it easier, and most importantly it does not require any skilled manpower. The next-generation sequencing has brought a revolution in the field of genome analysis, disease identification and diagnosis, and drug discovery. The process of obtaining NGS data is very cheaper compared to the other existing sequencing techniques.

The major issues associated with NGS bioinformatics are discussed in light of future advances. Even with the tremendous advances in NGS technology and bioinformatics, more bioinformatics algorithm advancements are needed to cope with complicated and genetically heterogeneous illnesses.

NGS GENE EXPRESSION DATA (STRUCTURE, CHARACTER, AND CHALLENGES)

NGS, also known as massively parallel sequencing, is rapidly revolutionizing biomedical and biological research from the level of a single gene to the level of the entire genome [20]. In comparison to gene expression microarrays established in the late 1990s and early 2000s, NGS technologies have a far greater influence on a wide range of biological applications, particularly clinical diagnostics. The NGS data for genomics and proteomics research/analysis comes in two forms nucleotide sequences and gene expression. The data in NGS are stored in the data file with extensions like.BCL, .FASTQ, .FASTA and the view of these datasets are shown in Fig. (**7**). The most commonly used file extension for NGS gene expression data is .FASTQ [19].

(a)

```
Header ──● >VIT_201s0011g03530
Sequence ──● AATTAAGCATAAATACTCACTCTTACCCCCTTATTTTCTTATCTCTCATCACTTTTGGTGCGAAG
         ● GACCATGAGAACAAGCTGCAATGGGTGTAGGGTTCTTCGCAAGGCATGCAGCCAAGACTGCATCA
Header ──● >VIT_201s0011g03540
Sequence ──● CAGGTAGCGTGAAGTTAAACCCTAGCGCTTTAGACAAACAGCTGTAGTCACCGCCCACAAACACC
         ● AGCCTCTGAGACACCACCTCAAACCTTTCCACTTAAATACACATCCCTCACACCCTTTTCAATTC
Header ──● >VIT_201s0011g03550
Sequence ──● CATGCAAAGCTGAACGCGATGCTGTGATTGGTGGTAAGTGGTAGTTGAGTAAATTTGACAGTGAA
         ● GCCGAAATGGTAAAAGACTAAGGCTAGAAGTAGAATACCACTGTTCTTCTCATCACGTGGGCCCA
```

(b)

```
Name        @ERR194146.1 HSQ1008:141:D0CC8ACXX:3:1308:20201:36071/1
Sequence    ACATCTGGTTCCTACTTCAGGGCCATAAAGCCTAAATAGCCCACACGTTCCCCTTAAAT
            +
Base qualities  ?@@FFBFFDDHHBCEAFGEGIIDHGH@GDHHHGEHID@C?GGDG@FHIGGH@FHBEG:G
```

(c)

```
FCID,Lane,SampleID,SampleRef,Index,Description,Control,Recipe,Operator,SampleProject
FLOWCELL,1,samp1,a,TAAGGCGA-TAGATCGC,,N,,,proj2
FLOWCELL,2,samp1,a,TAAGGCGA-TAGATCGC,,N,,,proj1
FLOWCELL,3,samp1,a,TAAGGCGA-TAGATCGC,,N,,,proj1
FLOWCELL,4,samp1,a,TAAGGCGA-TAGATCGC,,N,,,proj1
FLOWCELL,5,samp1,a,TAAGGCGA-TAGATCGC,,N,,,proj1
FLOWCELL,6,samp1,a,TAAGGCGA-TAGATCGC,,N,,,proj1
FLOWCELL,7,samp1,a,TAAGGCGA-TAGATCGC,,N,,,proj1
FLOWCELL,8,samp1,a,TAAGGCGA-TAGATCGC,,N,,,proj1
#_IEMVERSION_3_Nextera XT
```

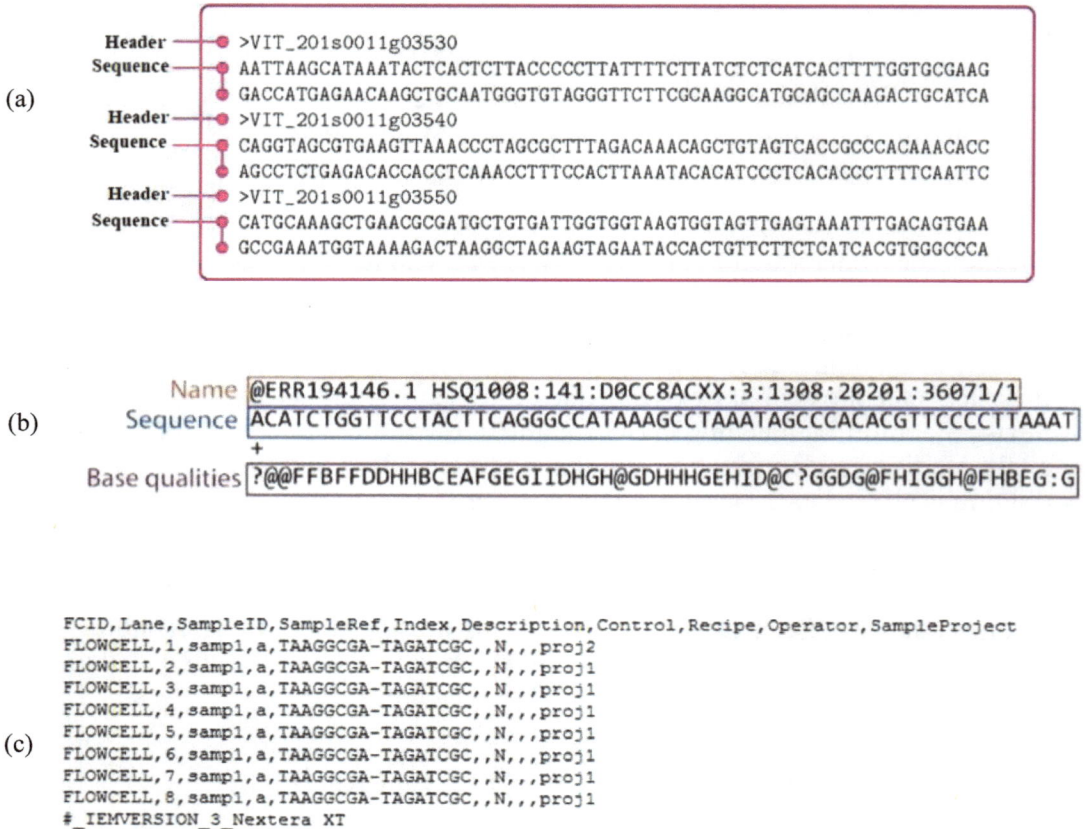

Fig. (7). NGS sequence data with (a).FASTA (b).FASTQ (c).BCL file extensions.

Fastq (*i.e.* fastq.gz) files are commonly used to store Illumina sequence readings. Fastq, circular consensus sequences (ccs), FASTA, or BAM files are used to store PacBio sequence readings. CCS file contains the error-corrected sequence reads. During a PacBio run, shorter sequence fragments are read many times (circled), and the accuracy improves with each pass. The PacBio BAM recipes can convert the BAM file to fastq format. The raw data from Oxford Nanopore (ONT) is delivered as fast5 files, which must be base called by using the Guppy to obtain fastq files. FASTQ is a standard file format for transmitting sequencing read data that includes both the sequence and a per-base quality score, the basic pipeline to obtain the FASTQC file is shown in Fig. (**8**). You should have a FASTQ file for each sample (Illumina single-end (SR), PacBio, and Nanopore data). You should have two FASTQ files (R1 and R2) per sample for an Illumina paired-end (PE) experiment.

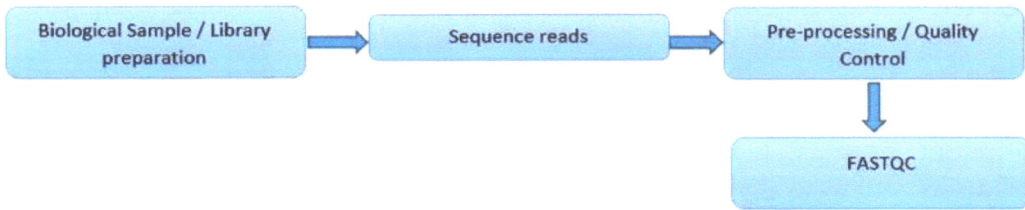

Fig. (8). Process to obtain FASTQC data format.

Each NGS system generates its own set of sequencing errors and biases, which must be recognized and addressed. High-frequency idle polymorphisms, homopolymeric areas, GC- and AT-rich regions, replication bias, and substitution errors are all linked to substantial sequencing errors [21, 22]. Another issue with the NGS, in terms of solving the mounting hurdles of storage, analysis, and interpretation of NGS data, bioinformatics is a crucial rate-limiting step for NGS technology [23].

QC TOOLS FOR NGS DATA PRE-PROCESSING

The high-throughput sequencing data generated in Next generation sequencing technology are vast and complex. To obtain a useful downstream analysis, it is important to pass the raw NGS data into a quality control (QC) phase. The QC provides a standardize NGS sequence that is suitable for subsequent analysis models/tolls. The Raw NGS data needs to feed to the quality control pipeline to generate the subsequent .FASTQ file. The primary work of the QC process starts with extracting the built-in quality of the raw reads by implementing the metrics (quality score) obtained from the sequencing platform. On the other way, the same can be done by calculating the base composition from raw reads. However, there is a limitation to the QC pipeline for NGS data pre-processing [2]. Various QC tools used in NGS data pre-processing are briefly discussed in the following section;

i. **Rapid Identification of PCR Primers Pairs for Unique Core Sequences (RUCS 1.0)**

It takes 50 genomes in each submission for processing and all raw NGS data must be in .FASTA format. The user needs to create two different folders named positive and negative, the positive and negative folders contain the target genome and not the target genome in the FASTA format respectively [24]. The zip file of these two folders is the input to the RUCS 1.0 tool for pre-processing and finding the PCR primer pairs.

i. OmicsBox

Different statistics charts and reports aid in the biological interpretation of the results as well as evaluating the genome assembly and characterization processes. It provides the facility like annotation visualization in the form of tracks by combining the genome sequences (.fasta) with alignments (.bam), intron-exon structure (.gff), and variation data. The user interface makes it simple to process large genome annotations. Gene annotations can be filtered, sorted, and integrated with other result sets using the General Feature Format style [10].

Software packages and installation tools for specific languages or systems are collected in package suites, bioinformatics software is one of them. From the literature, we have some bioinformatics software for various biomedical data analyses.

- Bioconductor – It is a tool for high-throughput sequencing genomic data and includes 1500+ software packages. It is an open-source application [12].
- Biopython – It is an open-source tool for computational biology in python. It contains various packages including Entrez, which helps with API access to the NCBI databases [13].
- Bioconda – It is a bioinformatics software with a package manager of conda application. It includes more than 3000 ready-to-install packages which can be installed with conda [14].
- BioJulia – It runs with Julia programming language and has various computational biology and bioinformatics applications [25].
- SegAn – It is used for sequence analysis and uses the programming language C++ [12].
- RustBio – It helps in the implementation of various parts of the bioinformatics model especially the algorithm and data structure [26].

In current research trends for NGS data analysis, a few of the popular commercial software tools are described in Table **1**. However, it is found that most of the pre-processing and analysis tools for NGS data are commercial software as seen in Table **2**, and the cost of usage of these tools is too high for individuals. The high cost of this software creates a huddle for biomedical (genomic) researchers and these resources are confined to limited places (laboratories). In the last few years, the emerging trends of ML and DL encourage the researcher to take advantage of these methods while dealing with the NGS data analysis. Most importantly the accuracy, cost-effectiveness, and biological relevance results of these model make them more popular among biomedical researchers.

Table 2. Most Popular Tools for NGS data Analysis.

S. No.	Tool	Input File formats/ Technology Supports	Major Functionality	Compatibility	URL
1	Strand NGS	ELAND (Illumina-specific format), BAM, and SAM.	Alignment, RNA-seq, Chip-seq, DNA-seq, Biological annotation, and visualization	Windows/Linux	https://www.strand-ngs.com/
2	CLC Genomics Workbench (**QIAGEN**)	VCF, FASTA, BED, Cosmic, GTF/GFF/GVF, Wiggle, and UCSC data variants.	Read mapping, re-sequencing, variant detection, genome browser, chip-seq.	Windows/Linux	https://digitalinsights.qiagen.com/desktop-applications/top-features/
3	Laser-gene Genomics Suite (LGS)	BCL, FASTA, FASTQ. Supports major NGS technologies like Illumina, Pac Bio, Ion Torrent and Roche 454	Alignment, variant call, and Analysis of NGS data. Transcriptome analysis, targeted sequencing, assembly of metagenomics samples, exome alignment.	Windows, Mac OS X, Linux, and Amazon Cloud	https://www.dnastar.com/software/lasergene/genomics/
4	Partek Genomics Suite	BCL, FASTA, FASTQ, Microarray file format, text file, and GEO soft files.	NGS data analysis work flow: RNA-Seq, miRNA-Seq, ChIP-Seq, DNA-Seq, and Methylation. Powerful visualization and statistical analysis capacity.		https://www.partek.com/partek-genomics-suite/
5	NextGENe	BCL, FASTA, FASTQ	Useful for high-throughput sequencing data analysis produced from Illumina®, Ion Torrent Proton, Applied BioSystems SOLiD™, and Roche FLX platforms.	Windows	https://softgenetics.com/NextGENe.php

(Table 2) cont.....

S. No.	Tool	Input File formats/ Technology Supports	Major Functionality	Compatibility	URL
6	Partek Flow	NGS- FASTA, SAM, BAM and Micorarray from Illumina an Affymetrix.	Alignment, base trimming, quantification, statistics, quality analysis, and visualization. Best fit for variant calling, fusion detection, pathway enrichment, WGS, RNA-Seq, and small RNA-Seq.	Linux (cloud/local server)	https://www.partek.com/partek-flow/
7	Golden Helix	TXT, XLSX, XLS, CHP, Plink PED, CEL, BED, VCF, Impute2 GWAS...*etc*.	Analysis and visualization of Phenotype and genotype data. Genomic prediction, genome-wide association, copy number analysis, large and small sequence DNA-Seq analysis.		https://www.goldenhelix.com/products/SNP_Variation/index.html
8	Biodatamics	BED	Drag and drop interface, genomic data visualization, and it is integrates more than 4000 open source tolls and pipelines for genomic analysis.	Open source and have private as well as public cloud.	https://www.biodatomics.com/
9	Basepair	BCL, FASTA, FASTQ	Cloud based with high computational efficiency. No limitations in computing and storage usages. Large projects are managed with the help of REST and Python API.	Cloud based application.	https://www.basepairtech.com/

MACHINE LEARNING TECHNIQUES FOR NGS DATA ANALYSIS

Machine Learning (ML) techniques to deal with vast dataset make it popular among researchers. The promising approach of ML in every part of research proves its capability and robustness. The application of ML for big data analysis starts from pre-processing of data, classification, feature selection, and result diagnosis. This approach of ML insists the biomedical researchers to apply various machine learning techniques for the analysis of NGS data. In the last decade, machine learning has proved its prominent use for NGS data analysis resulting in the identification of diseases, finding of mutations, and drug design with more biological significance and high accuracy [1].

There are several methods (models) found in ML to perform different tasks in the process of NGS data analysis. The ML models for NGS data can solve the specific task without being instructed in detail from outside. ML methods can build statistical models by using the available NGS data to solve a particular task [7]. The supervised and un-supervised ML techniques are having different problem-solving approaches to solve a particular problem assigned to them. In the case of significant gene identification from NGS data, the supervised ML uses the labelled training data for model inference where the annotation process takes place between the data points with the true outcome.

Machine Learning (ML) is a significant part of current business and research. It utilizes calculations and neural organization models to help computers continuously work on their performance. Machine Learning techniques can build some mathematical models which can take decisions by using some sample datasets.

The application of Machine Learning techniques can be considered for many areas, but can be described with the major functionality as follows:

a. **Classification:** One of the most researched tasks in machine learning is classification. The classification concept is based on the predicted attribute to forecast the class of the user-specified target attribute. Genome classification and sequence annotation are the most important concerns in genomics. Fuzzy sets, neural networks, evolutionary algorithms, and rough sets are all commonly used methods in the mining of biological sequences. There are also a variety of general categorization models available, including naïve Bayesian networks, decision trees, neural networks, and rule learning with evolutionary algorithms [17 - 28].

b. **Feature selection:** When creating a predictive ML model, feature selection is the process of minimizing the number of input variables. The number of input variables should be reduced to lower the computational cost of modelling and, in some situations, to increase the model's performance [29].

c. **Clustering:** Machine learning's clustering technique can group sequences with similar features and investigate the effective information of unknown sequences using existing functions and structures. As a result, grouping biological sequences is extremely important in bioinformatics research. Clustering differs from classification in that it does not use a fixed category. Each cluster has its own set of traits in common. The goal of cluster analysis is to group data with similar features into one category, then evaluate the data using various approaches [17, 30].

d. **Dimensionality Reduction:** Dimension reduction is to change the primary depiction of items into a lower-dimensional depiction while saving a few informative characteristics of the primary depiction.

Various Datamining Methods for Sequence data

Mining sequential patterns in sequence datasets is a complex data mining problem. In literature, several algorithms, such as AprioriAll, GSP, FreeSpan, PrefixSpan, SPADE, and SPAM, have been presented for more than two decades. These algorithms can be classified as employing a horizontal database (namely, AprioriAll, GSP, FreeSpan, and PrefixSpan) or a vertical database (*e.g.*, SPADE and SPAM) [31].

The advantage of a vertical representation is that it allows you to calculate pattern frequencies without having to undertake time-consuming database scans. Vertical mining algorithms can now perform better on dense databases or extended sequences than horizontal feature extraction techniques [31].

Taxonomy of Datamining, ML, and DL Techniques used for NGS data Analysis

Although there are numerous machine learning and deep learning techniques available, the most commonly used technique for NGS and high-throughput gene expression data analysis is shown in Fig. (**9**).

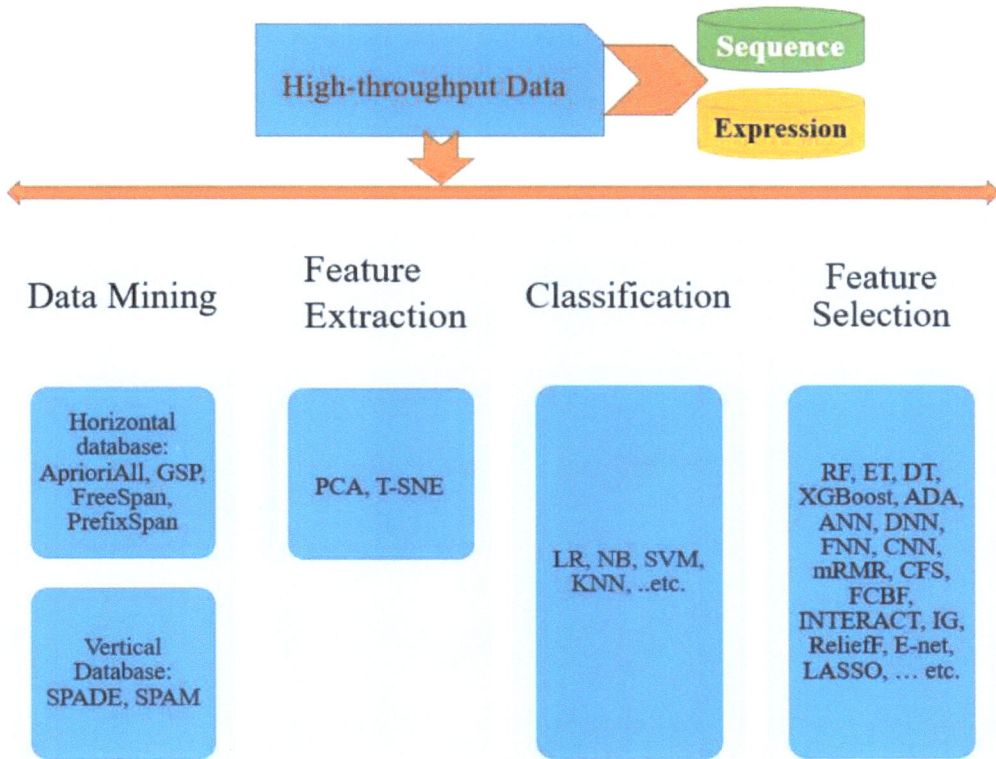

Fig. (9). Commonly used Datamining, ML, and DL techniques for NGS data analysis.

MACHINE LEARNING TECHNIQUES FOR NGS FEATURE SELECTION

The fast advancement of next-generation sequencing (NGS) technology, as well as its use in large-scale cohorts in biomedical research, has resulted in common big data concerns. It brought about a new field of study that combines systems biology with machine learning. The important factor associated with NGS data analysis is the selection of significant features to predict, and diagnose the disease and thus can further help in drug design. Most importantly while extracting the features it should indulge in the scene that the process is cost-effective, accurate, and biologically relevant [32].

One of the most crucial processes in Machine Learning is feature selection. Feature selection in Machine Learning is broadly divided into three different groups. The first one is known as the supervised feature selection method where features relating to the class are chosen first. The second type of feature selection method is Unsupervised where data distribution, classification, and data variance are the key factors for selecting any features. The third kind is the semi-supervised element determination strategy which considers both the named and unlabelled information for choosing the segregate features. Different norms are set to compute the pertinence of an element which is the primary reason for the component forecast step. Contingent upon the unique search boundaries and methods, the feature selection is categorized into five groups as shown in Fig. (10).

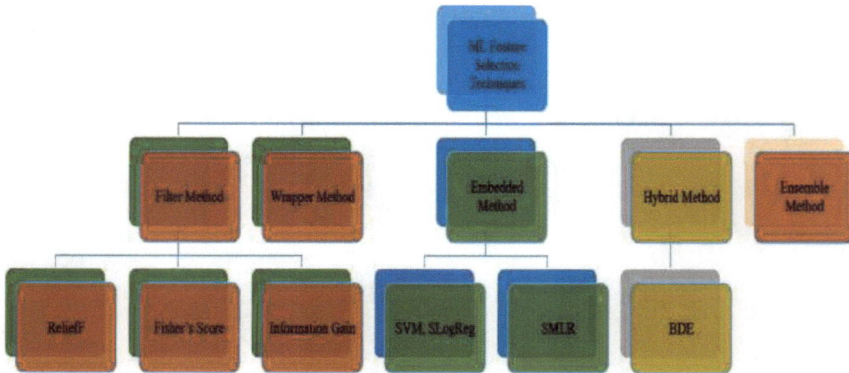

Fig. (10). Few commonly used feature selection techniques for NGS data analysis.

Filter Method

Filter Methods get the inborn properties of the provisions estimated by employing univariate measurements rather than cross-approval execution. These strategies are quicker and less computationally costly than covering techniques. When managing high-dimensional information, it is computationally less expensive to utilize Filter Methods. For feature evaluation, filter method does not acquire any classification algorithm. In the filter method, we follow only two steps for selecting the features. The first step includes the selection of features based on evaluation standards and in the second step, we follow the classification process based on top-scoring features. Different types of Filter Methods are used in Machine Learning for next-generation data analysis. Some of the methods are Chi-Square, Relief, Correlation-based feature selection, Fisher's Score, information gain, and Consistency based filter [17]. In this method, there is a disadvantage in that it does not look over the correlated features. This limitation is overcome by a subset search method where the features are evaluated in the cluster [33].

Key points:

- Filter methods are a type of pre-processing that is not dependent on the learning algorithms that follow.
- They choose characteristics using distinct methodologies.
- An assessment criterion, or a score, is used to choose the set of features by assessing the degree of relevance of each characteristic to a target variable.

Wrapper Method

Wrapper methods require some strategy to look through the space of all potential subsets of provisions, surveying their quality by learning and assessing a classifier that includes a subset. The element determination measure depends on a particular Machine Learning algorithm that we are attempting to fit on a given dataset. It follows a greedy search approach by thinking about every one of the potential combinations of features in contrast to the assessment standard. The covering techniques ordinarily bring about preferable prescient precision over filter methods. Fundamentally, in this technique, the module identified with feature search creates the feature set followed by the assessment of features through execution assessment of the picked subset utilizing the classifier. The wrapper procedure additionally utilizes different strategies like direct forward determination, re-positioning based feature choice, non-parametric thickness assessment strategy, and numerous channels and different wrapper techniques for effective feature choice.

Key points:

- Wrappers are feature selection approaches that assess a subset of characteristics based on the correctness of a predictive model that has been developed alongside them.
- The evaluation is carried out with the help of a classifier that calculates the importance of a subset of attributes.
- This type of approach is efficient, but it is computationally expensive, which is why it is not often used.

Embedded Method

Feature expectation frames the premise of the learning algorithm in the inserted approach alongside picking the feature subset. There are different algorithms utilized in inserted strategy which are sparse multinomial logistic regression

(SMLR), Bayesian logistic regression (BLogReg), recursive feature disposal for support vector machines (SVM-RFE), sparse logistic regression (SLogReg), feature optimization (JCFO) and joint classifier. While going through the course of arrangement, the choice of feature choice is finished by the algorithm. An illustration of the implanted methodology is the choice trees. This strategy chooses the subset of features alongside the arrangement procedure to assess the proficiency regarding incorrectly grouping rate.

Key points:

- Embedded Combine the benefits of both the filter and wrapper approaches.
- Because the Filter methods are faster but inefficient, and the Wrapper methods are more effective but computationally expensive, especially with large datasets, a solution that combines the benefits of both methods was required.

Hybrid Method

The Crossover strategy takes in the joined benefit of the channel and wrapper technique to achieve better effectiveness. This strategy decreases the intricacy of the wrapper method and limits overfitting. Apolloni *et al.* [8], and Mohapatra *et al.* [34] have proposed a viable crossover model known as the binary differential evolution (BDE) algorithm for choosing the significant features. Wrapper strategies tend to the downside of discovering the relationship between the features in channel technique by advancing the feature subset. BDE assesses the wellness work based on the occasions the features are available and expressed that the feature subset discovered has a precision close to 100%.

Ensemble Method

The principle point of this strategy is to give information about the variety and to increase the routineness of the cycle to choose the feature. This facilitates considering the strength of each selector, as well as the constraints. The assessment of the features should be possible in two distinctive manners. One way is the individual assessment where each feature has been relegated to a position by assessing the degree of significance of individual features. Yet, in this cycle, the repetitive features are not eliminated as they might have a comparative positioning.

The current research trends in biomedical research especially the fields like proteomics, genomics, metagenomics, and transcriptomics implement various machine learning methods as discussed above to achieve the desired analysis result as shown in Fig. (**11**).

MACHINE LEARNING APPLICATION TO DIFFERENT TYPES OF NGS DATASETS

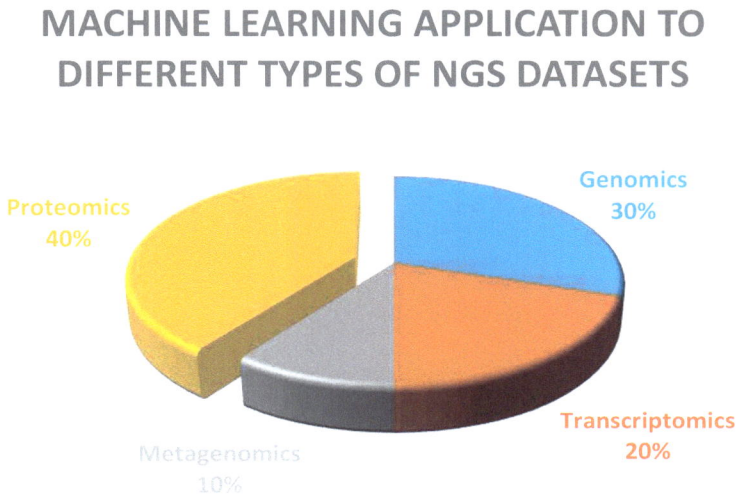

Fig. (11). Application of various ML techniques to different fields of biomedical research.

Several ML feature extraction techniques are proposed in the literature, here we described the widely used feature extraction techniques which can best fit NGS data analysis.

FEATURE EXTRACTION TECHNIQUES FOR NGS DATA

Next-generation sequencing (NGS) technologies have opened up a world of possibilities for researchers in a variety of biological and biomedical fields. For large-scale comparative and evolutionary studies to be undertaken on the vast volumes of data obtained from the NGS platform, efficient data mining technologies are in high demand. Using NGS data to extract features is a crucial step in predicting the disease and thus makes disease diagnosis easier. The different ML methods discussed in the previous section can be applied to NGS data for classification, and informative feature selection. For NGS data, multiple feature extraction approaches are employed in machine learning [35]. ML algorithms like CFS, FCBF, INTERACT, Information Gain, ReliefF, mRMR, LASSO, E-Net, and RF are some of the widely used approaches discussed in this section. The list of most commonly used feature selection methods for NGS data analysis is shown in Fig. (**12**).

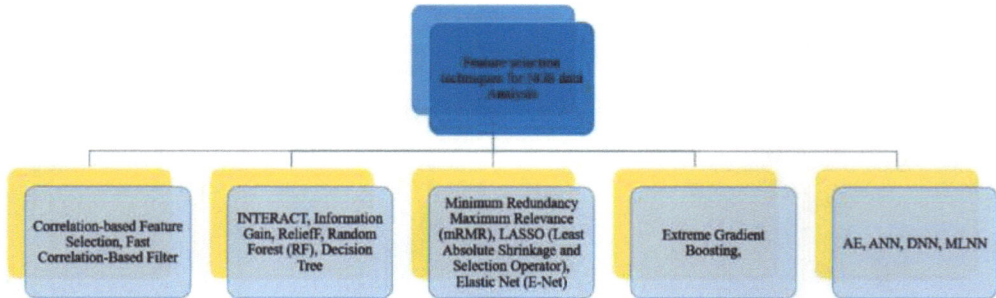

Fig. (12). Feature selection methods used for NGS data analysis.

Correlation-based Feature Selection (CFS)

The CFS algorithm is a multivariate algorithm. It uses a correlation-based heuristic evaluation function to rank the feature subset. The bias of the evaluation function is held by the subset that contains strongly correlated characteristics with the class and uncorrelated features with each other in this method [36]. Irrelevant features should be removed because they have a very low association with the class. Because redundant characteristics are strongly related to the remaining features, they should be eliminated. The selected feature's further analysis is based on their projected classes, which should not be predicted by other characteristics.

Fast Correlation-Based Filter (FCBF)

A multivariate algorithm is FCBF. This algorithm calculates the correlation between a feature and its class, as well as between features. The highly correlated characteristic to the target and uncorrelated with others is selected based on symmetrical uncertainty (SU) in this technique, which is independent of the classifier (SU). This algorithm's main task is to select features that are greater than the SU's chosen threshold. The ratio of the entropy of two characteristics to the information gain is known as SU [36].

It uses three heuristics to get rid of the irrelevant features, keeping the features that are more important to the class and removing the ones that aren't. For high-dimensional datasets, FCBF is effective at removing unnecessary and redundant features. This approach has the drawback of being unable to map the relationship between multiple features.

INTERACT

The INTERACT algorithm acts as a supplement to the FCBF filter algorithm in terms of measuring its efficacy, particularly the SU, by accounting for consistency contribution. By removing numerous noisy features, consistency contribution is required to achieve the desired level of consistency. This algorithm's operational mode is divided into two parts. The first section consists of a downward list of traits based on their SU value. The second section consists of evaluating features one by one, beginning at the bottom of the sorted feature list and progressing to the top. If the consistency contribution is less than the threshold, the feature is disabled; otherwise, it is enabled. This strategy is useful in feature interaction and feature selection for high-dimensional datasets [37].

Information Gain

The information gain (IG) algorithm is a single-variate filtering method. This algorithm operates on the evaluation of information gain for each variable (features), and feature selection is based on the largest information gain, resulting in reduced entropy and a more effective grouping of datasets [37].

ReliefF

The relief algorithm's original application is limited to binary classification problems. It works by taking a random sample of the data and then selecting neighbors from both the correlated and uncorrelated classes. The traditional approach is unable to deal with the missing values [37]. The advanced version of relief (ReliefF) is called extended relief. The comparison values of the attributes of the sample instance's closest neighbors are used to update the relevance score of each attribute. It improves the original relief by giving it the ability to handle multiclass problems. Furthermore, it is robust and capable of handling incomplete and noisy data.

Minimum Redundancy Maximum Relevance (mRMR)

The mRMR method is used to accurately identify gene and phenotypic traits. It also offers a description of feature selection relevance. The subset frequently comprises features that are relevant but redundant, the mRMR acts on this issue and eliminates the redundant feature. This approach selects features that are mutually far apart and has a high correlation between them.

LASSO (Least Absolute Shrinkage and Selection Operator)

Lasso regression is a type of regularization. For a more accurate forecast, it is preferred over regression approaches. Shrinkage is used in this model. Data values are shrunk towards a central point known as the mean in shrinkage. Simple, sparse models are encouraged by the lasso approach. This type of regression is ideal for models with a lot of multicollinearities or when you wish to automate elements of the model selection process, such as variable selection and parameter removal [38].

Elastic Net (E-Net)

Like the technique LASSO, Elastic net is a variable selection approach that does the work for you, shrinks it continuously, and allows you to select groups of corresponding features [5]. In the Elastic net, shrinking is accomplished by combining LASSO's L1 (norm penalty) with the ridge's L2 (norm penalty). The goal of L1 is to create a scattered model by reducing some regression coefficients to zero, and the goal of L2 is to balance the L1 regularization route by encouraging associated effects and relaxing constraints on the selected features [38].

Random Forest (RF)

Random Forest is an ensemble technique that is efficient at processing massive datasets. This algorithm generates numerous decision trees by selecting a subset of variables at random. Poor bias, high volatility, and low correlation between generated trees are all advantages of Random Forest [36].

ISSUES AND OPPORTUNITIES WITH TRADITIONAL MACHINE LEARNING

Machine learning is the most extensively used data processing approach and is at the heart of data mining. Machine learning algorithms have the advantage of being able to filter enormous amounts of data to hunt for patterns that might otherwise go unnoticed. Machine learning is critical in uncovering predictable patterns in biological systems in the era of huge data in biomedical research. The followings are the primary issues and opportunities with existing machine-learning applications in biological data:

a. Machine learning models trained on one data set may not generalize effectively to other data sets due to variations in biological data. If the fresh data differs significantly from the training data, the machine learning model's analysis outputs are likely to be incorrect.

b. Most biological data sets (NGS) are very huge and complex. However, the results obtained from the ML methods are not significant and lose biological relevance when applied to these datasets. Even though the total amount of biological data is enormous and growing by the day, the data is collected from several platforms. Integrating multiple data sets is extremely difficult due to technological and biological differences.

c. Machine learning models' black-box nature poses significant challenges for biological applications. The output of a given model is typically difficult to comprehend from a biological point of view, which limits the model's application.

d. There is a need to develop a method for converting machine learning's "black box" into a biologically meaningful and easily understandable "white box."

The feature selection techniques used in ML performs excellently while applied over small dataset but, the prediction and selection result is affected when applied to dataset having huge values or big dataset [7]. There are a lot of possibilities at the junction of machine learning and biomedical data integration, but there are also a lot of barriers to overcome. In the domain of biological research, machine learning is still far from fulfilling its maximum potential, and we have a long way to go [17]. Missing values in high-throughput sequencing or expression dataset is also a threat to the performance of ML models. So, the ML algorithms for clustering need to be automated to handle incomplete datasets [39]. However, to overcome these issues with ML, DL techniques like deep neural network (DNN) applied over large-scale complex data (NGS) analysis improved the accuracy of a computational model for molecular subtyping [40, 41], mutation prediction [59, 60] and drug design [42, 43].

DEEP LEARNING (THE EMERGING TREND)

The recent advancement in the research areas of biomedical and computational technologies gives tremendous opportunity for researchers to explore more by dealing with numerous and huge biological data like next-generation sequencing (NGS) of genomic and protein, medical images, and electroencephalography (identifying the electrical activity features of a different region of the brain). The analysis of these datasets provides the researcher the detailed knowledge about human health and the associated diseases, the same can be considered for single-cell bacteria to multicellular living objects [44]. The deep learning techniques are based on the concept inherited from the functions of human neurons and developed using an artificial neural network (ANN). The algorithms used in deep learning are advanced and able to extract learning patterns and features from complex data like NGS.

The Deep learning technique is the current trend in biomedical research for model abstraction from large-scale, complex data by implementing multi-layer deep neural networks (DNN) and gives meaning to a complex dataset like text, image, and sound [26]. The operational procedure of DL has two wings (i) a Non-linear processing unit of multiple layers, and (ii) a learning type like un-supervised or supervised imposed on the features presented in each layer. The evolution of deep learning comes with the framework that contains artificial neural networks (ANN) in the early 1980s [18], but the remarkable impact of deep learning in various research areas started in 2006 [45]. During the journey from 2006 deep learning is applied in numerous fields including image processing, speech recognition, natural language processing, bioinformatics, and drug design [46, 47].

The growth of quantity, quality, and availability of data in all the research fields are exponential since the last decade. It can be observed that the data growth in the field of biomedical especially the protein structure data, medical images, and genomic sequences data has massively increased in the last decade and this is possible due to the advancement in high-throughput sequencing technology. The large and complex datasets in the biomedical field thus required high-performance and advanced computational techniques to pre-process, analyze, interpret, and storing of these data. It is also important to adopt effective and efficient computational techniques which come in terms of less time with minimal cost [46, 48]. To face this issue, deep learning is one of the best solutions due to its standard algorithmic framework which is designed to handle such complex problems. The state-of-art applications of deep learning make it more popular among biomedical, and bio-computational experts especially due to the more robustness compared to machine learning and the training of the deep learning framework requires minimal manpower interference.

The Revolution of Deep Learning

The fundamental principle of deep learning (DL) was inspired by the biological process of ANN in the early 1960s. The computational advancement gives a new wing to the development of DL techniques. Deep learning (DL) refers to a group of techniques that have recently achieved state-of-the-art performance in computer vision, pattern recognition, and natural language processing, such as multi-layer neural networks (MLNN), convolutional neural networks (CNN), deep auto-encoders (AE), and recurrent neural networks (RNN). In the instance of high-throughput genomics, DL is capable of tracking the internal structure of biological data and extracting high-level abstract characteristics from high-dimensional sequencing or expression data [49].

Specialized neural network architectures such as convolutional neural networks (CNN) and recurrent neural networks (RNN) with long short-term memory cells (LSTM) can now be trained efficiently and have been successfully applied to a variety of problems, including image recognition [50] and natural language processing tasks like speech recognition [51]. The success of neural networks has prompted the creation of several programming frameworks for creating and training neural networks. PyTorch (http://pytorch.org/), Caffe (http://caffe.berkeleyvision.org), and TensorFlow (https://www.tensor flow.org) were a few examples.

In literature, there are several DL techniques are proposed for NGS data analysis and it is found that the results are more significant with less computational power and cost-effectiveness. In the following section various DL techniques (architecture) for NGS data analysis are discussed.

DEEP LEARNING APPROACH FOR NGS DATA ANALYSIS

Artificial Neural Network (ANN)

The ANN was discovered in the early 1960s and uses the working principle of the eyes and cells of the visual cortex. It is inspired by the information processing concept which is layer by layer in the case of the connection between the human eyes and cells of the visual cortex [52]. The same principle is followed by the ANN with the help of placing artificial neurons within the layers for extracting the feature of the visualized object. But, the actual revolution in the advancement of the ANN technique comes after its invention due to a lack of computational resources during that time.

The ANN model contains artificial neurons (Fig. **13**), the artificial neurons are the scalar functions of n+1 input variables $x_i, 0 \leq i \leq n$, and these are treated as input to a non-linear function. The non-linear function is also called the activation function or transfer function. The activation function used in ANN helps to learn the complex data patterns, without the activation function, the ANN can only act as a linear regression model. The activation function applied to the weighted sum $= \sum_{i=0}^{n} w_i x_i = w^t x$ of the vector x, which is the input vector. To make the w_0 to act as bias in s, generally, the value of x_0 is constant to 1 ($x_0=1$).

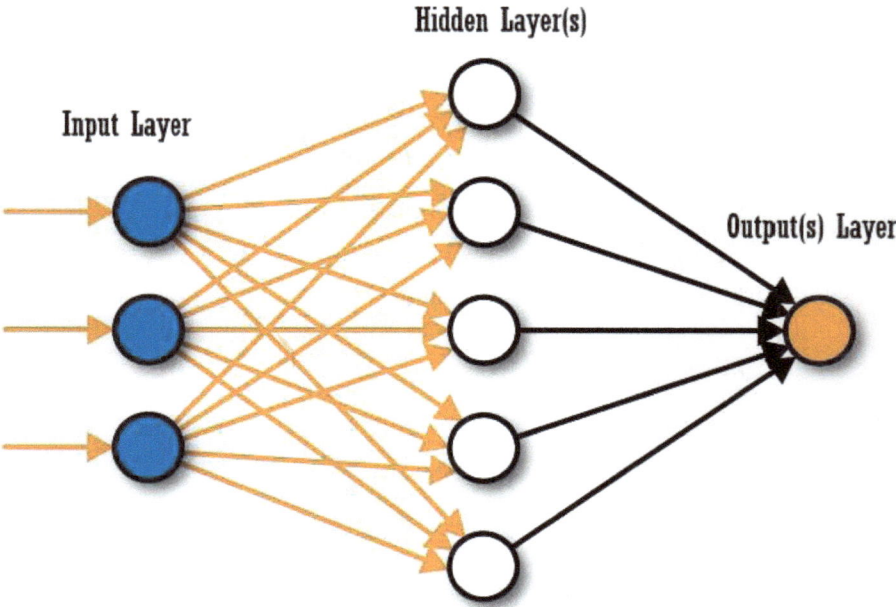

Fig. (13). Architecture of a Simple ANN with one hidden layer.

In general, three kinds of activation functions are the most common. The first is biologically inspired action potential approximations. These functions are frequently sigmoidal, and they're usually represented by a hyperbolic tangent with the symbol φx tanh (x). The second type of activation function is linear or nearly linear, such as the popular rectified linear units or ReLU [35], which are defined as φx max{x,0}.The so-called softmax function [38, 39], the third type of popular activation function, is neither scalar nor uses a weighted sum of the input variables. Instead, it uses the Boltzmann distribution φx exi∑i=1nexi to simulate a probability distribution for k different outcomes or classes.

For all neurons in the network, sigmoidal activation functions have traditionally been the most preferred choice. They're mostly employed in the final output layer nowadays. The fundamental rationale for this approach is that sigmoidal activation functions saturate readily into either an on- or off-state when gradients vanish during gradient-based training. As a result, learning such functions is difficult. As a result, the default activation function for deep network inner layers is typically a ReLUs version, whereas the output layer is controlled by (actually) linear, sigmoidal, or softmax functions [32].

Convolutional Neural Network (CNN)

The accuracy in object detection and classification has touched an ultra-high pick in the last few years due to the advancement of deep learning and especially convolutional networks [53]. In CNN the artificial neurons are responsible to extract the features from the small part of the input image, the small part is also called the receptive field. This feature extraction is based on the working principle of the visual mechanism of living being, where a small portion of the visual field is focused by the cell in the visual cortex [50]. The architecture of CNN is shown in Fig. (**14**).

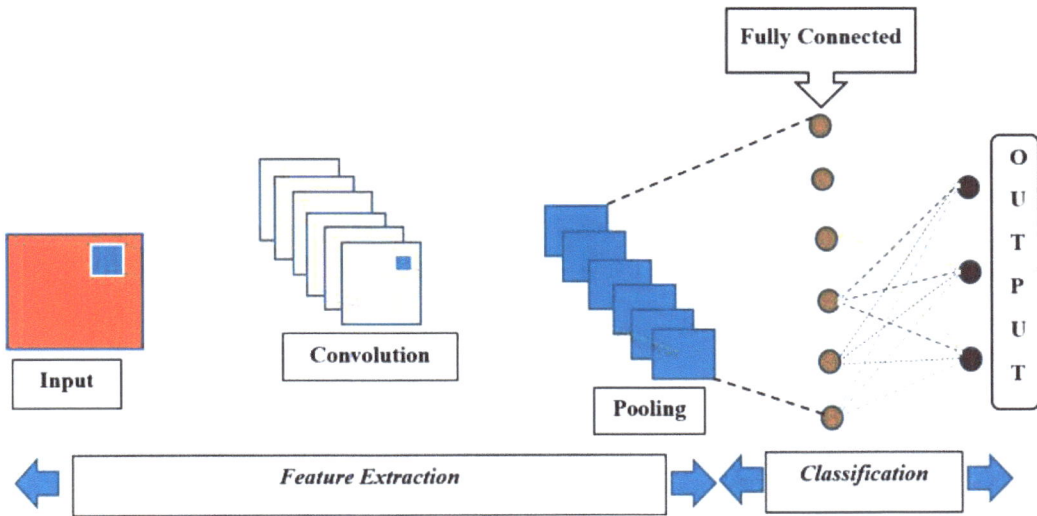

Fig. (14). Workflow diagram of Convolutional Neural Network (CNN).

Training a CNN using gene-expression data entails not just rearranging the data to give it structure so that convolutional filters may take advantage of local information patterns, but also coping with the dimensionality problem that genomics data entails. Training a CNN architecture—or, more broadly, a DL model—with a small set of samples containing a large number of features (*i.e.* N > M) might result in significant over-fitting. Several ways have been presented in the literature to address the huge imbalance between the number of samples and characteristics, which can be grouped into two main categories: data augmentation (DA) and transfer-learning (TL) procedures.

Deep Neural Network (DNN)

In recent years, deep neural network architectures such as convolutional and long short-term memory networks have grown in popularity as machine learning tools. The availability of increased computer resources, more data, new techniques for training deep models, and easy-to-use frameworks for neural network installation and training are the driving forces behind this advancement.

Deep networks are made up of numerous artificial neurons organized in a common topology. The neurons are conceptually structured into layers, with the output of one layer feeding into (at least) one other layer. Hidden layers are those that are underneath the final output layer as shown in Fig. (**15**).

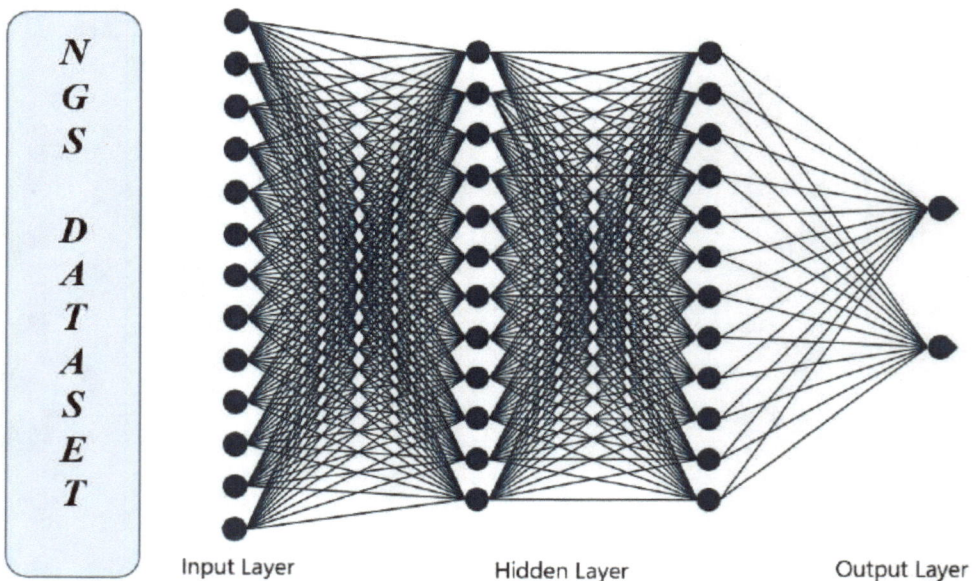

Fig. (15). Architecture of Deep Neural Network.

Feedforward Neural Network (FNN)

An input layer, a hidden layer, and an output layer are the three layers that form the FNN architecture. The predictions are generated by the output layer, which accepts the input feature vector. The prediction model must be captured by the hidden layer. Each layer is made up of several nodes, and each node in one layer connects to the nodes in the next layer as shown in Fig. (**16**).

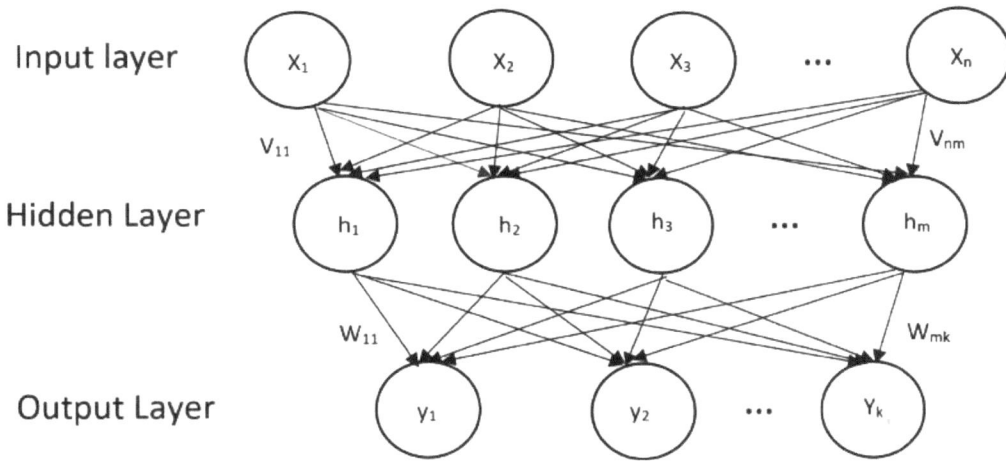

Fig. (16). FNN architecture with N input node, m hidden node, and k output node.

The weights v_{ij} and w_{ij} between the ith node in one layer and the jth node in the next layer are used to connect the nodes. Activation functions are used to process the input values, which are computed as the weighted sum of values supplied from the preceding layer.

The following are the two most commonly utilized activation functions:

$$\emptyset(v_i) = \tanh(v_i)$$

$$\emptyset(v_i) = (1 + e^{v_i})^{-1}$$

Where {v_i is the weighted sum of the inputs}

The former hyperbolic tangent function has values between -1 and 1, while the latter logistic function has values between 0 and 1. Radial basis activation functions are also used in some situations. Adjusting the connection weight values to minimize the prediction error on training data is how the FNN-based prediction model is learned. The observations are indicated by {y_i} for a given input feature vector {x_i}.

The FNN's purpose is to discover a function:$=X \rightarrow Y$, it describes the relationship between inputs X and observations Y. A cost function C=[(f(xi-yi))2] is used to evaluate the merit of function f. The cost function for a training dataset with n samples is

$$C = \sum_{i=1}^{n} \frac{[(f(x_i - y_i)]^2}{n}$$

A backpropagation algorithm is used to alter the link weights based on the amount of error associated with the network's outputs concerning the intended outcome (cost function). The n input feature vectors are fed several times (each presentation of the whole training dataset is referred to as an epoch) until the weight values do not change or the cost function has reached the desired value. In protein bioinformatics, FNN is the most extensively used of the NN designs [32].

Recurrent Neural Network (RNN)

A recurrent neural network (RNN) is a variant of a feed-forward neural network (FNN). In this scenario, a "context" layer is added, which keeps information consistent between observations. A fresh feature vector is fed into the input layer with each iteration. In the next iteration, the previous contents of the hidden layer are copied to the context layer and then fed back into the hidden layer. The detailed architecture of RNN is shown in Fig. (**17**).

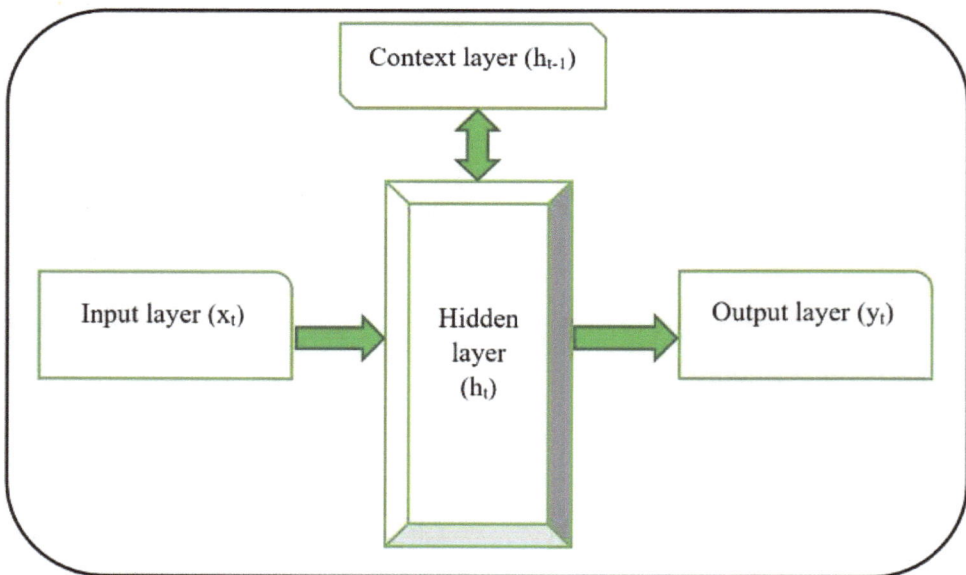

Context layer (h_{t-1})

Input layer (x_t)   Hidden layer (h_t)   Output layer (y_t)

Fig. (17). RNN's architecture. RNN has an input layer, a hidden layer, and an output layer, the same as FNN.

The RNN operations are as follows when an input feature vector is fed into the input layer:

1. Paste the values of the input vectors into the input nodes.

2. Compute hidden node activations based on net input from input nodes and context layer nodes.

3. Calculate the activation of output nodes.

4. Backpropagation process is used to calculate the new weight values.

5. In the context layer, copy the updated hidden node weights.

The normal backpropagation technique is used to learn the weight values since the trainable weights, that is, weights between the input and hidden layers and between the hidden and output layers, are feedforward only. In calculating the cost function, the weights between the context and hidden layers play a crucial role. They get error values from hidden nodes, hence they are dependent on the error at the hidden nodes in the tth iteration. During the RNN model's training, we take into account the gradient of a cost (error) function, which is determined by the activations in both the current and prior iterations.

RNN is widely used to predict protein structure, including the secondary structure and content, contact maps, structural contacts, structural domain boundaries, and specific types of local structures such as beta-turns [9].

SIGNIFICANT GENE IDENTIFICATION AND ANNOTATION

Fig. (**18**) depicts the blueprint for major gene selection utilizing multiple DL approaches. The sequence generated by the sequencer is fed to the mapping stage, which only considers the mapped reads for further processing. The sequence file with selected reads is then converted into FASTA/bam files and passed on to the next stage of analysis. The next step is to choose significant features (genes) and apply several DL algorithms to the input NGS dataset.

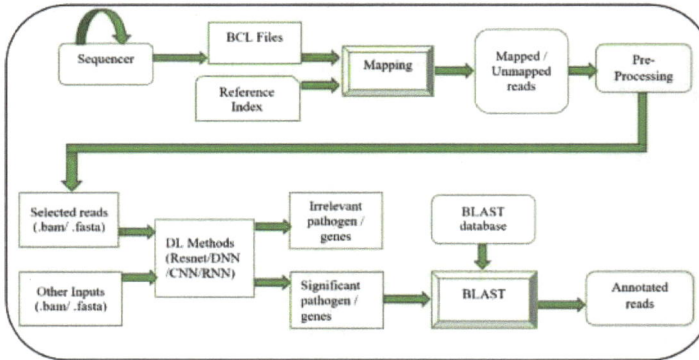

Fig. (18). Blueprint of hybrid DL model for NGS data analysis and significant gene identification and annotation.

SUMMARY OF DL METHODS USED FOR NGS DATA ANALYSIS

There are various DL techniques used so far for biomedical NGS data analysis. Table (**3**) lists the different DL approaches that were utilized to analyze the NGS data. Fig. (**19**) depicts the use of several DL approaches for NGS data in various disciplines such as genomics, medical imaging, biomedical data, and infectious disease analysis. It is observed that the DL techniques used for various application areas of biomedical research like transcriptomics, metagenomics, epigenetics, and variant calling are produced more accurate and biologically significant results. Most importantly the DL models are robust and show great potential while dealing with NGS data analysis. Thus, DL approaches are used in almost all areas of biomedical research, and this trend is growing exponentially day by day.

Table 3. Summarization of DL methods applied on various biomedical research areas.

S. No.	Methods	Architecture	Framework	Application Area
1	DCA [54]	AE	Tensorflow/Keras	
2	DeepImpute [55]	MLP	Tensorflow/Keras	
3	sclGain [56]	GAN	PyTorch	
4	scDeepCluster [57]	AE	Tensorflow/Keras	Transcriptomics
5	scScope [58]	AE	Tensorflow	
6	scvis [59]	AE	Tensorflow	
7	AutoImpute [60]	AE	Tensorflow	

(Table 3) cont.....

S. No.	Methods	Architecture	Framework	Application Area
8	GeNet [61]	CNN	Tensorflow	
9	DeepMicrobes [62]	LSTM	Tensorflow	
10	Seq2species [63]	CNN	Tensorflow	Metagenomics
11	Meta^2 [61]	MIL	NA	
12	DanQ [64]	CNN/LSTM	Tensorflow/Keras	
13	DeepBind [65]	CNN	Python/C++	
14	DeepHistone [66]	CNN	PyTorch	
15	DeepSEA [65]	CNN	Torch	Epigenetics
16	DeepLift [67]	CNN	Tensorflow/Keras	Epigenetics
17	DeepCpG [68]	RNN/CNN	Theano/Keras	
18	FunDMDeep-m^{6}A [69]	CNN	Tensorflow/Keras	
19	MRCNN [70]	CNN	Tensorflow/Keras	
20	CNNScoreVariance [71]	CNN	Tensorflow	
21	Deep Variant [72]	CNN	Tensorflow/Nucleus	
22	Clair [73]	RNN	Tensorflow	
23	Clairvoyante [74]	CNN	Tensorflow	Variant calling
24	DeepSC [75]	CNN	Tensorflow	
25	NeuSomatic [75]	CNN	Pytorch	

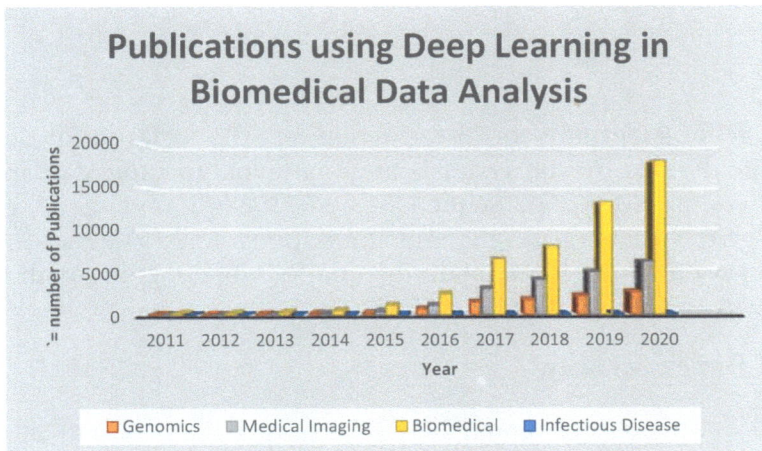

Fig. (19). Studies addressing deep learning in medicinal applications that have been published.

CRITICAL OBSERVATION

ML and DL techniques are popular among biomedical researchers due to their potential to deal with NGS data analysis. However, ML methods can determine if single reads are from more distant, undiscovered viruses, but they require relatively large input sequences and processed data from a completed sequencing run. Because incomplete sequences include less information, there is a trade-off between sequencing time and detection accuracy when using them. However, the hybrid deep learning methods can efficiently identify the features (pathogen/genes) from the complex dataset (NGS) of various infectious diseases. Apart from this, the hybrid DL methods may be implemented beyond the NGS datasets to any other dataset to achieve the desired result without affecting the accuracy. In the case of traditional ML, however, the accuracy is decreased / constant while applied over complex datasets like NGS [76].

During the literature, it is found that the following valid points are associated with NGS data analysis and should be taken care of.

Data Volume

The major issue associated with NGS data is the size of the dataset, it's huge and complex. The growing number of molecular approaches that transition into an experimental data set generated by NGS is incredible, and it acts as a significant 'big' multiplier. The heterogeneous structure of NGS data also gives the researcher a new challenge to deal with such complex data and its pre-processing [77].

Data Quality

As we deal with subgroups of the population, the data in most genomic applications are diverse. At the system's biology level, genomic data includes (i) gene or non-coding transcript sequencing, (ii) quantitative gene expression profiles, (iii) gene variants, (iv) genome alternations, and (v) gene interactions [78]. So, it is very difficult to maintain the quality while dealing with these data from one state to another.

The Curse of Dimensionality

The so-called "curse of dimensionality" of omics data is the most egregious artificial intelligence constraint in genomics. Even though genomics is a massive data domain in terms of volume, genomic datasets typically contain a significant number of variables and a limited number of samples.

Interpretability

The interpretation of the model is one of the primary challenges with DL designs in general. If one wants to extract the causation relationship between the data and the output, it is difficult to understand the rational and learned patterns due to the structure of the DL models.

Domain Complexity

There is no universally applicable strategy, so to apply DL approaches, we need to be problem-specific. Another drawback of DL is its increased complexity, which affects both model design and the processing environment required [78].

Biological Annotation

External model validation and clinical trials are required before ML models may be used in clinical practice. While clinical outcomes (*e.g.*, survival, length of stay in the hospital, duration of antimicrobial therapy, rate of complications, readmission rate) are vital to establishing, insights into how doctors will integrate ML into clinical practice are also required [29].

The DL models are well-known and can deal with NGS data analysis and generate significant results at a low cost. However, for the analysis of NGS data from various biomedical research areas, a suitable DL model based on the desired conclusion (result) is necessary.

The key functionality of DL methods in various fields of biomedical research are listed below,

- Deep learning (DNN) models can handle a large amount of data in a variety of formats. It's a fantastic tool to utilize [7].
- In various DL research, completely interconnected NN and CNN models were used to predict cancer prognosis and performed well.
- Current deep-learning models in biomedical research, including genomes, cancer prognosis, and infectious disease analyses, still need to be tested and validated in larger datasets [7].

Apart from the advancement of ML and DL techniques, there are still some open issues for the researchers:

i. When processing massive amounts of NGS data, there are still efficiency issues.
ii. It's critical to understand how to extract sequence characteristics from next-

generation sequences and how to construct an appropriate quality measure to assess sequence quality [51].

iii. According to the relevant background knowledge and sequence features, appropriate ML and DL algorithms for NGS data should be built for various biological needs [79].

CONCLUSION AND FUTURE SCOPE

The successful story of DL in the field of language processing and computer vision has inspired many researchers to apply these methods in the field of bioinformatics. Deep neural network topologies have reawakened interest in machine learning sectors like image and speech recognition, but it is only slowly extending into biology and bioinformatics. One possible reason for this is a dearth of examples or code templates targeted to bioinformatics challenges, as well as the perception that deep learning methods are difficult to implement and train due to their computational complexity. Whole genome and exome sequencing are associated with high costs and a significant computing burden, as well as difficult data interpretation. Data interpretation is a serious impediment to widespread clinical sequencing by NGS for cancer diagnosis and therapy. Large servers and trained bioinformaticians are required for big data administration and interpretation.

Traditional analysis tools, on the other hand, are inefficient in terms of computing time as data volumes grow, and how to design efficient calculation methods is an important research topic. Mining efficiency will be considerably improved by combining distributed computing and parallel computing. Despite its potential, implementing AI in the healthcare sector still faces numerous challenges. Big data and prices are increasing as a result of the automated computation. Due to their reliance on specialized computational requirements for fast data processing, AI systems can be costly. When working with biological sequencing data, how the data is represented numerically has an impact on model performance. With developments in AI technology, AI in healthcare and infectious disease analysis will greatly benefit from addressing these hurdles and constraints.

CONSENT FOR PUBLICATION

Not applicable.

CONFLICT OF INTEREST

The authors declare no conflict of interest, financial or otherwise.

ACKNOWLEDGEMENT

Declared none.

REFERENCES

[1]   L. Koumakis, "Deep learning models in genomics; are we there yet?", *Comput. Struct. Biotechnol. J.,* vol. 18, pp. 1466-1473, 2020.
        [http://dx.doi.org/10.1016/j.csbj.2020.06.017] [PMID: 32637044]

[2]   U.H. Trivedi, T. Cézard, S. Bridgett, A. Montazam, J. Nichols, M. Blaxter, and K. Gharbi, "Quality control of next-generation sequencing data without a reference", *Front. Genet.,* vol. 5, no. MAY, p. 111, 2014.
        [http://dx.doi.org/10.3389/fgene.2014.00111] [PMID: 24834071]

[3]   S. Chae, S. Kwon, and D. Lee, "Predicting infectious disease using deep learning and big data", *Int. J. Environ. Res. Public Health,* vol. 15, no. 8, p. 1596, 2018.
        [http://dx.doi.org/10.3390/ijerph15081596] [PMID: 30060525]

[4]   G. López-García, J.M. Jerez, L. Franco, and F.J. Veredas, "Transfer learning with convolutional neural networks for cancer survival prediction using gene-expression data", *PLoS One,* vol. 15, no. 3, p. e0230536, 2020.
        [http://dx.doi.org/10.1371/journal.pone.0230536] [PMID: 32214348]

[5]   J. Lewis, M. Raff, and K. Roberts, *Molecular Biology of the Cell (4th Ed)*, 2002.
        [http://dx.doi.org/10.1080/00219266.2002.9655847]

[6]   S.C. Schuster, "Next-generation sequencing transforms today's biology", *Nat. Methods,* vol. 5, no. 1, pp. 16-18, 2008.
        [http://dx.doi.org/10.1038/nmeth1156] [PMID: 18165802]

[7]   B. Schmidt, and A. Hildebrandt, "Deep learning in next-generation sequencing", *Drug Discov. Today,* vol. 26, no. 1, pp. 173-180, 2021.
        [http://dx.doi.org/10.1016/j.drudis.2020.10.002] [PMID: 33059075]

[8]   T. Eltaeib, and A. Mahmood, "Differential evolution: A survey and analysis", *Appl. Sci. (Basel),* vol. 8, no. 10, p. 1945, 2018.
        [http://dx.doi.org/10.3390/app8101945]

[9]   J. Cheng, A. Z. Randall, M. J. Sweredoski, and P. Baldi, *SCRATCH: A protein structure and structural feature prediction server g these hurdles and constrain,* vol. 33, no. SUPPL. 2,, pp. 72-76, 2005.
        [http://dx.doi.org/10.1093/nar/gki396]

[10]   K. Mahmood, J. Orabi, P.S. Kristensen, P. Sarup, L.N. Jørgensen, and A. Jahoor, "De novo transcriptome assembly, functional annotation, and expression profiling of rye (*Secale cereale* L.) hybrids inoculated with ergot (*Claviceps purpurea*)". *Sci. Rep.,* vol. 10, no. 1, p. 13475, 2020.
        [http://dx.doi.org/10.1038/s41598-020-70406-2] [PMID: 32778722]

[11]   Z. Wang, M. Gerstein, and M. Snyder, "The transcriptome is the complete set of transcripts in a cell, and their quantity", *Nat. Rev. Genet.,* vol. 10, pp. 57-63, 2009.
        [http://dx.doi.org/10.1038/nrg2484] [PMID: 19015660]

[12]   https://www.bioconductor.org/'https://www.bioconductor.org/

[13]   https://biopython.org/'https://biopython.org/

[14]   https://bioconda.github.io/'https://bioconda.github.io/

[15]   D.S.K. Nayak, S. Mahapatra, and T. Swarnkar, *'Gene Selection and Enrichment for Microarray Data—A Comparative Network Based Approach.',* *Prog. Adv. Comput. Intell. Eng.* Springer: Singapore, 2018, pp. 417-427.
        [http://dx.doi.org/10.1007/978-981-10-6875-1_41]

[16]   M. Barba, H. Czosnek, and A. Hadidi, "Historical perspective, development and applications of next-generation sequencing in plant virology", *Viruses,* vol. 6, no. 1, pp. 106-136, 2014.
[http://dx.doi.org/10.3390/v6010106] [PMID: 24399207]

[17]   A. Yang, W. Zhang, J. Wang, K. Yang, Y. Han, and L. Zhang, "Review on the Application of Machine Learning Algorithms in the Sequence Data Mining of DNA", *Front. Bioeng. Biotechnol.,* vol. 8, no. September, p. 1032, 2020.
[http://dx.doi.org/10.3389/fbioe.2020.01032] [PMID: 33015010]

[18]   K. Fukushima, "A neural network model for the mechanism of selective attention in visual pattern recognition", *Syst. Comput. Jpn.,* vol. 18, no. 1, pp. 102-113, 1987.
[http://dx.doi.org/10.1002/scj.4690180110]

[19]   https://www.labiotech.eu/interview/next-generation-sequencing-n-ck-mccooke/'https://www.labiotech.eu/interview/next-generation-sequencing-nick-mccooke/

[20]   M.L. Metzker, "Sequencing technologies — the next generation", *Nat. Rev. Genet.,* vol. 11, no. 1, pp. 31-46, 2010.
[http://dx.doi.org/10.1038/nrg2626] [PMID: 19997069]

[21]   S.M. Huse, J.A. Huber, H.G. Morrison, M.L. Sogin, and D. Welch, "Accuracy and quality of massively parallel DNA pyrosequencing", *Genome Biol.,* vol. 8, no. 7, p. R143, 2007.
[http://dx.doi.org/10.1186/gb-2007-8-7-r143] [PMID: 17659080]

[22]   L.M. Bragg, G. Stone, M.K. Butler, P. Hugenholtz, and G.W. Tyson, "Shining a light on dark sequencing: characterising errors in Ion Torrent PGM data", *PLOS Comput. Biol.,* vol. 9, no. 4, p. e1003031, 2013.
[http://dx.doi.org/10.1371/journal.pcbi.1003031] [PMID: 23592973]

[23]   D.S. Horner, G. Pavesi, T. Castrignanò, P.D. De Meo, S. Liuni, M. Sammeth, E. Picardi, and G. Pesole, "Bioinformatics approaches for genomics and post genomics applications of next-generation sequencing", *Brief. Bioinform.,* vol. 11, no. 2, pp. 181-197, 2010.
[http://dx.doi.org/10.1093/bib/bbp046] [PMID: 19864250]

[24]   M.C.F. Thomsen, H. Hasman, H. Westh, H. Kaya, and O. Lund, "RUCS: rapid identification of PCR primers for unique core sequences", *Bioinformatics,* vol. 33, no. 24, pp. 3917-3921, 2017.
[http://dx.doi.org/10.1093/bioinformatics/btx526] [PMID: 28968748]

[25]   https://biojulia.net/'https://biojulia.net/

[26]   https://github.com/rust-bio/rust-bio'https://github.com/rust-bio/rust-bio

[27]   A. Pati, M. Parhi, and B.K. Pattanayak, "IDMS: An integrated decision making system for heart disease prediction", *1st Odisha Int. Conf. Electr. Power Eng. Commun. Comput. Technol. ODICON 2021,* 2021.
[http://dx.doi.org/10.1109/ODICON50556.2021.9428958]

[28]   A. P. B, M. Parhi, and B. K. Pattanayak, 'IADP : An Integrated Approach for Diabetes', 2022.

[29]   E. H. Weissler, 'Correction to: The role of machine learning in clinical research: transforming the future of evidence generation (Trials, (2021), 22, 1, (537), 10.1186/s13063-021-05489-x)', Trials, vol. 22, no. 1, pp. 1–15, 2021.
[http://dx.doi.org/10.1186/s13063-021-05489-x]

[30]   D.T. Dinh, B. Le, P. Fournier-Viger, and V.N. Huynh, "An efficient algorithm for mining periodic high-utility sequential patterns", *Appl. Intell.,* vol. 48, no. 12, pp. 4694-4714, 2018.
[http://dx.doi.org/10.1007/s10489-018-1227-x]

[31]   M. Zihayat, H. Davoudi, and A. An, *Mining significant high utility gene regulation sequential patterns BMC Syst. Biol,* vol. 6, pp. 1-14, 2017.
[http://dx.doi.org/10.1186/s12918-017-0475-4]

[32]   Y. Park, D. Heider, and A.C. Hauschild, "Integrative analysis of next-generation sequencing for next-

generation cancer research toward artificial intelligence", *Cancers (Basel),* vol. 13, no. 13, p. 3148, 2021.
[http://dx.doi.org/10.3390/cancers13133148] [PMID: 34202427]

[33] M.A. Ambusaidi, X. He, P. Nanda, and Z. Tan, "Building an intrusion detection system using a filter-based feature selection algorithm", *IEEE Trans. Comput.,* vol. 65, no. 10, pp. 2986-2998, 2016.
[http://dx.doi.org/10.1109/TC.2016.2519914]

[34] D. S. K. Mohapatra, D., Tripathy, J., Mohanty, K. K., & Nayak, 'Interpretation of Optimized Hyper Parameters in Associative Rule Learning using Eclat and Apriori', *2021 5th Int. Conf. Comput. Methodol. Commun.,* vol. In 2021 5t, pp. 879–882, 2021.

[35] L. Yu, and H. Liu, "Redundancy based feature selection for microarray data", *KDD-2004 - Proc. Tenth ACM SIGKDD Int. Conf. Knowl. Discov. Data Min,* no. 2, pp. 737-742, 2004.
[http://dx.doi.org/10.1145/1014052.1014149]

[36] B.M. Sabbar, and M.R. Sulyman, "Analysising of DNA Microarray data using principle component analysis (PCA)", *J. Theor. Appl. Inf. Technol.,* vol. 70, no. 1, pp. 130-139, 2014.

[37] J.K. Peeters, *Microarray Bioinformatics and Applications in Oncology.* 2008.

[38] S. Shukor, A. Tamayo, L. Tosi, H.B. Larman, and B. Parekkadan, "Quantitative assessment of LASSO probe assembly and long-read multiplexed cloning", *BMC Biotechnol.,* vol. 19, no. 1, p. 50, 2019.
[http://dx.doi.org/10.1186/s12896-019-0547-1] [PMID: 31340783]

[39] D.T. Dinh, V.N. Huynh, and S. Sriboonchitta, "Clustering mixed numerical and categorical data with missing values", *Inf. Sci.,* vol. 571, pp. 418-442, 2021.
[http://dx.doi.org/10.1016/j.ins.2021.04.076]

[40] K. Chaudhary, O.B. Poirion, L. Lu, and L.X. Garmire, "Deep learning–based multi-omics integration robustly predicts survival in liver cancer", *Clin. Cancer Res.,* vol. 24, no. 6, pp. 1248-1259, 2018.
[http://dx.doi.org/10.1158/1078-0432.CCR-17-0853] [PMID: 28982688]

[41] F. Gao, W. Wang, M. Tan, L. Zhu, Y. Zhang, E. Fessler, L. Vermeulen, and X. Wang, "DeepCC: a novel deep learning-based framework for cancer molecular subtype classification", *Oncogenesis,* vol. 8, no. 9, p. 44, 2019.
[http://dx.doi.org/10.1038/s41389-019-0157-8] [PMID: 31420533]

[42] X. Zeng, S. Zhu, X. Liu, Y. Zhou, R. Nussinov, and F. Cheng, "deepDR: a network-based deep learning approach to *in silico* drug repositioning". *Bioinformatics,* vol. 35, no. 24, pp. 5191-5198, 2019.
[http://dx.doi.org/10.1093/bioinformatics/btz418] [PMID: 31116390]

[43] N.T. Issa, V. Stathias, S. Schürer, and S. Dakshanamurthy, *Machine and deep learning approaches for cancer drug repurposing,* 2021.
[http://dx.doi.org/10.1016/j.semcancer.2019.12.011]

[44] C. Cao, F. Liu, H. Tan, D. Song, W. Shu, W. Li, Y. Zhou, X. Bo, and Z. Xie, "Deep Learning and Its Applications in Biomedicine", *Genomics Proteomics Bioinformatics,* vol. 16, no. 1, pp. 17-32, 2018.
[http://dx.doi.org/10.1016/j.gpb.2017.07.003] [PMID: 29522900]

[45] A.J. Holden, *Reducing the Dimensionality of,* 2006.

[46] M. Längkvist, L. Karlsson, and A. Loutfi, "A review of unsupervised feature learning and deep learning for time-series modeling", *Pattern Recognit. Lett.,* vol. 42, no. 1, pp. 11-24, 2014.
[http://dx.doi.org/10.1016/j.patrec.2014.01.008]

[47] B.A. Krizhevsky, I. Sutskever, and G.E. Hinton, "ImageNet classification with deep convolutional neural networks", *Commun. ACM,* vol. 60, no. 6, pp. 84-90, 2012.
[http://dx.doi.org/10.1145/3065386]

[48] E. Asgari, and M.R.K. Mofrad, "Continuous distributed representation of biological sequences for deep proteomics and genomics", *PLoS One,* vol. 10, no. 11, p. e0141287, 2015.

[http://dx.doi.org/10.1371/journal.pone.0141287] [PMID: 26555596]

[49] R. Miotto, F. Wang, S. Wang, X. Jiang, and J.T. Dudley, "Deep learning for healthcare: review, opportunities and challenges", *Brief. Bioinform.,* vol. 19, no. 6, pp. 1236-1246, 2018.
[http://dx.doi.org/10.1093/bib/bbx044] [PMID: 28481991]

[50] D.C. Cires, U. Meier, J. Masci, and L.M. Gambardella, *Flexible, High Performance Convolutional Neural Networks for Image Classification.* Proc. Twenty-Second Int. Jt. Conf. Artif. Intell. Flex, 2013, pp.   1237-1242.   [Online].   Available: https://www.aaai.org/ocs/index.php/IJCAI/IJCAI11/paper/viewFile/3098/3425

[51] F. Bewicke-Copley, E. Arjun Kumar, G. Palladino, K. Korfi, and J. Wang, "Applications and analysis of targeted genomic sequencing in cancer studies", *Comput. Struct. Biotechnol. J.,* vol. 17, pp. 1348-1359, 2019.
[http://dx.doi.org/10.1016/j.csbj.2019.10.004] [PMID: 31762958]

[52] D.H. Hubel, and T. Wiesel, *'And functional architecture in the cat's visual cortex From the Neurophysiolojy Laboratory, Department of Pharmacology central nervous system is the great diversity of its cell types and inter- receptive fields of a more complex type (Part I) and to.* Most, 1962, pp. 106-154.

[53] R.H.R. Hahnloser, R. Sarpeshkar, M.A. Mahowald, R.J. Douglas, and H.S. Seung, "Digital selection and analogue amplification coexist in a cortex-inspired silicon circuit", *Nature,* vol. 405, no. 6789, pp. 947-951, 2000.
[http://dx.doi.org/10.1038/35016072] [PMID: 10879535]

[54] D. Talwar, A. Mongia, D. Sengupta, and A. Majumdar, "AutoImpute: Autoencoder based imputation of single-cell RNA-seq data", *Sci. Rep.,* vol. 8, no. 1, p. 16329, 2018.
[http://dx.doi.org/10.1038/s41598-018-34688-x] [PMID: 30397240]

[55] T. Tian, J. Wan, Q. Song, and Z. Wei, "Clustering single-cell RNA-seq data with a model-based deep learning approach", *Nat. Mach. Intell.,* vol. 1, no. 4, pp. 191-198, 2019.
[http://dx.doi.org/10.1038/s42256-019-0037-0]

[56] C. Arisdakessian, O. Poirion, B. Yunits, X. Zhu, and L.X. Garmire, "DeepImpute: An accurate, fast and scalable deep neural network method to impute single-cell RNA-Seq data", *bioRxiv,* pp. 1-14, 2018.
[http://dx.doi.org/10.1101/353607]

[57] J. Ding, A. Condon, and S.P. Shah, "Interpretable dimensionality reduction of single cell transcriptome data with deep generative models", *Nat. Commun.,* vol. 9, no. 1, p. 2002, 2018.
[http://dx.doi.org/10.1038/s41467-018-04368-5] [PMID: 29784946]

[58] G. Eraslan, L.M. Simon, M. Mircea, N.S. Mueller, and F.J. Theis, "Single-cell RNA-seq denoising using a deep count autoencoder", *Nat. Commun.,* vol. 10, no. 1, p. 390, 2019.
[http://dx.doi.org/10.1038/s41467-018-07931-2] [PMID: 30674886]

[59] Y. Deng, F. Bao, Q. Dai, L.F. Wu, and S.J. Altschuler, "Massive single-cell RNA-seq analysis and imputation *via* deep learning", *bioRxiv,* pp. 1-11.
[http://dx.doi.org/10.1101/315556]

[60] Y. Xu, Z. Zhang, L. You, J. Liu, Z. Fan, and X. Zhou, "scIGANs: single-cell RNA-seq imputation using generative adversarial networks", *Nucleic Acids Res..* vol. 48, no. 15, p. E85, 2020.
[http://dx.doi.org/10.1093/nar/gkaa506] [PMID: 32588900]

[61] M. Rojas-Carulla, I. Tolstikhin, G. Luque, N. Youngblut, R. Ley, and B. Schölkopf, "GeNet: Deep Representations for Metagenomics", arXiv:1901.11015, 2019.
[http://dx.doi.org/10.1101/537795]

[62] Q. Liang, P.W. Bible, Y. Liu, B. Zou, and L. Wei, "DeepMicrobes: taxonomic classification for metagenomics with deep learning", *NAR Genom. Bioinform.,* vol. 2, no. 1, pp. 1-13, 2020.
[http://dx.doi.org/10.1093/nargab/lqaa009] [PMID: 33575556]

[63]   A. Busia, "A deep learning approach to pattern recognition for short DNA sequences", *bioRxiv,* pp. 1-12.
        [http://dx.doi.org/10.1101/353474]

[64]   D. Quang, and X. Xie, "DanQ: a hybrid convolutional and recurrent deep neural network for quantifying the function of DNA sequences", *Nucleic Acids Res.,* vol. 44, no. 11, p. e107, 2016.
        [http://dx.doi.org/10.1093/nar/gkw226] [PMID: 27084946]

[65]   J. Zhou, and O.G. Troyanskaya, "Predicting effects of noncoding variants with deep learning–based sequence model", *Nat. Methods,* vol. 12, no. 10, pp. 931-934, 2015.
        [http://dx.doi.org/10.1038/nmeth.3547] [PMID: 26301843]

[66]   Q. Yin, M. Wu, Q. Liu, H. Lv, and R. Jiang, *DeepHistone: A deep learning approach to predicting histone modifications BMC Genomics,,* vol. 20, no. 2, 2019.
        [http://dx.doi.org/10.1186/s12864-019-5489-4]

[67]   Ž. Avsec, M. Weilert, A. Shrikumar, S. Krueger, A. Alexandari, K. Dalal, R. Fropf, C. McAnany, J. Gagneur, A. Kundaje, and J. Zeitlinger, "Base-resolution models of transcription-factor binding reveal soft motif syntax", *Nat. Genet.,* vol. 53, no. 3, pp. 354-366, 2021.
        [http://dx.doi.org/10.1038/s41588-021-00782-6] [PMID: 33603233]

[68]   C. Angermueller, H.J. Lee, W. Reik, and O. Stegle, "DeepCpG: accurate prediction of single-cell DNA methylation states using deep learning", *Genome Biol.,* vol. 18, no. 1, p. 67, 2017.
        [http://dx.doi.org/10.1186/s13059-017-1189-z] [PMID: 28077169]

[69]   S.Y. Zhang, S.W. Zhang, X.N. Fan, T. Zhang, J. Meng, and Y. Huang, "FunDMDeep-m6A: identification and prioritization of functional differential m6A methylation genes", *Bioinformatics,* vol. 35, no. 14, pp. i90-i98, 2019.
        [http://dx.doi.org/10.1093/bioinformatics/btz316] [PMID: 31510685]

[70]   Q. Tian, J. Zou, J. Tang, Y. Fang, Z. Yu, and S. Fan, *MRCNN: A deep learning model for regression of genome-wide DNA methylation BMC Genomics,,* vol. 20, no. 2, pp. 1-10, 2019.
        [http://dx.doi.org/10.1186/s12864-019-5488-5]

[71]   S. Friedman, L. Gauthier, Y. Farjoun, and E. Banks, "Lean and deep models for more accurate filtering of SNP and INDEL variant calls", *Bioinformatics,* vol. 36, no. 7, pp. 2060-2067, 2020.
        [http://dx.doi.org/10.1093/bioinformatics/btz901] [PMID: 31830260]

[72]   R. Poplin, P.C. Chang, D. Alexander, S. Schwartz, T. Colthurst, A. Ku, D. Newburger, J. Dijamco, N. Nguyen, P.T. Afshar, S.S. Gross, L. Dorfman, C.Y. McLean, and M.A. DePristo, "A universal SNP and small-indel variant caller using deep neural networks", *Nat. Biotechnol.,* vol. 36, no. 10, pp. 983-987, 2018.
        [http://dx.doi.org/10.1038/nbt.4235] [PMID: 30247488]

[73]   R. Luo, C-L. Wong, Y-S. Wong, C-I. Tang, C-M. Liu, C-M. Leung, and T-W. Lam, "Exploring the limit of using a deep neural network on pileup data for germline variant calling", *Nat. Mach. Intell.,* vol. 2, no. 4, pp. 220-227, 2020.
        [http://dx.doi.org/10.1038/s42256-020-0167-4]

[74]   R. Luo, F.J. Sedlazeck, T.W. Lam, and M.C. Schatz, "A multi-task convolutional deep neural network for variant calling in single molecule sequencing", *Nat. Commun.,* vol. 10, no. 1, p. 998, 2019.
        [http://dx.doi.org/10.1038/s41467-019-09025-z] [PMID: 30824707]

[75]   S.M.E. Sahraeian, R. Liu, B. Lau, K. Podesta, M. Mohiyuddin, and H.Y.K. Lam, "Deep convolutional neural networks for accurate somatic mutation detection", *Nat. Commun.,* vol. 10, no. 1, p. 1041, 2019.
        [http://dx.doi.org/10.1038/s41467-019-09027-x] [PMID: 30833567]

[76]   W. Zhu, L. Xie, J. Han, and X. Guo, "The application of deep learning in cancer prognosis prediction", *Cancers (Basel),* vol. 12, no. 3, p. 603, 2020.
        [http://dx.doi.org/10.3390/cancers12030603] [PMID: 32150991]

[77]   E.R. Mardis, "The challenges of big data", *Dis. Model. Mech.,* vol. 9, no. 5, pp. 483-485, 2016.

[http://dx.doi.org/10.1242/dmm.025585] [PMID: 27147249]

[78]   C.F. Luz, M. Vollmer, J. Decruyenaere, M.W. Nijsten, C. Glasner, and B. Sinha, "Machine learning in infection management using routine electronic health records: tools, techniques, and reporting of future technologies", *Clin. Microbiol. Infect.,* vol. 26, no. 10, pp. 1291-1299, 2020. [http://dx.doi.org/10.1016/j.cmi.2020.02.003] [PMID: 32061798]

[79]   J. Punetha, and E.P. Hoffman, "Short read (next-generation) sequencing: a tutorial with cardiomyopathy diagnostics as an exemplar", *Circ. Cardiovasc. Genet.,* vol. 6, no. 4, pp. 427-434, 2013. [http://dx.doi.org/10.1161/CIRCGENETICS.113.000085] [PMID: 23852418]

CHAPTER 10

Breast Cancer Detection Using Machine Learning Concepts

Fahmina Taranum[1,*] and **K. Sridevi**[1]

[1]*Computer Science and Engineering Department, Muffakham Jah College of Engineering and Technology, Hyderabad, India*

Abstract: Machine learning is applied in medical diagnosis to do early prediction of diseases, for increasing the possibility of recoverability around the globe. Cancer is a disease, which spreads quickly and would be difficult to control in advanced stages. The idea is to diagnose the disease at an early stage, so as to increase the chances of fast recovery. Breast cancer is common in women, and is a disease that causes the death of women in the age of fifty years or older. The purpose is to apply machine learning concepts to do early detection of disease. The system is fed with the images of all stages of cancer patients and the classification tools are used to train the system with the cases. This helps to predict the stage of cancer. After the prediction of the stage, the patient is prescribed with the medication or other appropriate treatment processes by the doctor. The right time diagnoses help to improve the prognosis and increase the chances of survival. The type of the tumour, size and its re-occurring nature need to be monitored from time to time to check it in control. The Data Mining algorithm in collaboration with Deep learning or Machine learning concepts can be used to design a system for early predictions. The proposal is to use the machine learning concepts to do performance comparison using different classifiers, such as Support Vector Machine (SVM), Decision Tree and K-Nearest Neighbour (KNN) on the Wisconsin Diagnostic Breast Cancer (WDBC) dataset [1]. The main aim of cancer detection is to classify tumours into malignant or benign, thus we use machine learning techniques to improve the accuracy of diagnosis.

The main objective is to assess the efficiency, effectiveness and correctness of the algorithm using performance metrics like Accuracy, Precision, F1 score and Recall Experimentation is done using Jupyter Notebook.

Keywords: Cancer, Classifiers, Machine Learning, WDBC.

---

[*] **Corresponding author Fahmina Taranum:** Computer Science and Engineering Department, Muffakham Jah College of Engineering and Technology, Hyderabad, India; E-mail: ftaranum@mjcollege.ac.in

INTRODUCTION

Background

Breast Cancer is a disease responsible for majority of women's deaths 50 years or older. It is the second most dangerous disease after lung cancer. The statistics provided by the World Cancer Research Fund (WCRF) in 2018, stated that a record of 626,679 deaths were reported of two million cancer cases. Breast cancer is 24.2% of all the other types of cancers found in women.

The prediction helps in recovering the disease more easily; hence either deep or machine learning approaches can be applied. The process of patient's consultation with the doctor can be arranged in an online mode for quick treatment. The recent technology supports online consultation with the doctors for senior or weak patients, who have difficulty reaching the hospital. The method for consultation fee payment is also made easier with services like PAYTM, GPAY, PhonePe and BHIM.

Undertaking Thorough Medical History

The admission process proceeds with the discussion of the patient's medical history collection process; the medical supervisor creates a record containing the medical history of the patient. The Physical examination along with the prescribed test would be performed to rule out the doubts and get a clear picture of the patient's health after diagnosis. The screening of the area is done using Magnetic resonance imaging (MRI), Ultrasound, Tissue biopsy, X-ray or manual examination by an expert. On confirming about the disease based on removal of the tissue from the infected area showing the results as cancerous, or by Sentinel node biopsy test, the patient may be forwarded through multiple examinations, if required. The hospitals must be well equipped with the facilities and machineries to conduct the diagnosis as the delay may spread the disease and deteriorate patients' condition. Avoiding all these processes by using machine learning algorithms for detecting the state as Benign or Malignant makes the job easier and would definitely increase the survival rate to some extent as the pre diagnosis has helped to control the disease on time. The screening or testing used is listed in this subsection.

Imaging Tests

Mammogram is an examination of the breast, which is a special medical testing of images extracted using a low-dose X-ray system to check the inside tissues and nerves of the breast and note any abnormal changes. Screening can be done based on symptoms like a lump in the breast, irritation in the breast epidermis, thickened parts of the breast, redness or flaky skin. The type of screening based on symptoms is named Diagnostic mammogram, otherwise screening mammogram.

Advanced Test

The use of computers to store images is a part of advanced technology named Digital mammography. These records are portable and sharable. The quality of the image is good with respect to sharpness and contrast. The 3-dimensional (3-D) breast imaging or breast to tomosynthesis is another type of advanced technology. These are known as efficient techniques as they capture images from different angles in less time. The collected information is filtered by a computer to create manifold thin section of the breast, which helps the radiologist to do accurate analysis.

Classification Using the Techniques

The machine learning tools help to declare the severalty of the case in advance. The input with multiple cases trains the system perfectly to detect any abnormalities in the initial stage itself. The prognosis and prediction of the disease are done based on ML approaches for modelling the succession of melanoma, which recognize the attributes that help guide towards accurate results. The research helps to design an efficient and fast-tracking system to categorize the type of infection into either malignant and benign class.

Dataset

Further accurate classification of benign tumours can prevent patients from undergoing additional treatments. Thus, the proper diagnosis of BC and classification of patients into cancerous or non-cancerous tumours is the major aim of research. Because of its unique advantages in critical features and analysis of complex BC datasets, machine learning (ML) is majorly used as the methodology of choice in BC pattern classification and forecast modelling. Classification and data mining algorithms are effectively used for classifying data. Especially in the medical field, where these algorithms are widely used in prediction and prognosis to make decisions. Machine learning classifiers use the patterns in the images from the huge dataset to perform testing, training and validations for producing accurate results. These complex working principles and quick execution of the testing results are benefitted over a minimized cost of medicines (as it helps to detect cancer at an early stage), upgrade healthcare and its value in rescuing lives of humans. Most of these classification techniques deliver a high degree of accuracy in the prediction of the kind and stage of tumours.

The International collaboration on cancer reporting (ICCR) works on the updates as responses to the World Health Organization (WHO) classification of cancerous tumours. Features for selection are computed from a digitized image extracted a from breast mass using a fine needle aspirate (FNA). To synchronize the ICCR, with the updates to the WHO Classification of Tumours, ICCR has developed the four datasets as listed below:

   i. Lymph nodes extracted from the breast tumours surgically.
  ii. The duct of the breast and low grade lesions have become cancerous.
 iii. Aggressive carcinoma of the breast.
 iv. Use of Neoadjuvant therapy, before the main treatment of the radical intervention, to reduce the extent of cancer effect to make the treatment easier.

The first three datasets are ready for publication. Public consultation of the residual dataset will instigate in the third sector of 2021.

PROPOSED SYSTEM

The system is used to detect cancer in its early stage by using prediction algorithms. The system is trained using a selected percentage of training and testing datasets, to finely generate an accurate prediction.

Problem Statement

Screening of breast cancer is very common in women of younger age, as the chances of women getting infected with cancer are increasing ; and it is taken as a topic of intense attention and mandatory consideration. The components of the topic like the screening process, conversion probabilities, rechecking, monitoring and stopover time distributions are appraised for women in the age limit of 40-59 years, using different breast screening studies with the help of the dataset. Factors held responsible for the delay in diagnosis are ignorance, unawareness, poverty and geographical isolation in most of the humans. These reasons have enlightened the researchers to choose this topic to work on.

The challenging task is to find factors to categorize the types of tumours into malignant or benign. Machine learning techniques have dramatically increased the accuracy of diagnosis by training the machine in an efficient way.

Objectives

- Accurate classification of existing tumours as Benign and Malignant using different machine learning techniques.
- Determining which classification technique is the best.
- Dividing the dataset into parts and observing the change in the accuracy using each part against the actual accuracy achieved using the complete dataset.

Why WDBC?

The reason for selecting WDBC for proposal execution is the relevance of characteristics with the requirement. The enhancement in the dataset is listed in Table. **1**. Before it is made publicly available, the dataset had 701 points, and revision was made in January 1989 with 2 instances from group 1 after removing the inconsistencies. Later revisions were made to remove noise, substitute value zero with one, and extend the features from 1-10.

Table 1. Group of instances.

Group Id.	Instances	Date
Group 1	369 instances	January 1989
Group 2	70 instances	October 1989
Group 3	31 instances	February 1990
Group 4	17 instances	April1990
Group 5	48 instances	August 1990
Group 6	49 instances	January 1991
Group 7	31 instances	June 1991
Group 8	86 instances	November1991
Total 701 instances		

The information in the Wisconsin Breast Cancer Diagnosis was extracted from the UC Irvine Machine Learning Repository. The features in this dataset characterise the Cell nucleus properties, which were generated from the image analysis of fine needle aspirates (FNA) of breast masses.

The proposal has used a large dataset Wisconsin Breast Cancer Diagnosis (WDBC) to evaluate the patterns using classification techniques for all applied on 569 instances and to find the most accurate technique for predicting cancer.

LITERATURE SURVEY

Machine learning is a branch of Artificial Intelligence that deals with the planning, designing and development of algorithms that are in agreement with the processors to for supporting empirical data, generated from sensor data.

Technological Development

The advancement in disease is proportionate to the advancement in technologies. The era is an introduction to robots replacing humans, for safe and fast service. Recent developments of 5 robots have shown an improvement in the quality of care and treatment that are listed below:

a. The daVinci Surgical Robot is a multi-armed wonderbot, used in surgeries to reduce the errors, make surgery less invasive and have a faster recover or healing. It makes small or tiny and exact incisions in the surgical area using advanced 3-D magnified high clarity vision, to improve the possibility of the success rate as this helps to reach an area; which cannot be reached by a human hand.

b. The Xenex Germ-Zapping Robot: The reason for death could also be non-cleanliness. The rooms cannot be made completely sterile as the germs are not visible with human eye. To quicken the process of cleaning because of the time constraints, a robot invented in 2011 helps to kill microorganisms using full-spectrum UV rays. It helps to reduce germs, bacteria, hospital-acquired infections, and Methicillin-resistant Staphylococcus Aureus (MRSA).

c. The PARO Therapeutic Robot: It is designed to recover excellence of life during recovery on post-surgery for mental illness. The PARO Therapeutic Robot is an interactive gadget with an appearance of a baby harbor stick, designed to give the benefits of animal rehabilitation. It is used for senior people with dementia to reduce stress. PARO naps, blinks, wiggles and makes funny little noises to entertain elders.

d. The Cyber-Knife: The Cyber knife is a robotic used to do radiation to tumours with less precision in units of milli-meters, by targeting the beam of radiotherapy on the tumour area for appropriate treatment by keeping the patient stationary.

e. The TUG: This robot is used for transportation operations and to supply meals, deposable and material in the hospital and provide fast and safe service.

The robot Cyber Knife is used for the treatment of tumours, and many classifiers help to know the type of tumour. The classification is based on the features selected for training a system with a balanced dataset. If the input is un-balanced, then the training will be problematic, hence filtering and pre-processing are applied to convert it to a balanced form.

Dataset used in the Research

In this work, the dataset used to do analysis is Wisconsin Diagnostic Breast Cancer (WDBC) dataset obtained from the UCI Machine Learning Repository. This dataset was produced by Dr. William and H. Wolberg, physicians at the University of Wisconsin, Hospital in Madison, Wisconsin, USA. To generate the dataset, Dr.Wolberg worked on the fluid samples and solid mass extracted from a patient's breast. A user-friendly graphical computer program Xcyt was used to do the analysis of cytological component based on a digital scan. It uses a curve fitting algorithm to calculate the mean, value and standard error for an image using the selected and extracted features (Radius, Texture, Perimeter, Area, Smoothness, Compactness, and Concavity, Concave points, Symmetry and fractal dimension). The mean, standard error and "worst" or the largest (mean of the three largest values) of these features were computed for each image, resulting in 30 features. For instance, field 3 is the Mean Radius, field 13 is the Radius SE, and field 23 is the Worst Radius. In WDBC dataset, there are 569 records in which there are 357 Benign and 212 Malignant which can be shown in Fig. (**1**). Some other types of datasets applicable for cancer detection are shown in Table. **2**, which represent the number of supporting instances, attributes, and types.

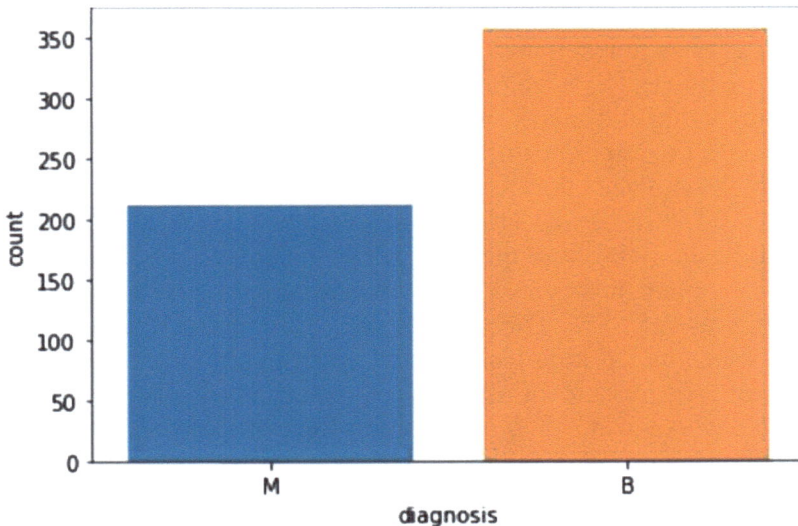

Fig. (1). Graph showing the number of benign and malignant tumor in the total dataset.

Table 2. Description of Cancer related Dataset.

Dataset	Instances	Attributes	Benign/ Non-Recurrent	Malignant/ Recurrent
WBC	699	11	458	241
BC	256	10	201	85
WPBC	198	34	151	47
WDBC	569	32	357	212
Open ML-Breast Cancer	286	10	201	85

Related Work

The related work done by other researchers is quoted in the references. The analysis can be done using the datasets available in Table **2**. According to the studies in the literature related to this classification application, it is observed that various methods give varying results. J.R. Quinlan [2] have obtained 94.74% accuracy with 10-fold cross validation with the classifier as decision-tree method. Hamilton *et al.*, [3]. observed 96% accuracy with the RIAC method. Ster and Dobnikar [4] obtained 96.8% accuracy with the linear discrete analysis (LDA) method. The accuracy obtained by Bennett and Blue [5] with support vector machine (SVM) (5 × CV) method was 7.2%. Nauck and Kruse [6] interpreted that the accuracy was 95.06% with neuro-fuzzy techniques. Pena-Rayes and Sipper [7] came up with the proposal of 97.36% accuracy using the fuzzy-GA method.

R. Setiono sight has reached an efficiency of 98.1% using neuro-rule method [8]. William and Wolberg [9] have proposed some methods for the rejection of noisy training exam using automatic way of selecting model n in linear regression. Goodman *et al.*, [10] applied three different methods to obtain a solution to the problem which showed the following accuracies: optimized-LVQ method's performance: 96.7%, big-LVQ method: 96.8% and AIRS: 97.2%, which is proposed on the artificial immune system. Nevertheless, Abonyi and Szeifert [11] discussed and applied supervised fuzzy clustering (SFC) technique and obtained a major finding as 95.57% Djebbari *et al.*, [12] considered the effect of an ensemble of machine learning techniques to predict and detect the survival time in breast cancer. Aruna and Kishore [13] interpreted the comparison of the performance analysis of C4.5, Naïve Bayes, Support Vector Machine (SVM) and K- Nearest Neighbor (K-NN) to explore the best classifier in WBC. SVM proves to be the most accurate classifier with an accuracy of 96.99%. Angeline Christobel Y and Sivaprakasam [14] explained the major finding, achieving an accuracy of 69.23% using decision tree classifier (CART) in breast cancer datasets. Chaurasia and Pal [15] proposed a comparison of the performance of supervised learning classifiers; such as Naïve Bayes, SVM-RBF kernel, RBF neural networks, Decision trees (J48) and simple CART; for finding the best classifier in breast cancer datasets. The experimental result shows that the SVM-RBF kernel has given more accurate results than other classifiers; i-e. 96.84% in Wisconsin Breast Cancer (original) datasets. Dinh *et al.*, [16] have used a clustering technique to define categorical and numerical attributes. To find the proximity among data object information, Euclidean distance is applied. To enhance the results, DT based method is collaborated with categorical attributes. Duy-Tai Dinh [17] used k-PbC to initially obtain the greatest frequent itemset. Followed by that, he used a kernel-based method to create cluster centres with an information-theoretical founded divergence degree to calculate the expanse between cluster centres and data objects. The proposal of Mahin *et al.* [18] was to generate the dataset from the network simulator and validate the results using classifiers of machine learning algorithms.

METHODOLOGIES

Learning Algorithms

Our research work includes a performance comparison between different machine learning algorithms: K-Nearest Neighbours (KNN), Support Vector Machine (SVM) and Decision Tree, and aims to assess the correctness in classifying data with respect to the efficiency and effectiveness of these three algorithms in terms of Accuracy, Precision, Recall and F1 score. Applied classification techniques of machine learning used in Architecture are: SVM: Support Vector Machine, KNN: K-Nearest Neighbour, NB: Naïve Bayes, DT: Decision Tree, LR: Logistic Regression, RF: Random Forest, CNN: Convolution Neural Network and LSTM: Long Short-Term Memory. In this module, the deep learning algorithms are analysed in terms of accuracy in identifying the malware family present in the given input data by calculating performance metrics.

Measuring the Effectiveness of the Models

After data cleaning, pre-processing and training, the models depicted in Fig. (**2**) are used to get the probable outputs. The effectiveness is linearly proportional to the performance. In order to determine the effectiveness of the three classification techniques, maximum correct predictions are determined, with the following performance metrics.

Actual Values

Fig. (2). Confusion Matrix.

A. A Confusion matrix is a table used to analyze the performance of an algorithm or classification model or classifier on a dataset with the realistic values in Fig. (**2**).
B. Precision: Precision is the fraction of retrieved documents that are relevant to the query. Precision = TP/(TP+FP)
C. Recall: Recall is the fraction of the relevant documents that are successfully Retrieved. Recall = TP / (TP + FN)
D. F-measure: The traditional F-measure or balanced F-score (F1 score) is the Harmonic mean of precision and recall. F-Measure= 2*(Recall * Precision) / (Recall + Precision)
E. Accuracy: The accuracy is the proportion of correct predictions (both true Positives and true negatives) among the total number of cases examined.

TP: True Positive, FP: False Positive, TN: True Negative, FN: False Negative.

Accuracy = (TP+TN)/(TP+FP+FN+TN)

Processing of Patterns

The patters are processed by supplying the dataset from Table **2**. Filtering, pre-processing or re-sampling of data is done to remove duplicates and missing data. This transformation helps to process the patterns quickly, from a balanced form. The cross validation helps to evaluate the algorithms on a limited sample to make predictions for un-used training data. The classifications tools are selected from the section "Learning Algorithms" and are interpreted in Fig. (**3**). J48 is a licensed version of Rolls-Royce Tay, an extension of ID3 generated by C4.5 and invented by Ross Quinlan. It is declared as the best machine leaning approach to generate decision trees. It works by splitting the huge data into a smaller size. Naive Bayes work on the concept of entropy information. SMO works on the approach of John

Platt's approach for training support vector to generate optimized sequential results

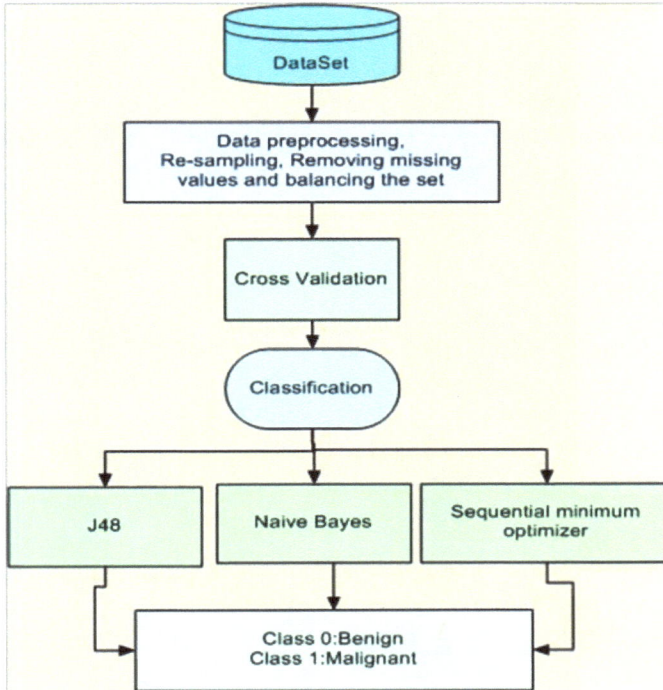

Fig. (3). Process of recognizing state from dataset.

RESULTS AND DISCUSSION

After training all the three models, the confusion matrix of each model and the values of all the performance metrics are acquired using the below code as shown in Fig. (**4**).

Here,

Model [0] is the KNN classifier

Model [1] is the SVM classifier

Model [2] is the Decision Tree classifier

Output of the above code is shown in Fig. (**5**).

```
#Show the confusion matrix and paramters for all of the models on th

from sklearn.metrics import confusion_matrix
for i in range(len(model)):
    cm = confusion_matrix(Y_test, model[i].predict(X_test))

    TN = cm[0][0]
    TP = cm[1][1]
    FN = cm[1][0]
    FP = cm[0][1]

    Accuracy = (TP + TN) / (TP + TN + FN + FP)
    Precision = (TP / (TP+FP))
    Recall = (TP / (TP+FN))
    F1Score = (2*Precision*Recall) / (Precision+Recall)


    print(cm)
    print('Model[{}] Testing Accuracy = '.format(i),Accuracy)
    print('Model[{}] Testing Precision = '.format(i),Precision)
    print('Model[{}] Testing Recall = '.format(i),Recall)
    print('Model[{}] Testing F1-Score = '.format(i),F1Score)

    print()# Print a new line
```

Fig. (4). Snippet of our code calculating the performance metrics.

```
[[89  1]
 [ 5 48]]
Model[0] Testing Accuracy =  0.958041958041958
Model[0] Testing Precision =  0.9795918367346939
Model[0] Testing Recall =  0.9056603773584906
Model[0] Testing F1-Score =  0.9411764705882353

[[87  3]
 [ 2 51]]
Model[1] Testing Accuracy =  0.965034965034965
Model[1] Testing Precision =  0.9444444444444444
Model[1] Testing Recall =  0.9622641509433962
Model[1] Testing F1-Score =  0.9532710280373832

[[84  6]
 [ 1 52]]
Model[2] Testing Accuracy =  0.951048951048951
Model[2] Testing Precision =  0.896551724137931
Model[2] Testing Recall =  0.9811320754716981
Model[2] Testing F1-Score =  0.9369369369369369
```

Fig. (5). Snippet showing the Accuracy, Precision, Recall and F1 Score values.

Accuracy can be misleading because sometimes it may be desirable to select a model with a lower accuracy because it has a greater predictive power on the problem. In some cases, where there is a large class imbalance, a model can predict the value of the majority class for all predictions and achieve high classification accuracy. This is called the Accuracy Paradox. Hence, accuracy can be used when the class distribution is similar while F1-score is a better metric when there are imbalanced classes.

As we can see in Fig. (**6**), the F1 score value of the SVM classifier model is high. Hence we conclude that the SVM is the best among the three algorithms. (Decision Tree, KNN and SVM).

Fig. (6). Comparison of the algorithms with respect to each performance metrics.

Now let us observe by dividing the dataset into parts or subsets and check if the results are still the same for all the subsets or not. When we trained our models using first 25% of the dataset in which there were 114 records and 32 columns with 68 instances as Malignant and 46 as Benign, the results are as shown below in Fig. (7).

```
[[10  3]
 [ 1 15]]
Model[0] Testing Accuracy =  0.8620689655172413
Model[0] Testing Precision =  0.8333333333333334
Model[0] Testing Recall =  0.9375
Model[0] Testing F1-Score =  0.8823529411764706

[[11  2]
 [ 1 15]]
Model[1] Testing Accuracy =  0.896551724137931
Model[1] Testing Precision =  0.8823529411764706
Model[1] Testing Recall =  0.9375
Model[1] Testing F1-Score =  0.9090909090909091

[[11  2]
 [ 0 16]]
Model[2] Testing Accuracy =  0.9310344827586207
Model[2] Testing Precision =  0.8888888888888888
Model[2] Testing Recall =  1.0
Model[2] Testing F1-Score =  0.9411764705882353
```

Fig. (7). Snippet showing results for the first 25% of the total dataset.

When we trained our models using 25% of the dataset in which there are 114 records and 32 columns with 68 instances as Malignant and 46 as Benign. The results are shown in Fig. (**8**). As we can see in Fig. (**9**), the F1 score value of the Decision Tree classifier (DT) is high for 25% of the total dataset.

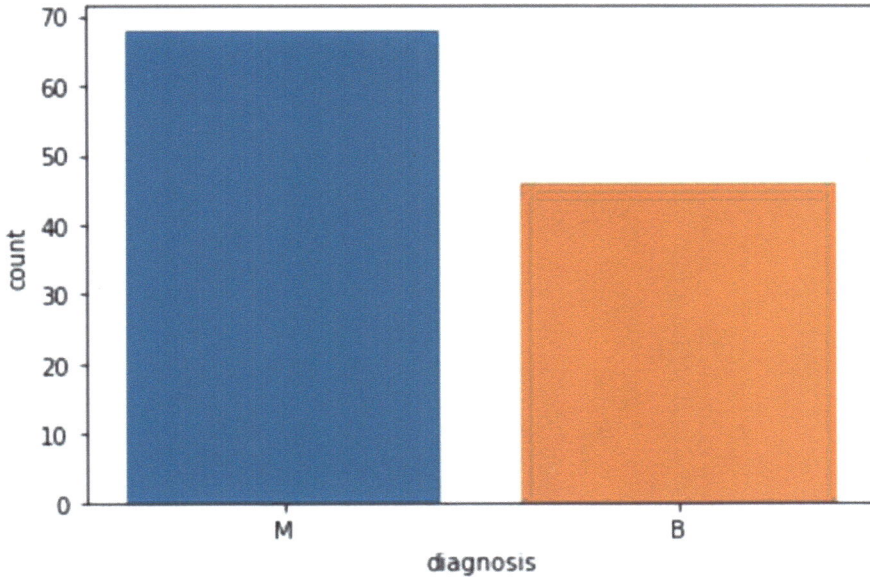

Fig. (8). Graph with benign and malignant tumour in 25% of the total dataset.

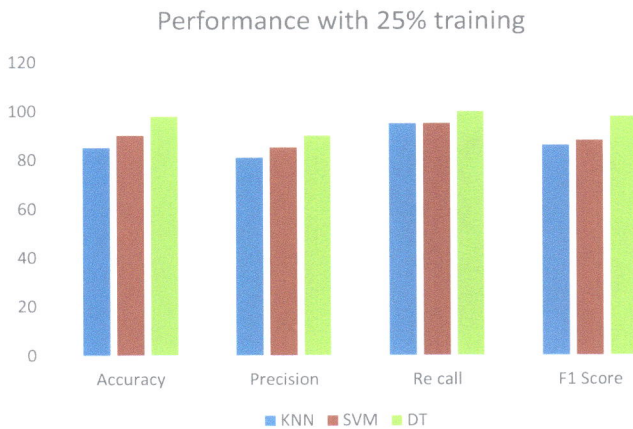

Fig. (9). Comparison of the algorithms with performance metrics for 25% of the dataset.

When we trained our models using 40% of the dataset, there were 228 records and 32 columns with 117 instances as Malignant and 111 as Benign. The results are shown below in Fig. (**10**).

```
[[31  0]
 [ 2 24]]
Model[0] Testing Accuracy =  0.9649122807017544
Model[0] Testing Precision =  1.0
Model[0] Testing Recall =  0.9230769230769231
Model[0] Testing F1-Score =  0.9600000000000001

[[31  0]
 [ 3 23]]
Model[1] Testing Accuracy =  0.9473684210526315
Model[1] Testing Precision =  1.0
Model[1] Testing Recall =  0.8846153846153846
Model[1] Testing F1-Score =  0.9387755102040816

[[29  2]
 [ 7 19]]
Model[2] Testing Accuracy =  0.8421052631578947
Model[2] Testing Precision =  0.9047619047619048
Model[2] Testing Recall =  0.7307692307692307
Model[2] Testing F1-Score =  0.8085106382978723
```

Fig. (10). Snippet showing results for the 40% of the total dataset.

When we trained our models using 40% of the dataset, there were 228 records and 32 columns with 117 instances as Malignant and 111 as Benign. The results are as shown in Fig. **(11)**.

Out[9]: <matplotlib.axes._subplots.AxesSubplot at 0x1ca81380908>

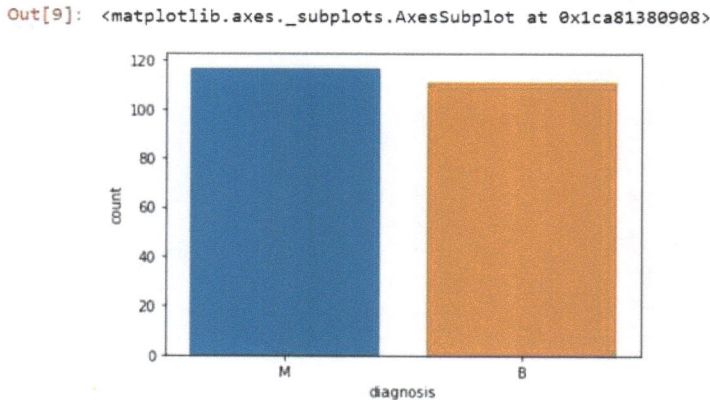

Fig. (11). Graph with benign and malignant tumour in the 40% of the total dataset.

As we can see in the above Fig. **(12)**, the F1 score value of the K-Nearest Neighbour (KNN) is high for 40% of the total dataset for all the performance metrics.

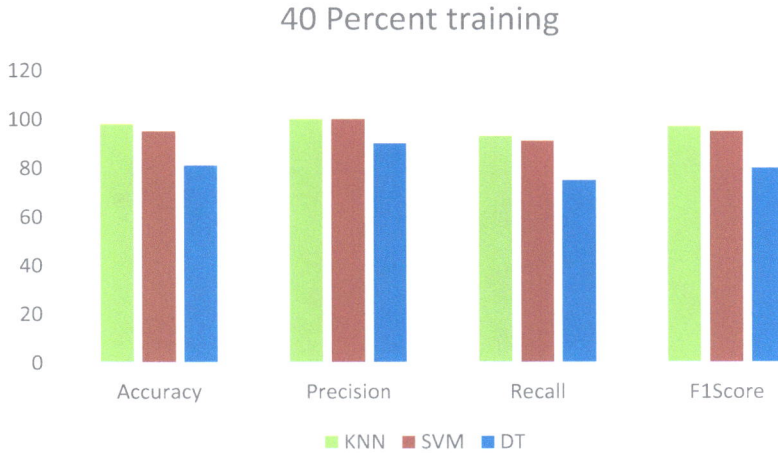

Fig. (12). Comparison of the algorithms with performance metrics for 40% of the dataset.

Fig. (**13**) shows epochs, when testing is done on all the considered performance metrics on 60% of the dataset used.

```
[[52  1]
 [ 2 31]]
Model[0] Testing Accuracy =  0.9651162790697675
Model[0] Testing Precision =  0.96875
Model[0] Testing Recall =  0.9393939393939394
Model[0] Testing F1-Score =  0.9538461538461539

[[51  2]
 [ 1 32]]
Model[1] Testing Accuracy =  0.9651162790697675
Model[1] Testing Precision =  0.9411764705882353
Model[1] Testing Recall =  0.9696969696969697
Model[1] Testing F1-Score =  0.955223880597015

[[49  4]
 [ 2 31]]
Model[2] Testing Accuracy =  0.9302325581395349
Model[2] Testing Precision =  0.8857142857142857
Model[2] Testing Recall =  0.9393939393939394
Model[2] Testing F1-Score =  0.9117647058823529
```

Fig. (13). Snippet of our output showing results for the 60% of the total dataset.

When we trained our models using 60% of the dataset, there were 342 records and 32 columns with 157 instances as Malignant and 185 as Benign. The results are as shown in Fig. **(14)**. Fig. **(14)** shows the Benign and Malignant cases with 60% training.

```
Out[9]:  <matplotlib.axes._subplots.AxesSubplot at 0x1fb35f68288>
```

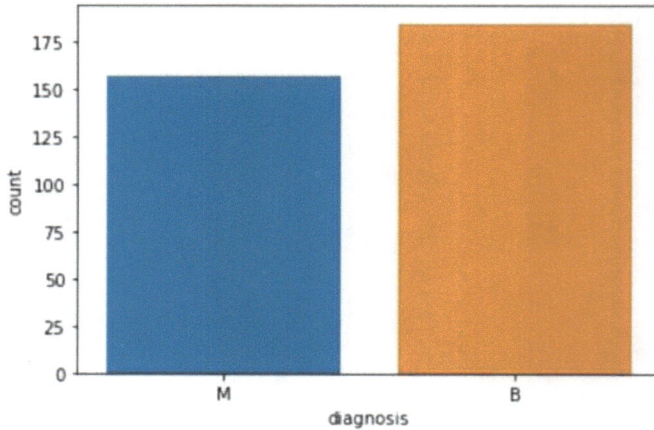

Fig. (14). Graph showing benign and malignant tumour in the 60% of the total dataset.

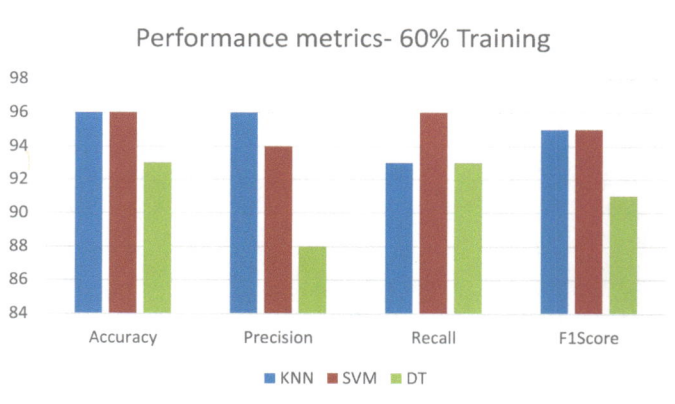

Fig. (15). Comparison of the algorithms with performance metrics for 60% dataset.

As we can see in Fig. **(15)**, the F1 score value of the K-Nearest Neighbor (KNN) and Support Vector Machine (SVM) is high for 60% of the total dataset.

Fig. **(16)** shows epochs, when testing is done on all the considered performance metrics on 80% of the dataset used. When we trained our models using 80% of the dataset, there were 456 records and 32 columns with 186 instances as Malignant and 270 as Benign. The results are as shown in Fig. **(17)**.

```
print('Model[{}] Testing Recall = '.format(i),Recall)
print('Model[{}] Testing F1-Score = '.format(i),F1Score)

print()# Print a new line
[[70  0]
 [ 5 39]]
Model[0] Testing Accuracy =  0.956140350877193
Model[0] Testing Precision =  1.0
Model[0] Testing Recall =  0.8863636363636364
Model[0] Testing F1-Score =  0.9397590361445783

[[69  1]
 [ 1 43]]
Model[1] Testing Accuracy =  0.9824561403508771
Model[1] Testing Precision =  0.9772727272727273
Model[1] Testing Recall =  0.9772727272727273
Model[1] Testing F1-Score =  0.9772727272727273

[[65  5]
 [ 4 40]]
Model[2] Testing Accuracy =  0.9210526315789473
Model[2] Testing Precision =  0.8888888888888888
Model[2] Testing Recall =  0.9090909090909091
Model[2] Testing F1-Score =  0.8988764044943819
```

Fig. (16). Snippet of showing results for the 80% of the total dataset.

```
Out[9]:  <matplotlib.axes._subplots.AxesSubplot at 0x1d3e833c4c8>
```

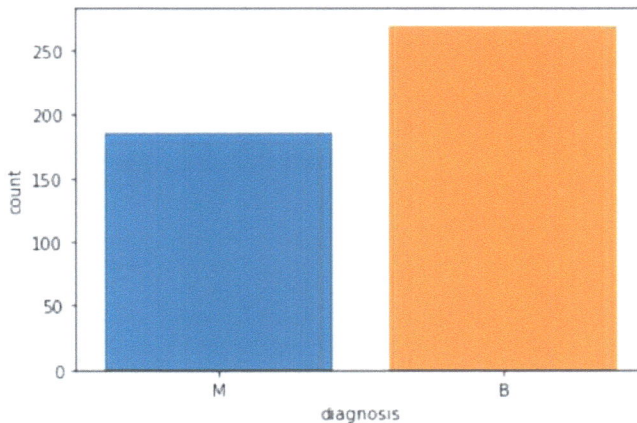

Fig. (17). Graph showing benign and malignant tumour in the 80% of the total dataset.

As we can see in Fig. (**18**), the F1 score value of the Support Vector Machine (SVM) is high for 80% of the total dataset.

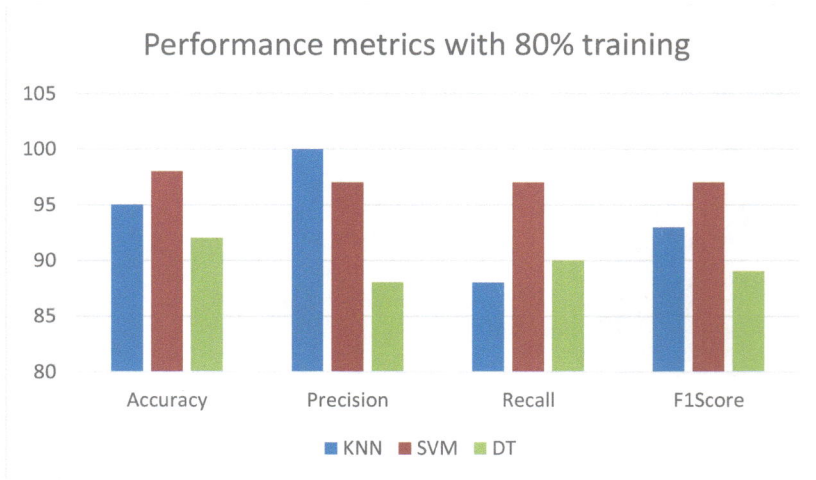

Fig. (18). Comparison of the algorithms with performance metrics for 80% of the dataset.

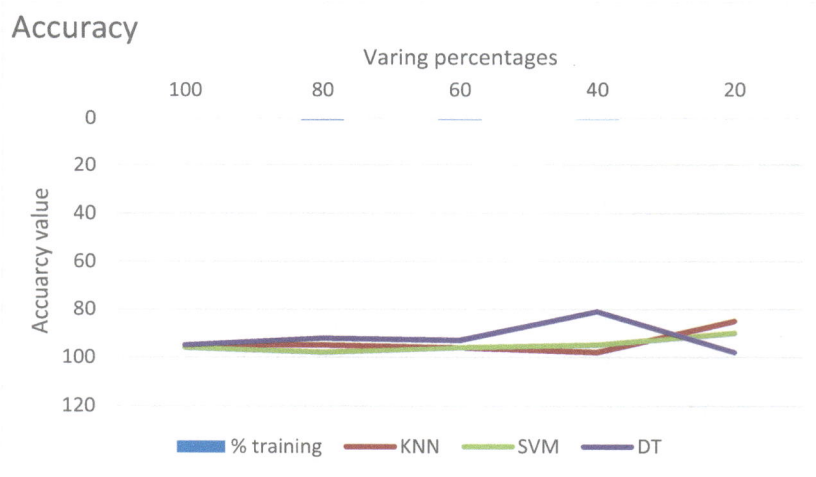

Fig. (19). Accuracy on different levels.

Accuracy of the different classifiers is shown in Fig. (**19**). SVM and KNN are close to each other in comparison.

CONCLUSION

After reviewing all the results from the four subsets and total dataset, we observe that 4 out of 5 times, the SVM classifier showed us the best performance based on the F1 score value. Hence we conclude that the SVM classifier is the best classifier used for breast cancer detection using Wisconsin Diagnostic Breast Cancer (WDBC) dataset, when the experiment is conducted on different percentages for testing and training. Further extension of the proposal is to experiment and validate with other available datasets of breast cancer.

CONSENT FOR PUBLICATION

Not applicable.

CONFLICT OF INTEREST

The authors declare no conflict of interest, financial or otherwise.

ACKNOWLEDGEMENT

Declared none.

REFERENCES

[1]   H. William, *Wolberg, W Nick Street, and L. Olvi, "Mangasarian. Breast cancer Wisconsin (diagnostic) data set.* UCI Machine Learning Repository, 1992. [http://archive. ics. uci. edu/ml/]

[2]   J.R. Quinlan, "Improved use of continuous attributes in C 4.5", *J. Artif. Intell. Res.,* vol. 4, pp. 77-90, 1996.
        [http://dx.doi.org/10.1613/jair.279]

[3]   H.J. Hamilton, N. Shan, and N. Cercone, *"RIAC: A rule induction algorithm based on approximate classification", Technical Report CS.* University of Regina, 1996, pp. 96-06.

[4]   B. Ster, and A. Dobnikar, "Neural networks in medical diagnosis: Comparison with other methods", *Proceedings of the International Conference on Engineering Applications of Neural Networks (EANN '96),* 1996pp. 427-430

[5]   K.P. Bennet, and J.A. Blue, A support vector machine approach to decision trees.*Math. Report.* Rensselaer Polytechnic Institute, 1997, pp. 97-100.

[6]   D. Nauck, and R. Kruse, "Obtaining interpretable fuzzy classification rules from medical data", *Artif. Intell. Med.,* vol. 16, no. 2, pp. 149-169, 1999.
        [http://dx.doi.org/10.1016/S0933-3657(98)00070-0] [PMID: 10378442]

[7]   C.A. Peña-Reyes, and M. Sipper, "A fuzzy-genetic approach to breast cancer diagnosis", *Artif. Intell. Med.,* vol. 17, no. 2, pp. 131-155, 1999.
        [http://dx.doi.org/10.1016/S0933-3657(99)00019-6] [PMID: 10518048]

[8]   R. Setiono, "Generating concise and accurate classification rules for breast cancer diagnosis", *Artif. Intell. Med.,* vol. 18, no. 3, pp. 205-219, 2000.
        [http://dx.doi.org/10.1016/S0933-3657(99)00041-X] [PMID: 10675715]

[9]   H. William and Wolberg "Sparsity through Automated Rejection," University Col-lege London, 2001.

[10]   D.E. Goodman, L. Boggess, and A. Watkins, "Artificial immune system classification of multiple-class problems", *Proceedings of the ArtificialNeural Networks in Engineering ANNIE,* pp. 179-183, 2002.

[11]   J. Abonyi, and F. Szeifert, "Supervised fuzzy clustering for the identification of fuzzy classifiers", *Pattern Recognit. Lett.,* vol. 24, no. 14, pp. 2195-2207, 2003.

[http://dx.doi.org/10.1016/S0167-8655(03)00047-3]

[12]   A. Djebbari, Z. Liu, and S. Phan, "International journal of computational biology and drug design", *21ˢᵗ Annual Conference on Neural Information Processing Systems,* 2008.

[13]   S. Aruna and L. V NandaKishore, "Knowledge Based Analysis of various Sta-tistical Tools in Detecting Breast", pp. 37–45, 2011.

[14]   Angeline Christobel and Sivaprakasam, "An Empirical Comparison of Data Mining Classification Methods", Vol. 3, no. 2, pp. 24-28, 2011.

[15]   V. Chaurasia, and S. Pal, *Data Mining Techniques: To Predict and Resolve Breast Cancer Survivability,* vol. 3, no. 1, pp. 10-22, 2014.

[16]   D-T. Dinh, V-N. Huynh, and S. Sriboonchitta, "Clustering mixed numerical and categorical data with missing values", *Inf. Sci.,* vol. 571, pp. 418-442, 2021.
[http://dx.doi.org/10.1016/j.ins.2021.04.076]

[17]   D.T. Dinh, and V-N. Huynh, "k-PbC: an improved cluster center initialization for categorical data clustering", *Appl. Intell.,* vol. 50, no. 8, pp. 2610-2632, 2020.
[http://dx.doi.org/10.1007/s10489-020-01677-5]

[18]   Syeda Hajra Mahin,Fahmina Taranum, and Reshma Nikhat, "Case study- Intru-sion Detection System Using Machine Learning,"Machine Learning and Big Data: Con-cepts, Algorithms, Tools and Applications, July 2020.
[http://dx.doi.org/10.1002/9781119654834.ch16]

SUBJECT INDEX

Communication 40, 41, 45, 51, 57, 58, 60, 62,
    141, 146, 156
  diagnostic 58
  network 51
  process 45
  technologies 141, 156
Computational 28, 92, 178, 199
  Intelligence techniques 92
  power 199
  techniques 178
  mechanisms 28
Computer networks 49
Computing, hybrid edge-cloud 93
Consumption, fuel 140
Convolutional neural network (CNN) 93, 198,
    199, 201, 225
Correlation-based feature selection (CFS) 190,
    193, 194
COVID-19 pandemic 112
Crop(s) 73, 87
  damage 73
  healthy 87
Cryptographic algorithms 61, 62
Cryptography 45, 54
Crypto Interface 61
Cybersecurity 40, 71, 75
Cyclonic storm 145

D

Data 74, 88
  clustering 88
  transmit attacks 74
Data analysis 110, 111, 114, 115, 206
  biomedical NGS 206
Data mining 7, 118, 176, 196, 217, 219
  algorithms 219
Data sets 34, 37, 197
  biological 197
  desired clustered 37
Databases 35, 36, 188
  dense 188
  systems 35, 36
Decision tree(s) 11, 14, 15, 17, 23, 85, 86, 98,
    99, 217, 225, 226, 227, 229, 231
  and k-nearest neighbour 217
Decryption methods 51
Deep learning 3, 76, 156, 172, 173, 175, 179,
    197, 198, 199, 201, 209, 210, 217
  algorithms aids 172

and large data analysis 156
  approach 199
  framework 198
  methods 210
Deep networks 200, 202
Deep neural network (DNN) 197, 198, 202,
    209, 210
  architectures 202
  topologies 210
Denoising process 161, 162
  wavelet-based 161
Deoxyribonucleic acid 179
Depressions 123, 125
Detecting learning algorithm 90
Detection 76, 186
  crop diseases 76
  fusion 186
Development activities 123, 124, 126
Developmental programs 125
Devices, mobile computing 113, 114
Disaster prevention agencies 2
Disease 137, 157, 170, 172, 173, 177, 187,
    189, 193, 217, 218, 219, 222
  contagious 172
  dangerous 218
  waterborne 137
DL techniques for NGS data analysis 189
DNA sequence(s) 176, 179, 180
  analysis 176
  data 179

E

ECG 149, 153, 157
  applications 153
  denoising algorithms 149
  waveforms 157
ECG signal 149, 150, 161, 166
  denoising 149, 161
  filtering techniques 166
  processing 150
Ecosystems, fragile 123
ECU 51, 68
  development 51
  NVM memory 68
Electrical signals 151, 157
Electric consumption data 91
Electricity 1, 90, 91, 95
  consumption 91, 95
  management 91

W

www.ingramcontent.com/pod-product-compliance
Lightning Source LLC
Chambersburg PA
CBHW050822220326
41598CB00006B/296